THE PORTABLE

ROUTER BOOK

No. 2869
$24.95

THE PORTABLE

ROUTER
BOOK

R. J. DE CRISTOFORO

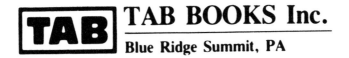

TAB BOOKS Inc.
Blue Ridge Summit, PA

FIRST EDITION
FOURTH PRINTING

Library of Congress Cataloging in Publication Data

DeCristoforo, R. J.
The portable router book.

Includes index.
1. Routers (Tools) 2. Woodwork.   I. Title.
TT203.5.D43   1987   684'.083   86-30019
ISBN 0-8306-0869-9
ISBN 0-8306-2869-X (pbk.)

TAB BOOKS Inc. offers software for
sale. For information and a catalog,
please contact TAB Software Department,
Blue Ridge Summit, PA 17294-0850.

Questions regarding the content of this book
should be addressed to:

Reader Inquiry Branch
TAB BOOKS Inc.
Blue Ridge Summit, PA 17294-0214

Cover photograph courtesy of
Porter-Cable Corporation, Jackson, Tennessee 38302.

Contents

Introduction

I've produced a number of magazine stories about the portable router and have included chapters on it in books dealing with power tools. Many times I introduced the topic by saying something like, "You don't know what you are missing if you don't own a portable router," or "Even if you own a portable router, it's possible that you are not exploring its capabilities." I feel that expressing these same thoughts is a good way to get started with this project.

You can't do justice to this interesting tool in a three or four-page magazine article or even in a lengthy book chapter. That fact is what prompted production of this book that deals exclusively with portable router techniques. For information concerning router projects, see *24 Router Projects*, TAB book No. 9062, by Percy W. Blandford.

The portable router is something of an enigma. It is a deceptively simple concept: not much more than a motor driving a shaft, or spindle, that has a chuck-type device at its free end. On its own, it can't do more than spin its chuck,

a comparison you can make with a table saw or radial arm saw that isn't equipped with a saw blade or a drill press without a boring bit. By adding cutters (router bits) the router can turn with suitable power and speed, and a host of accessories and jigs that you can make or buy, the tool transforms into a multipurpose unit that allows anyone to accomplish a full range of practical woodworking chores and to do them professionally.

Too often, like the fairly common view of a stationary shaper, the tool is viewed as a means of producing decorative edges on projects like tabletops, trays, picture frames, and so on. It can do such work superbly, but the limitation is like using a jigsaw just to produce jigsaw puzzles.

The modern router has types, sizes, and price ranges to fit any level of interest and size of pocketbook. It just about eliminates the dividing line between amateur and expert in many areas. For example, with a dovetail jig, anyone can produce precisely fitted, classic dovetail joints. Some of the jigs limit the user to equally spaced units, but others allow spacing that suits the worker's view of how the connection should look. Thus, individual craftsmanship becomes part of the scene. The work isn't accomplished simply by saying "abracadabra," but the possibility of human error is greatly reduced and apprenticeship time is practically nil. If you follow the instructions supplied with the jigs and handle the router correctly, the first joint you make will be perfect. The same happy thought applies to other classic joints like the mortise-tenon and to more prosaic connections like dadoes, grooves, and rabbets.

The router is a super tool for forming woodworking joints, but there is much more. Its capabilities include shaping edges on project components either before or after assembly, hollowing for trays and chair seats, piercing for decorative effects or for producing duplicate parts, leveling slabs, decorative panel routing, 3-D or bas-relief carving, pattern routing—the list goes on.

Manufacturers have become aware of router potential and are now offering unique accessories that allow, among other things, bowl making, decorative work on spindle turnings, controlled letter and number shaping, duplicating from stencils or drawings using pantograph devices, even cutting precise screw threads in wood.

The router is a portable tool, so most times it is applied to work that is held stationary in some fashion. But there are times when it is more convenient to use the tool like a stationary unit. The use method is then reversed; the work is applied to the tool. There are even situations, usually created by the types of router bits being used, where such an arrangement is mandatory. Cutters like Freud's "Panel Door Set," Zac Products' "The Door Shop," and Sears' "Crown Molding Kit" are never used in the freehand manner normally associated with portable router techniques.

This poses no problem for anyone who wishes to fully utilize the portable router. Many manufacturers offer a special stand in which the router can be installed and used like a stationary shaper. Chapter 12 shows a few commercial router/shaper stands and also offers construction drawings for a sophisticated, floor-model unit that you can make in your own shop.

The use of jigs, fixtures, and guides that you can make are as important to efficient and sometimes safer power tool use as the tools themselves. Often the homemade device allows the tool to function in a manner even the manufacturer didn't anticipate. Other times the device serves to reduce, if not eliminate, the possibility of human error. This is an important factor, especially in the area of guides. The user should adopt a mechanical means of guiding the tool to assure accuracy whenever possible. *The Portable Router Book* gives plans for many accuracy accessories that are useful and not difficult to make. When you encounter a situation that calls for a special setup, give some thought to what can be done to provide automatic precision. This is especially important when the router is used to make duplicate pieces and when the same cut is required on many project components.

The portable router is considered to be a fairly safe tool, but in my mind no tool, hand or powered, is *safe*. It's important to remember that safety is as much in the mind as it is in the tool or in particular procedures. Anything that can cut wood and even harder materials can cut you. Never lose your respect for the tool. The complacency that can accompany increased knowledge of the tool can spoil workshop fun. As many professionals as amateurs are hurt in workshops; expertise doesn't guarantee safety. Don't skip over Chapter 2. Obey the rules. "Thinking" is your job. Even tools that can make some decisions for you electronically can't tell whether they are confronting wood or a finger.

Two adages of mine . . .

"Think twice before cutting."

"Measure twice, cut once."

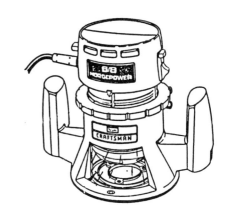

Chapter 1

The Tool

I'T'S FAIRLY CERTAIN THAT THE FIRST "ROUTER" was a hand tool—a hand plane or, specifically, a "hand router plane." A more sophisticated version of the original concept is seen in the modern Stanley version in Fig. 1-1. The tool, designed for a two-hand grip, has a husky base and a means of securing a cutter for a specific depth of cut. The idea was probably originated by someone using hand chisels to remove material to hollow a tray or to form a dado or groove. Chances are that all hand planes were visualized the same way—a means of doing a chore with less effort and with mechanical control for better results.

If you substitute an electrically powered rotary cutter for the stationary blade that is part of the hand tool, you'll have a basic idea of portable router advantages. The depth of cut is still controlled. The router does the work while you concentrate on being creative.

ROUTER BACKGROUND

The invention of the electric router is credited to a Mr. R. L. Carter, a respected wood and metal patternmaker with an inventive mind. Like many ingenious ideas, the powered router came about because of a chore that ordinarily required many tedious hours of work with a tool that resembled a spokeshave. The solution, which *sounds* simple, was to redesign a worm gear—removed from a barber's clipper—as a cutter and attach it directly to the shaft of an electric motor.

The improvisation worked impressively, especially after Mr. Carter added guides to provide accurate cut control. The new "hand shaper," having solved the on-hand problem, was stored for more than a year. Then a nephew, Julius A. Yates, rediscovered it to demonstrate to a cabinetmaker how much easier it was to use the electric tool in place of hand tools to carve some ornate curves in the walnut back of a sofa that was being constructed. The cabinetmaker became an enthusiastic first customer.

It was sometime later that the two men, working out of a machine shop set up in a ga-

Fig. 1-1. Earlier versions of this hand router plane preceded the development of the modern electric router. Note that the tool's base has been extended with an auxiliary base. This "extra span" technique is also used with powered routers.

rage, began to mass-produce the tool at about 15 a week, which did not satisfy the avid, waiting customers. Factory space was increased, employees were added, and in 10 years more than 100,000 tools were in use.

Stanley acquired the Carter business in 1929 and their improvements, plus those the originator had continued to develop over the years, resulted in the amazingly versatile machine that exists today. Stanley manufactured routers until about 1980 when their power tools division was passed on to the Bosch Power Tool Corporation.

Currently routers are being manufactured by such companies as Porter-Cable, Black & Decker, Sears Roebuck under the Craftsman name, Wen, Milwaukee, Ryobi, Makita, and others. Rockwell, which was commonly seen on portable router nameplates after the company had acquired Porter-Cable, is no longer seen on the tools. The line, together with other portable electric tools, has been returned to Porter-Cable.

There are more types and sizes around than you can "shake a stick at." This is a good situation because anyone can acquire exactly the

tool or tools needed to suit the area of woodworking interest. Many of the manufacturers offer exciting accessories, some of which are listed in Fig. 1-2. This is also a good deal because it allows you to utilize the tool beyond its basic functions.

BASIC NOMENCLATURE

The portable router, as it is usually purchased, consists of two major components: the upper housing, containing the motor and motor-driven spindle, and a base that receives the housing (Fig. 1-3). The base maintains the motor in vertical position and, by a means that can differ from tool to tool, allows the motor to be raised or lowered, which is how the cutter-projection below the base (depth of cut) is adjusted.

The router's base assembly includes a removable subbase that is usually made of an opaque black plastic (Fig. 1-4). Most router users agree that while the "standard" subbase is sturdy enough for long-lived use, its opacity and an often minimum-size hole for the cutter to poke through make it difficult to see what the cutter

ACCESSORY	
DOVETAIL JIGS AND TEMPLATES	many styles available for joinery or decorative work—made in high-speed steel, solid tungsten carbide, or carbide-tipped—most have integral or ball bearing pilots
ROUTER/SHAPER TABLES	allow quick, accurate forming of dovetail joints—more flexible units let operator decide joint spacing—used with dove-tail bits
HINGE-MORTISING TEMPLATE KITS	router can be mounted for use as a stationary shaper—usually equipped with adjustable fences and guards
PLANER ATTACHMENT	adjustable templates allow accurate routing of mortises for door hinges
EDGE GUIDE	the router can be used like a portable, powered plane—not available for all routers
CIRCLE CUTTING GUIDE	guides the router for cuts parallel to an edge—comes with the tooloris available as an accessory
	guides the router through circular grooves or disc cutting—some edge guides are designed so they can also be used for circular work
TEMPLATE GUIDES	used in router's base—many applications,including pattern routing, template work, dovetail cutting
LAMINATE TRIMMING PITS	for trimming plastic laminates and veneers—usually carbide-tipped
BIT SHARPENER	router attachment with special guides for maintaining sharp edges on router bits
LETTER AND NUMBER GUIDES	templates for routing house numbers, name plates—available in various sizes and styles
PANTOGRAPH	guides router through duplication of designs, letters, numbers, and so on—most have enlarging or reducing capability
DOOR AND PANEL KITS	adjustable guides and templates for decorative grooving of doors, panels, drawer fronts
EDGE-CRAFTER*	used with router/shaper table—for decorative shaping on edges of oval or round frames, and circular scalloped edges
ROUTER RECREATOR*	guides router through duplication of 3-D objects as well as letters or numbers
ROUTER CRAFTER*	lathe-type accessory for forming decorative furniture legs and posts
WOOD THREADER**	for cutting threads in any species of hard or soft wood—matching taps available
BOWL CRAFTER*	used with router for "turning" projects like bowls, goblets, plates, trays, boxes with fitted lids
*Sears (Craftsman) product	**Beall Tool Company

Fig. 1-2. Quick look at portable router accessories. Some, like bits, edge guides, circle cutting guides, and jigs for forming accurate joints, are essential, others you may choose to do without. Much depends on the scope of your router woodworking.

3

Fig. 1-3. The portable router consists of a motor and a base. The units are usually purchased together but they are offered separately by many manufacturers. Many users have an extra motor for use in a fixed position in a commercial or homemade jig.

is doing. This might not be a problem when the router is mechanically guided through a cut, but it is a nuisance when the router is guided freehand and the operator must follow a line. The fact that a company like Porter-Cable is now offering the see-through bases that are shown in Fig. 1-5 as accessories might indicate that manufacturers are listening.

A solution that is available to anyone is to make substitute subbases using a material like clear polycarbonate plastic. Acrylic-type plastics don't work too well because they scratch easily. The best material to use is available under the name "Lexan." It is shatterproof and scratch-resistant and, with an occasional cleaning with an antistatic cleaning solution formulated especially for plastics, will stay clear and last as long as any conventional subbase.

To make see-through subbases, use the original subbase as a pattern size and a template for locating the attachment screw holes. Countersink or counterbore the holes so attach-

ment screws do not project below the bottom surface of the homemade unit.

I have quite a few Lexan subbases in the shop. Many are duplicates of original equipment while others are designed for special applications. Those shown in Fig. 1-6 provide span support for the router when doing jobs like hollowing a tray. I usually increase the diameter of the center hole so I'm prepared to use bits that have a larger-than-normal cutting circle.

THE GRIPPING END

Router bits are secured with a chuck, usually a split-collet type, that is attached at the free end of the motor spindle (Fig. 1-7). The collet compresses around the shank of the bit when a threaded locknut is tightened. Sometimes two wrenches are required: one to hold the spindle still while the other turns the locknut. Some routers are equipped with a spindle lock. A lever or push button or some similar mechanism is used to hold the spindle in a fixed position so that only a single wrench, to turn the locknut, is needed.

Router sizes are usually called out in terms of horsepower, but it's the size of the collet that determines the maximum shank size of cutters that can be used. Small routers with a 1/4-inch collet are limited to cutters with 1/4-inch shanks, while larger units with 1/2-inch collets can handle larger bits. Often, a heavy router can be equipped with collets of different size, say 1/4 and 1/2 inch, or even 1/4, 3/8, and 1/2 inch. It's a feature to think about if your work scope covers a broad range of applications. Many production-type bits and special ones like those designed for use in a router/shaper setup have 1/2-inch shanks. Being able to handle heavy cutters as well as smaller shanked ones contributes much to router versatility.

A poor practice that can lead to injury is trying to increase depth of cut by not inserting the shank of the cutter as far into the collet as it should go. The standard procedure is to insert the shank as far as it will go and then retract it 1/16 to 1/8 inch before securing the locknut. Depth of cut is always controlled by the height position of the motor housing in the base. Be sure the shank of the cutter, the collet, and the locknut are clean.

HANDLES

Full-size routers are designed for a two-hand grip, but there is a lot of variation in the size, shape, and even the placement of handles. It's

Fig. 1-4. The base of the tool has a removable subbase that is usually an opaque black plastic. On many operations, the opacity of the subbase interferes with seeing what the cutter is doing, which is why it's a good idea to have several see-through substitutes on hand.

5

Fig. 1-5. Objections to standard opaque subbases seem to be getting through to manufacturers. A start in the right direction has been made by Porter-Cable. These transparent units are offered as accessories.

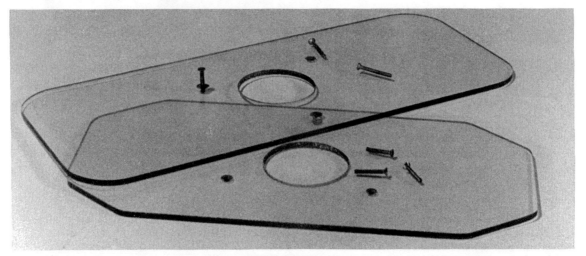

Fig. 1-6. If you can't buy them, make them. These extra-span subbases are made of Lexan, a shatterproof, scratch-resistant plastic that is available in many thicknesses. The original subbase was used as a template for locating the attachment holes.

Fig. 1-7. Bits are secured with a split collet that grips the shank of the cutter when a locknut is turned. Never try to use a cutter with a shank diameter that is smaller than the collet it is designed to take. Some routers can be used with various collet sizes.

a moot point whether handle styles will be a decisive factor when evaluating a router, but many expert users have preferences. It doesn't hurt to take a look at some typical designs.

The Milwaukee unit in Fig. 1-8 has husky, open-top handles placed low on the tool's base. Although the shape of the handles might differ—some units will have knobs—this is fairly typical. A possible disadvantage is that low-placed handles can cause some interference when the tool is guided along a straight edge, or when the edge of the subbase must be moved along a special template. Solutions include using a thinner material as a guide so the handle can pass over it, rotating the router about 90 degrees so there is no interference, or when possible, removing one of the handles. One of the favorable points advanced for low-placed handles is that the operator can get wrists and forearms flat on the bench and have better control when doing freehand work. Figure 1-9 shows a Porter-Cable tool with man-size control knobs positioned close to the base. Here the knobs can be removed, providing the best of two worlds.

In some cases the placement of the handles is affected by how the tool functions. The Black & Decker unit in Fig. 1-10 is a plunge router so handles are affixed to the motor housing because they are used to control the vertical movement of the tool. The design of the Makita tool

7

in Fig. 1-11 seems to oppose the view that low-placed handles provide better control. The handles are integral with the motor housing so, to some extent, their height above the work is affected by the depth-of-cut setting. Handles so placed, and spreading so wide beyond the motor, can be a nuisance in tight areas and might be in the way when making homemade jigs and fixtures. An advantage of this particular unit is the placement of the on-off switch in one of the

Fig. 1-8. Heavy-duty, 1 1/2-horsepower Milwaukee router has sturdy, open-top handles. The 8 1/2-pound unit has a no-load speed of 24,500 rpm and can be used with 1/4-, 3/8-, and 1/2-inch collets. Note the position of the slide switch and the flat top for steady positioning when changing bits.

Fig. 1-9. Porter-Cable 1 1/2-horsepower tool has removable, knobtype handles located low on the base. Being able to use just one handle, or none, can be an asset at times. This router turns at 22,000 rpm and can be used with three different size collets. Its net weight is 8 3/4 pounds.

handles. This allows starting with both hands firmly on the tool and with the router placed where you wish to start the cut.

Top-side handles are not standard on Makita routers. The unit in Fig. 1-12 has a "D"

handle plus a removable auxiliary knob. Good size "D" handles contribute a solid, secure feeling when the router is used, and they have the further advantage of usually containing a trigger on-off switch. A point against "D" handles made

9

by some operators is that the design can interfere with adapting the tool for use with a router table. This might apply to ready-made router/shaper tables, but when you make your own (see Chapter 12 "The Router as a Shaper"), the problem is solved by routing a groove to accommodate the handle.

There is more to router makeup than discussed so far. Figures 1-13 and 1-14, which are from Craftsman (Sears) Owner's Manuals, identify other router features. There is a point to be made here. Routers are the same, yet can be so different in the way depth-of-cut adjustments

are made, switch locations, how cutters are secured, how the base is locked, and so on. How a router is used and the extent of its applications might be universal, but the instructions that are supplied with the router should be bible for that particular unit. Study and restudy the Owner's Manual so you can appreciate and work hand in hand with the unit or units you own. Impatience is not conducive to good work procedures.

SIZE, POWER, SPEED

Routers differ not only in physical size and

Fig. 1-10. Black & Decker's 1 1/2-horsepower unit has man-size, pass-through handles. The trim-looking tool weighs 8 1/4 pounds and has a speed of 25,000 rpm. Features include a spindle lock, built-in work light, handle trigger switch, and a removable chip deflector.

Fig. 1-11. Makita's 3/4-horsepower 23,000-rpm router has top-side handles that are integral with the motor housing. Contoured handles provide a comfortable grip, but location and spread can interfere on some operations. The 5-pound tool has a handle switch and can be used with 3/8-inch or 1/4-inch collets.

weight (Fig. 1-15), but in horsepower and in motor speed, which is called out as *revolutions per minute* or simply *rpm*. High speed, which can range from 15,000 rpm to better than 30,000 rpm, is traditional with portable routers and takes the credit for the smooth cuts you expect. Theoretically, the higher the speed, the smoother the cut. A router spinning a cutter at 30,000 rpm makes twice as many cuts through a given inch or foot of work as a tool that works at 15,000 rpm.

But there are assumptions. The routers must be similar in horsepower, they must be moved through the cut at the same feed-speed, and they must be turning identical bits. It would not be fair for comparisons to move one tool faster than he other or to have one tool turning a single-flute bit while the other works with a double-flute bit. A double-flute bit makes twice as many cuts per revolution as a single-flute bit.

Feed speed has to do with how fast you

11

Fig. 1-12. "D" handles, like the one on this Makita 1 3/8-horsepower tool, are popular because they provide a solid, secure feeling. Another advantage is that they usually have a built-in trigger switch. This 8-pound tool has a speed of 23,000 rpm and can work with 1/4-, 3/8-, and 1/2-inch cutter-shank diameters. The guide shown with the tool is an optional accessory.

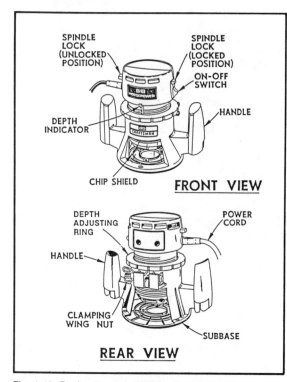

Fig. 1-13. Basic nomenclature of a router. Routers are similar but have different operational features. Studying the Owner's Manual is essential for efficient use of the tool.

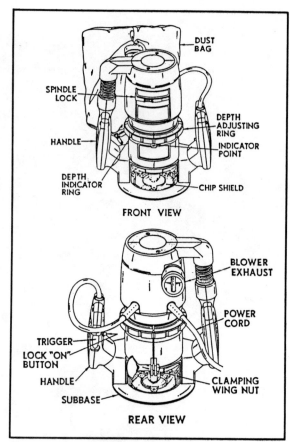

Fig. 1-14. Nomenclature of another router design. This one includes a dust collection system.

move the router through the cut. For example, if you moved the router at X feet per minute, it would make more cuts per inch of work than if you moved it 2X feet per minute.

Speed is important, but it's the horsepower of the tool that is the crucial factor when considering deep cuts, heavy cuts, and cuts through tough, dense materials. It's unfair to assume that the 5/8-horsepower unit shown in Fig. 1-16 could stand up to the operational "torture" that the 3-horsepower production router shown in Fig. 1-17 could abide. It's a mistake to think that high speeds go along with impressive horsepower. Often, the reverse is true. Some light-duty, low-horsepower routers have speeds of 30,000 rpm while bigger brothers turn a cutter at 20,000 to 25,000 rpm.

Fig. 1-15. The "big" and "small" of it. The 3-horsepower unit on the left weighs almost 19 pounds. The more easily handled, 7/8-horsepower one on the right weighs 7 pounds. Each one, and others that fall between, play important roles in the portable router picture. The extent to which you plan to use the tool is the crucial factor when making a choice.

The point, operationally, is that no router, or any power tool for that matter, should be subjected to stresses it was not designed for. If you insist on making a router work beyond its capacity, the results will be poor and the motor will fail before its time. This doesn't mean that low-horsepower routers should be ignored. Much depends on the extent of your workshop interests. If your interests are more toward gardening or golf, and you do woodworking when you must or are occasionally inclined to, then a light-duty product will be a good choice. The small tool can, when necessary, even emulate larger ones by adapting special procedures. For example, while a husky router might be able to cut a 1/2-inch wide × 1/2-inch deep dado or groove

in a single pass, a smaller unit can do the same by making repeat passes; that is, cutting to the same depth by going over the cut several times, an additional 1/8-inch or so with each pass. Each cut allows the tool to work efficiently. You get there, it just takes more time.

SWITCH LOCATION

Most routers have either a trigger-type switch located in a handle (Fig. 1-18) or a toggle, rocker, or slide mechanism placed somewhere on the body of the motor (Figs. 1-19 and 1-20). There are pros and cons, sometimes arguments, about the best location, with the major objection to motor-mounted switches having to do with safety.

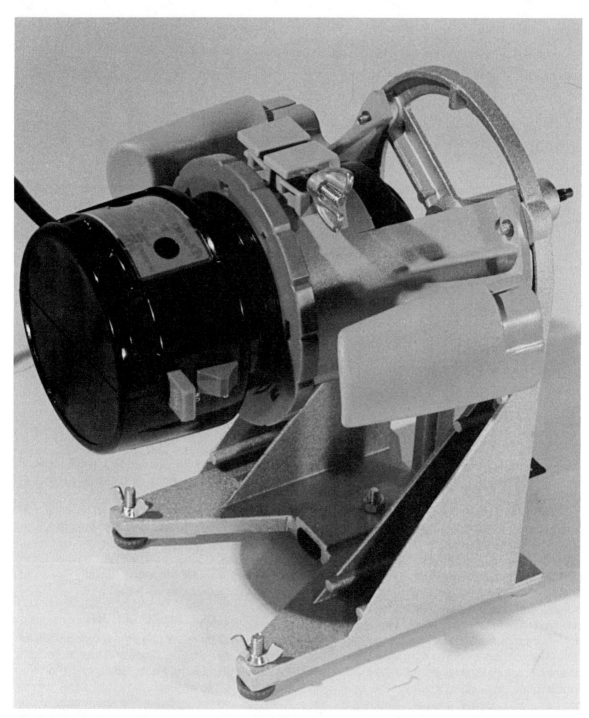

Fig. 1-16. This Craftsman 5/8-horsepower, light-duty router can't be expected to do the work of a powerful production model, but it's more than adequate for what it was designed to do. It turns at 25,000 rpm and works with 1/4-inch diameter bits. It's shown here mounted for use with a "Bowl Crafter," a major router accessory offered by Sears.

Fig. 1-17. The router to carve mountains with. This 18 3/4-pound, 3-horsepower machine can stand up to any kind of router work. Microprocessor-controlled electronics provide maximum torque at five selectable speeds that range from 10,000 to 22,000 rpm. A tool-mounted data chart tells what speed to use for general routing and when working on materials like plastics and nonferrous metals.

When the switch is located in a handle, the tool can be placed in firm operating position before it is activated. It can also be turned off and on at will during the procedure without relaxing your grip on the machine. Also, it's easier to oppose the motor's initial starting torque, which is generally characteristic of routers, when both hands are in holding position.

A disadvantage, unless the unit is equipped with two switches, is that it is difficult, if at all possible, to use the motor independently of the base. Separating the components is necessary

Fig. 1-18. 1 1/2-horsepower, 25,000-rpm Craftsman unit has a dust collection system. Waste is sucked up through a handle and into a top-side bag. The 9 3/4-pound tool has a trigger switch in one handle, a shaft lock, a removable chip deflector, and an internal work light.

when the motor alone is used somewhat like a high-speed grinder and when it is adapted for use in homemade jigs and in some commercial accessories.

Probably the switch arrangement that gets the most criticism is one that can't be used unless the operator removes one hand from the tool. This means that the starting torque must be opposed, and the tool's work position held firm, with one hand. Another thought is that the switch could inadvertantly be in the "on" position when the tool is plugged in. There's logic here, but it seems to be a moot point with amateur and professional router users. For one thing, knowing the characteristics of a particular tool is essential for using it safely and correctly. For another, a basic safety rule that applies to any power tool is to check the on-off switch before connecting to a power source. The word "inadvertant" in this case simply means forgetting that power tools can cut you as well as wood.

There are routers, like the Milwaukee unit displayed in Fig. 1-8, where the motor-mounted switch is placed where it can be reached without relaxing the basic grip. The thumb on the hand gripping the right-side handle can reach up to move the slide switch.

PLUNGE ROUTERS

Plunge routers are "in." If you have ever used

16

any conventional router to form a mortise or a stopped dado or groove, operations where the cutter must form its own starting hole, you'll quickly recognize the advantage of doing the job with a plunge router. A common technique with a nonplunging router is to hold the tool so its base is at an angle to the work surface and then slowly tilt it to get the bit started and until the base is in normal position. There's room here for human error and the safety factor of a projecting bit to consider.

The plunge router moves vertically, usually on posts that are part of the base. Thus it can be firmly planted on the work and pressed down so that the bit enters the work at 90 degrees. The distance the bit projects can be preset and maintained accurately with a level after full penetration. Because the units are spring loaded, the

Fig. 1-19. Toggle switches, like the one on this very popular, 7/8-horsepower, 22,000-rpm tool, are found on many routers. The point against them has to do with safety. The important safety factor is knowing the characteristics of the tool and using it accordingly.

Fig. 1-20. Some people also consider slide switches, like the side-mounted one on this 1-horsepower, 30,000-rpm router, as unsafe as toggle switches. Actually, on some routers, the nontrigger type switches *can* be reached without removing a hand from the grip position.

bit is easily retracted when the cut is complete simply by using the same lever.

Some of the tools have a turret-type device that allows presetting to several cut depths. This is an asset when it's necessary to make a few passes to achieve a particular depth of cut or, for example, when a project requires dadoes of different depths.

Plunge routers are relatively new to us, and those that were initially introduced were more costly than conventional designs. But they are exciting tools and interest is growing. Even at this writing, there are choices in price, horsepower, and physical size (see Figs. 1-21, 1-22, and 1-23).

A good conventional router *plus* a plunge router make a great team. If you are interested in a single-router shop and wish to check out a plunging tool, consider other pertinent router factors. Can the motor be separated from the base? Can the tool be adapted for use in a router/shaper table? What are its capacities?

ELECTRONICS

Routers haven't reached the point where they can function as independent robots, but many manufacturers are now thinking electronically and installing chips that help protect the router from abuse while guiding the user toward more efficient handling. A Black & Decker 1 1/2-horsepower, plunge-type router provides a digital display with a depth-of-cut readout that can "talk" to you in either English or metric. The Porter Cable unit that was shown in Fig. 1-17 provides maximum torque at five selectable speeds that range from 10,000 rpm to 22,000 rpm. A tool-mounted data chart suggests the most efficient speed in relation to the cutter and the material being worked on.

Fig. 1-21. Ryobi's 1-horsepower, 24,000-rpm plunge router has a 1/4-inch collect capacity and can make a plunge cut to 2 inches. Turret control allows presetting for three different cutting levels. The almost 6-pound tool has a handle-located switch and is supplied with an edge guide and a template guide.

Fig. 1-22. Ryobi's 2 1/4-horsepower, 22,000-rpm plunge router can be used with 1/4-, 3/8-, and 1/2-inch router bit shanks. A scale on the side of the tool is used to preset for a particular plunge depth. Maximum plunge depth on the 9.7-pound tool is 2 3/8 inches. Standard equipment includes three bit adapters, a template guide, roller attachment, and an edge guide.

The Craftsman electronic router shown in Fig. 1-24 features a display panel with touch controls. The tool's speed can be set to any of four material hardnesses and cutter size selections. The tool tells you if you are cutting too fast or too slow and alerts you to an overload condition.

A good feature on some of the electronic routers is a slow, "soft start." The motor accelerates smoothly to its operating speed without the initial starting torque that's characteristic of conventional units.

You will probably see more electronic controls on all power tools in the future, and you will profit from them. Nevertheless, it's nice to know that the tool can do only what you wish it to.

TRIMMERS

Trimmers are designed specifically for working on plastic laminates, but there is nothing wrong with viewing them as palm-size routers. In fact,

for some router work, like freehand signmaking, detailed carving, and some operations where it is convenient to use the motor without the base, the small units are easier to control than full-size routers. All of the products are light in weight, in the area of 3 to 4 pounds, and operate at speeds as high as 30,000 rpm. Some are actually miniature routers while others have features

Fig. 1-23. Among the big fellows in the plunge router area is Makita's 12.5-pound, 3-horsepower, 23,000-rpm unit. The 2 1/2-inch plunge capacity tool features a multiple depth adjustment mechanism and a shaft lock. It comes equipped with 1/2-, 3/8-, and 1/4-inch collet sleeves.

Fig. 1-24. You can "talk" to this new Craftsman router and it can "talk" back. The unit contains an electronic microprocessor that maintains a set speed under loaded conditions. The touch control panel sets the speed in relation to four material hardnesses and cutter sizes. The tool has a soft start and tells you when you are feeding too fast or too slow.

that make them particularly suitable for anyone, amateur or professional, doing a lot of work installing plastic laminates (Fig. 1-25). While motor design is similar, different base features make units particularly suitable for special oper-

ations. For example, a tilting base is fine for trimming odd angled corners that are less or more than 90 degrees, while an offset drive spindle makes it possible to trim in or out of 90-degree corners.

Fig. 1-25. An array of 3.8-amp Porter-Cable trimmers. They weigh from about 3 to less than 5 pounds, work at speeds in the area of 28,000 rpm, and have a motor diameter of 3 inches. All of them have a 1/4-inch collet capacity. The one on the left is much like a miniature standard router, while the others have special operational features. The center one can be tilted. The third one has an offset drive spindle so it can be moved in or out of 90-degree corners.

The idea that trimmers can often be used like full-size routers is indicated by some manufacturers who offer router-type accessories as standard equipment or at extra cost (Fig. 1-26). The base of the tool is designed to accept an edge guide, which is used to guide the unit when making a cut parallel to an edge. The trimmer guide, mounted as shown in Fig. 1-27, is used for laminate trimming.

BASIC EQUIPMENT

I like to make a distinction between router accessories, items you can choose to do without, and basic equipment that is necessary for routine router operation. Basic equipment, in addition to router bits, includes edge guides, trimming guides, and when applicable, additional collets. You're limited to a single bit shank diameter when the router is designed to work only with a 1/4-inch collet. Larger tools, like the one in Fig. 1-28 which has a 1/2-inch capacity, are usually able to handle smaller collets as well. Sometimes basic equipment includes an extra collet, but it's often necessary to spend more money to acquire additional ones.

The fact also applies to edge guides, examples of which are displayed in Figs. 1-29 and 1-30. Special multipurpose guides like the Black & Decker unit in Fig. 1-31 are always extra-cost items. This one lets you do more than cut parallel to an edge. It can be used for edge-decorating discs, forming circular grooves and arcs, even for some planing.

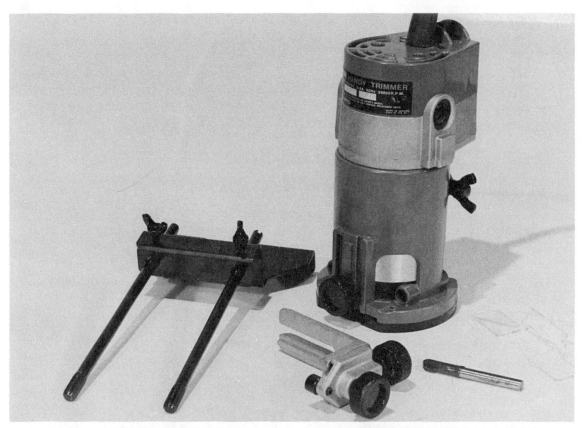

Fig. 1-26. Ryobi recognizes that a trimmer like its 3-pound 3.8-amp, 29,000-rpm unit can often function like a full-size router. As standard equipment, they provide an edge guide in addition to the roller guide that is used when trimming plastic laminates. Other accessories include template guides and high-speed steel or tungsten carbide cutters.

Some suppliers offer the router alone or the same router in kit form. The Wen router kit in Fig. 1-32 includes a 2/3-horsepower router and base plus an edge and circle cutting attachment, a straight bit, and a trimming accessory. Thus, while you're not extensively equipped, you can do some preliminary work right away. Another factor is that kits are usually cheaper than the total sum of the pieces when purchased separately.

THE DREMEL MOTO-TOOL

The Dremel Moto-Tool (Fig. 1-33), as the manufacturer states, is "A special tool for special jobs." Even the originator would be averse to classifying it as a "router." Any owner trying

Fig. 1-27. This is the way the trimming guide for the Ryobi router/trimmer is mounted. The cutting diameter of the bit and the outside diameter of the roller that rides against the edge of the work are the same. This is what produces the flush cutting that trimmers are noted for.

Fig. 1-28. Large routers like this 1 1/2-horsepower Porter-Cable unit with a 1/2-inch collet capacity can usually handle collets of different size. Sometimes an extra collet is provided as standard equipment. Other times they are offered as extra-cost accessories. This tool weighs 11 pounds and runs at 23,000 rpm.

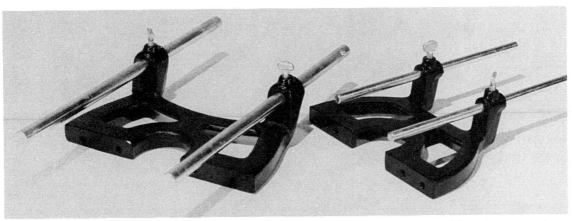

Fig. 1-29. This is what edge guides look like, although some are not manufactured as sturdily. Edge guides are not interchangeable, not even from tool to tool from the same manufacturer. So check for compatibility with the tool you own before you buy.

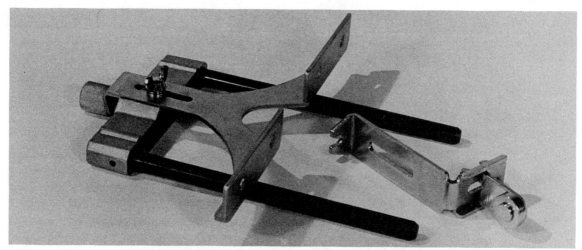

Fig. 1-30. This three-piece Ryobi accessory features an edge guide that can be replaced with a roller guide. Thus, the one tool can be used to guide a router along straight or curved edges and even for some trimming.

to use it for full-size router applications would be disappointed and would have a burned-out tool on his hands. Yet if the operator accepts its horsepower limitations and agrees that the proper way to use the tool is to combine its high speed with a light touch, allowing the cutter, not *force*, to do the work, the Moto-Tool alone or with accessories (like those shown in Figs. 1-34 and 1-35) can function like its larger counterparts. For getting into tight places or shaping the details required on sculptures (Fig. 1-36), the Moto-

Tool, which handles almost like a pencil, has few equals.

To understand the Dremel product, compare it with an electric drill. The drill is a relatively low-speed but high-torque tool. In order to form a hole, the drill must be applied with some pressure. The Moto-Tool is a high-speed, low-torque tool. To use it efficiently, you utilize a high-speed/cutter combination. Applying excessive pressure would simply slow up the tool. Keeping the cutter in position and guiding it, al-

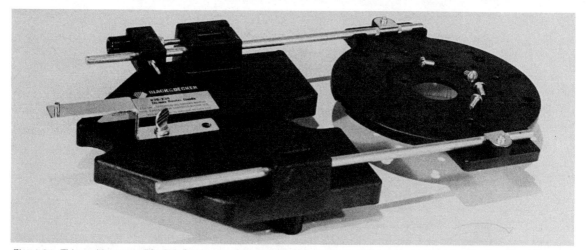

Fig. 1-31. This multipurpose Black & Decker product is designed so the router can be secured to the disc. It can be used as a guide on straight or circular edges and includes an adjustable pivot point for cutting discs or forming circular grooves.

Fig. 1-32. Some manufacturers offer routers in kit form and might even include a storage case. This Wen example includes a double-insulated, 2/3-horsepower, 25,000-rpm router plus edge and circle cutting attachments, a typical straight bit, and a veneer trimming unit.

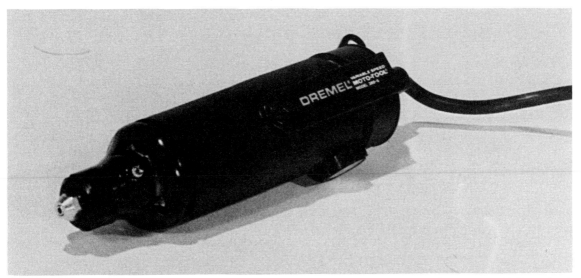

Fig. 1-33. The Dremel Moto-Tool is actually a high-speed grinder, but it can do router operations you wouldn't care to attempt with a full-size tool. It is available in single-speed models (about 30,000 rpm) or with variable speeds covering a range between 4,000 and 25,000 rpm.

Fig. 1-34. The Moto-Tool can be equipped with various accessories that make it more suitable for router-type operations. Among them is this base which has a knob-adjusted, depth-of-cut control.

Fig. 1-35. The accessory base provides for an edge guide that is used exactly like the edge guides on full-size routers. The same depth-of-cut rule applies. When necessary, arrive at full depth of cut by making repeat passes.

Fig. 1-36. The Moto-Tool is ideal for the detail work required on projects like this.

Fig. 1-37. These are typical accessories that are available for the Dremel product. With them you can carve, polish, sand, clean, drill, do cutoff work, and more. For efficient Moto-Tool use, it's critical to remember that it's speed that does the work, not heavy pressure.

lowing it to cut at its own pace, is the way to go.

Currently, the 1/8-inch and 3/32-inch collets for the Moto-Tool accommodate all cutting accessories (Fig. 1-37). These include high-speed burrs and tungsten carbide cutters, grinding points, miniature router bits, steel saws, cutting wheels, wire brushes, polishing wheels, and more. There are also major accessories like those pictured in Fig. 1-38. Thus the tool can be used like a small drill press or held firmly at almost any angle so work can be applied to the cutting tool.

Fig. 1-38. Accessories like this drill press and tool holder help make the Moto-Tool the versatile product it is. These units have been in my shop for a long time. Newer ones have a modern look and additional features.

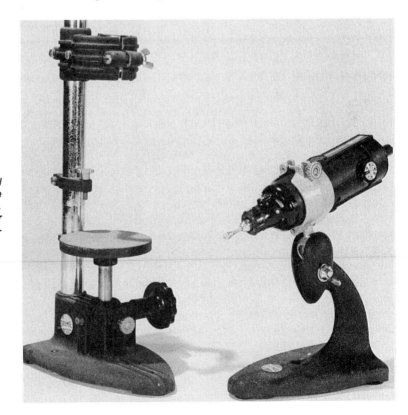

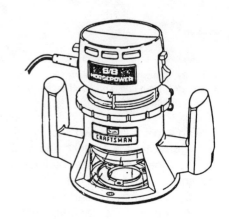

Chapter 2

Safety

"IT WON'T HAPPEN TO ME," IS OFTEN THE FIRM conviction of people who neglect to wear a seat belt when driving, feel a safety line when climbing a cliff is excess precaution, point a knife toward themselves when cutting, and who generally feel that taking measures to avoid injury is only for the accident prone. There is also the person who, because of initial respect and fear of a tool, starts right, but becomes complacement to danger as he acquires expertise. Records maintained by safety organizations prove that as many, if not more, professionals are hurt using power tools as amateurs. The point is that practice and expertise with a tool that grows with experience does not make you immune to injury. Safety is as much in the mind as it is in the tool and in correct procedures. Accepting that there is danger in a workshop is not different from being aware of the potential hazards of everyday life.

Tools are indifferent to what you present for them to cut. They can't think for you.

GENERAL SAFETY RULES

The safety equipment that is displayed in Fig. 2-1 should be standard equipment in all shops. It isn't difficult to convince workers about the logic of safety goggles, but the long-range effects of dust, and especially noise, are often overlooked.

Don't depend on prescription glasses for eye protection. Most safety goggles are made so they can be worn over lens you normally wear. Don't store the goggles where it will be a nuisance to get them. Keep them exposed as a constant reminder.

The word "dust" leads many workers into thinking that dust masks are worn only when sanding, but many woodworking tools, including routers, produce waste particles that should not enter your nose and lungs. Keep the filter in the mask clean; replace it as often as necessary.

OSHA (The Occupational Safety and Health Act) sets safety standards for business. One of

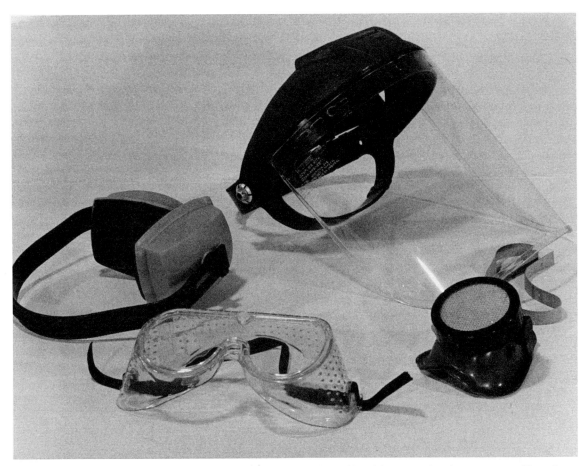

Fig. 2-1. Shown here are safety goggles, a face mask, a dust mask, and headphone-type hearing protectors. These items are as important to your safety and health as following operational procedures correctly. View them as important workshop equipment and use them—don't just store them!

these standards is that a worker's exposure time to power equipment must be in relation to the level of noise frequency. The higher the sound frequency, the shorter the time a worker should be exposed to it. OSHA isn't looking over your shoulder in a home workshop, but the rule is important enough for all of us to obey voluntarily.

The damaging effects of high frequencies, especially those produced by routing and shaping operations, are cumulative. Every prolonged exposure affects hearing—perhaps to a tiny degree, but it can build up to where hearing loss is obvious. Then it's too late to use a protective device. You don't want to block out sound completely. Good headphone-type hearing protectors, preferably of lightweight plastic, screen out hazardous frequencies while still allowing normal conversation. They also don't block out woodworking noises you should hear that might warn you of a malfunctioning tool or an incorrect operational procedure.

UNAUTHORIZED USE

Power tools are tempting items to children, and even some adults can't resist flicking a switch out of curiosity. Unplug the tool when you aren't using it. Store tools in cabinets, preferably ones that can be locked.

SHOPKEEPING AND SHOP DRESS

It's wise to have a special uniform for shop work. Trousers and shirts that fit snugly and nonslip shoes with steel toes make sense. Don't wear gloves or a necktie or any article of clothing that can catch on an idle tool or one that is in use. You don't need jewelry in a workshop. Wristwatches, bracelets, rings, and any other adornments should be removed. Cover your hair, for safety and protection against dust, regardless of whether it is long or short.

A clean environment contributes to better work as well as safety. Maintain benches, tools, and accessories in pristine condition. Don't allow waste to accumulate on a workbench. Litter and wood scraps on the floor are dangerous slipping or tripping hazards. It's a good idea to have a wide shop broom and a shop-type vacuum cleaner and to use them frequently.

SHOP PRACTICE

Don't overreach, no matter what tool you are using or what the operation is. It's very important to maintain firm footing and good balance at all times.

Don't work with dull cutting bits because they make it necessary to use more pressure to move the tool. This creates a situation where your hands might slip.

Disconnect the tool when it's necessary to change cutters or to add an accessory. Don't leave a power tool running when you turn to another chore regardless of how little time is involved. With a router, let the bit come to a stop before you set the tool down on its side or, if applicable, on its top.

Don't use tools as if they were stepladders. Serious injuries can result from slipping on a smooth surface or if the tool tips over. It's not likely that you will step on a portable router to stand taller, but I assume there will be other tools in the shop.

Recognize as a warning any operation where it becomes necessary to force a cutting action. Usually it indicates that the cutting tool is too dull or that you are trying to make a cut that is too deep for the tool to handle. Even super-horsepower routers have limits, so it's good practice to accomplish extra deep or oversize cuts by making repeat passes.

Socializing and tool use are a bad combination. Visitors should not be welcome when you are using tools. It's also a good idea to educate friends and neighbors about the danger of barging into your shop when they hear a tool running. The sudden entry can startle you and cause an accident.

Staying alert and keeping your mind on the job are critical safety precautions. Don't do shop work when you are tired or upset or have had an alcoholic drink.

TOOL PRACTICE

Become familiar with the tool *before* using it, whether it's a replacement item or a new addition. Learn the tool's applications and, especially, its limitations. Don't use a tool for operations it was not designed to accomplish efficiently and safely. Most manufacturers warn against using accessories that were not specifically designed for the tools they produce. The admonition doesn't always hold, but it's a good idea to be cautious before being adventurous.

Never work on a piece of wood that is too small to be held or clamped securely. When, for example, you need a small piece with a shaped edge, do the shaping on a large workpiece and then cut off the part you need.

Be sure you know the procedure you must follow before you start an operation. By previewing the chore, you can anticipate possible problems, determine safest hand positions, and plan most efficient feed direction for the tool. Often, and especially with a new procedure, it's wise to go through a dry run; that is, go through the operation but with the tool turned off. Practices like this help make you tool-wise.

Keep the body of the tool and its handles dry and clean and free from oil and grease. Clean tools with a lint-free cloth. Using solvents is not a good idea.

Check all parts of the tool, especially locking mechanisms, periodically to be sure no damage that can interfere with proper, safe operation has occurred. Switches that do not operate correctly should be replaced immediately, preferably by bringing the tool to an authorized service center. This suggestion is especially important if the tool is double insulated.

One of the most important safety factors I know is this—*always be a bit afraid of the tool*. Respect the fact that it is a machine. Whether you are in apprenticeship stages or have advanced to a more knowledgeable plateau, don't ignore that operator responsibility is the main ingredient for a safe workshop.

ELECTRICAL CONSIDERATIONS

Many of the routers that are available today are double insulated. This is a safety concept in electric tools that makes it unnecessary for the tool to have a grounded three-wire power cord. The design of a double-insulated tool provides two complete sets of insulation to protect the user. All exposed metal parts are isolated from the internal metal motor components with protecting insulation.

It is important with tools of this type that servicing be done with extreme care and only by qualified service technicians who have detailed knowledge of the system. An incorrect repair job can nullify the double insulation factor and place the user in danger.

Tools that are not double insulated will have a three-conductor cord and a three-prong grounding plug that is used in a *properly grounded* outlet box. When the tool is designed for use on less than 150 volts, the plug resembles the one shown in Fig. 2-2. The grounding blade, which is longer than the two current carrying prongs, slips into the third, specially shaped hole in the outlet.

An adapter (Fig. 2-3) can be used to connect a three-prong grounding plug to a two-prong receptacle providing that the outlet box is correctly grounded. This adapter is not allowed in Canada. It's recommended that adapters be viewed as temporary measures for use only until a correctly grounded outlet box is installed, preferably by a qualified electrician.

If the tool is designed for use on 150 to 250 volts, the power cord has a plug that has two flat current-carrying prongs in tandem and a grounding blade that might be round or U-shaped. The plug works only with a proper mating, three-conductor grounded receptacle (Fig. 2-4). Adapters are *not* used with plugs of this design.

Never remove the grounding blade from a

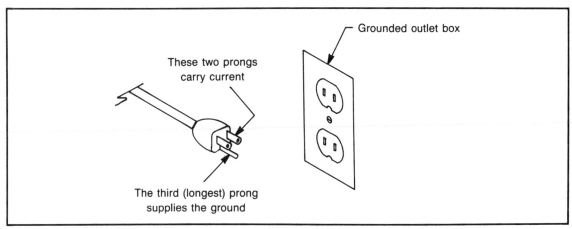

These two prongs carry current

Grounded outlet box

The third (longest) prong supplies the ground

Fig. 2-2. Tools that are not double insulated and are designed for use on less than 150 volts have a plug with two parallel, current-carrying prongs, plus a third one of different design, which is the grounding blade. Don't ever cut off the grounding blade so you can use the plug in a two-hole receptacle.

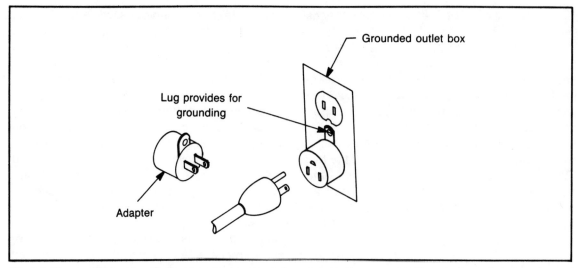

Fig. 2-3. It's possible to use a three-prong plug in a two-hole receptacle if you use this kind of adapter between plug and outlet. *But, this system does not provide protection unless the outlet box is properly grounded.*

three-prong plug so you can use it in a two-prong outlet. That's inviting trouble.

EXTENSION CORDS

The conductor size of an extension cord must be large enough to prevent an excessive voltage drop that will force the tool to work with less power and that can damage the motor. Recommended extension cord sizes in relation to

length and the ampere rating of the tool are shown in Table 2-1. Extension cords that are suitable for outdoor use are marked with the suffix W-A, which follows the designation that tells the type of cord. SJTW-A is a typical example.

SPECIAL CONSIDERATIONS

Safety factors that might apply especially to the portable router will be pointed out as you get into

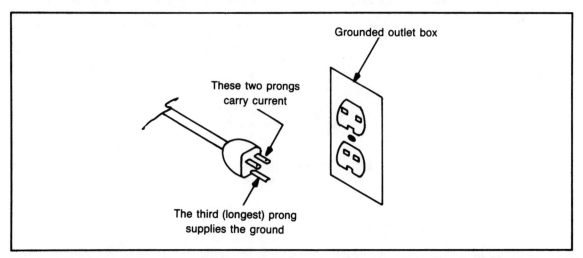

Fig. 2-4. Tools that are designed for use on 150 to 250 volts have this type of plug. It must be used with a proper, mating, three-conductor grounded receptacle. No adapter is available for this plug design.

Table 2-1. Recommended Extension Cord Sizes for Portable Electric Tools.

Voltage	Length of Cord (In Feet)								
115 V	25	50	100	150	200	250	300	400	500
230 V	50	100	200	300	400	500	600	800	1000

Amperage Rating (Check Nameplate)									
0-2	18	18	18	16	16	14	14	12	12
2-3	18	18	16	14	14	12	12	10	10
3-4	18	18	16	14	12	12	10	10	8
4-5	18	18	14	12	12	10	10	8	8
5-6	18	16	14	12	10	10	8	8	6
6-8	18	16	12	10	10	8	6	6	6
8-10	18	14	12	10	8	8	6	6	4
10-12	16	14	10	8	8	6	6	4	4
12-14	16	12	10	8	6	6	6	4	2
14-16	16	12	10	8	6	6	4	4	2
16-18	14	12	8	8	6	4	4	2	2
18-20	14	12	8	6	6	4	4	2	2

using the tool. Briefly . . .

☐ Always check to be sure the collet lock-nut is securely tightened before using the "on" switch. A loose bit can become a harmful projectile.

☐ Be sure the switch is in the "off" position before plugging into a power source.

☐ Don't have the tool plugged in when changing bits, making adjustments, or removing the base. Hold the tool firmly when you turn it off until the bit stops rotating. Then place it on its side with the bit pointing away from you. Don't make a bit change immediately after finishing a cut. The bit might be very hot.

☐ Check workpieces to be sure that nails or other foreign objects are not in the line of cut.

Use carbide-tipped bits when working on non-wood materials like plastics and plastic laminates and on man-made products like particleboard, hardboard, and plywood. High-speed steel bits work alright, but tungsten carbide blades cut smoother and stand up longer under abrasive abuse.

☐ Hold the router securely when you turn it on to oppose the twisting action that occurs. A two-handed grip is preferable. When this isn't possible, be sure to anticipate the initial action and be especially firm with one hand.

☐ Don't make depth-of-cut adjustments while the motor is running.

☐ Be sure the cord is free and can't snag on some nearby object during operation or trail across the cutting path.

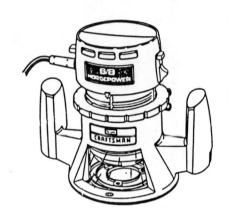

Chapter 3

Router Bits

THE PORTABLE ROUTER IS A FASCINATING TOOL, but on its own it's like an automobile without wheels. Without router bits (Fig. 3-1), it can't do more than whirr. Router bits are the stars of the show and are as intriguing as the tool itself. The number of bits that are available can be bewildering, even intimidating, and others that contribute to the versatility of the router are constantly being added. Among the latest sets to appear are those that allow the router owner to produce all the shapes that are required to make professional paneled doors. The bits, having 1/2-inch diameter shanks, are used with a heavy-duty router that is mounted in a shaper-type table.

Router bits can be placed in specific categories; for example, there are decorative bits and practical or utility bits. What you can accomplish with any bit, however, depends on whether you use it only for what it was designed to do or more creatively. Variations are possible with a single bit by following a first cut with a second one after the depth of cut or width of cut has been changed. The standard shape of one cutter takes on a new look when you repeat the operation using another cutter to add a detail. This kind of work can't be done haphazardly. It's always best to draw on tracing paper the profiles of the cutters you plan to use so results can be previewed by overlaying the drawings.

In the decorative bit area, you will find that the cutters often produce classic molding forms (Fig. 3-2). Here too, you can employ some control to alter results. If the bit is guided by the pilot, you get a full width of cut, but can opt for a depth of cut that puts only part of the cutter's profile into play. The width of the cut can also be varied by ignoring the bit's pilot and moving the router through the cut by using an edge guide. Figure 3-3 shows how shapes formed with decorative cutters and grooves formed with, for example, slotting cutters are combined to fabricate framed panels.

The greater your collection of router bits, the more work you can do with the tool, but buying everything right away would be exorbitant and

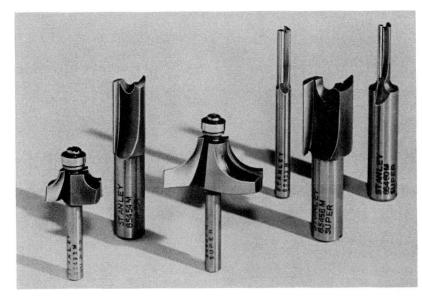

Fig. 3-1. Router bits are essential to portable router use. There are some accessories you can do without, but without bits, you might as well keep the tool displayed on a shelf. This drop-in-the-bucket display of what is available shows a few straight bits and two that have ball bearing pilots.

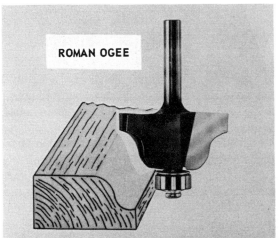

ROMAN OGEE

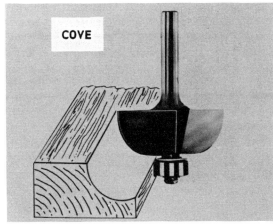

COVE

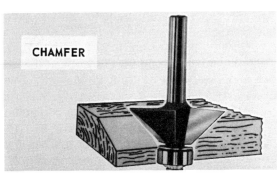

CHAMFER

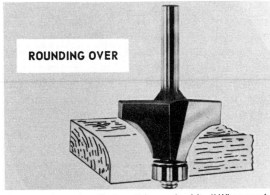

ROUNDING OVER

Fig. 3-2. Many available bits are used to produce classic molding forms and are classified as "decorative bits." When working with these bits, it is not imperative to always use the full profile of the cutter.

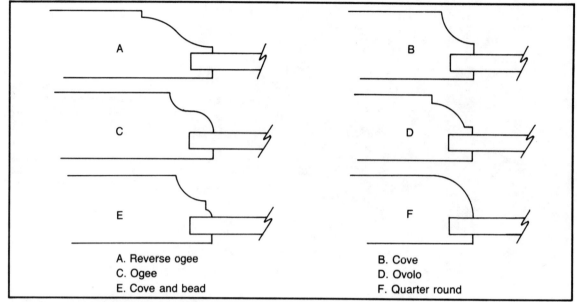

A. Reverse ogee
C. Ogee
E. Cove and bead

B. Cove
D. Ovolo
F. Quarter round

Fig. 3-3. Pieces that have been edge-shaped with decorative cutters are often grooved with slotting cutters, for example, and used as frame components for paneled doors. In this case, the frame is assembled with miter joints so the cope cuts and stile cuts normally associated with paneled doors are not needed.

unnecessary. It's much wiser to begin with some basic bits and occasionally add others as they are needed until the collection is something like the fairly typical one shown in Fig. 3-4. As always, what you buy should be determined by work on hand. For starters, several sizes of straight bits, a couple of decorative bits, with rabbeting and dovetail bits to follow seems to make sense.

TYPES OF ROUTER BITS

Router bits are made of high-speed steel (HSS) or have cutting blades of tungsten carbide, which is a tough, man-made material brazed onto a tool steel base (Fig. 3-5). Tungsten carbide bits can cost two to three times as much as their all-steel brothers, but quality units cut smoother and hold a cutting edge 15 to 25 times longer. Paying more is often logical then, especially for "workhorse" bits. For some router applications, like trimming abrasive materials such as plastic laminate and cutting through or shaping particleboard or hardboard, tungsten carbide

bits are almost mandatory. Better-quality carbide bits have edges that are thick enough to stand up to regrinding as many as fifteen times, while cheaper ones won't take more than four or five. Also, quality units can be retipped, which often costs less than a replacement.

Some small bits, where it might be difficult to braze carbide cutting edges in place, are made of solid carbide (Fig. 3-6). There is a factor to be aware of regarding tungsten carbide. It *is* a very tough material, but it is also brittle. Cutting edges can be chipped if the bits are not carefully stored or are banged against hard surfaces.

Carbide bits are not the only way to go. There is nothing wrong with buying good HSS bits, especially when selecting units you will only use occasionally.

There are other bits that home craftsmen won't use or can't be justified because of cost. Industry is now being offered disposable bits that are extremely low-cost units, when purchased in quantity, that can be discarded when they become dull. Diamond bits are cutters that have

38

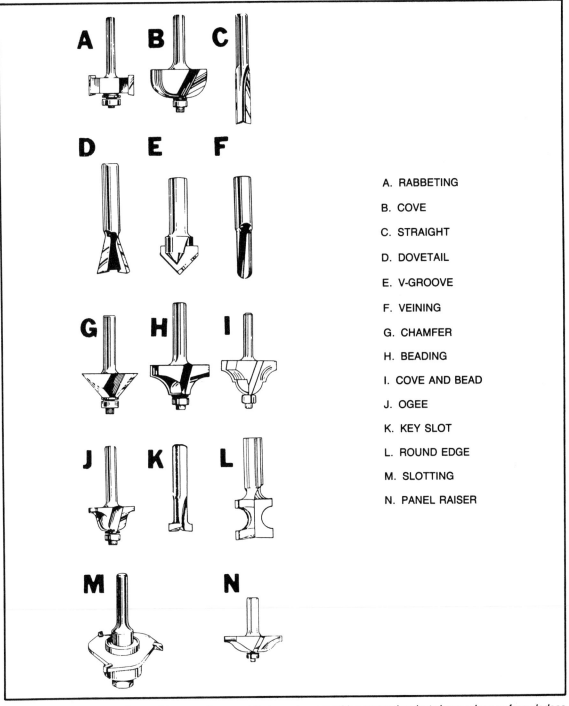

A. RABBETING

B. COVE

C. STRAIGHT

D. DOVETAIL

E. V-GROOVE

F. VEINING

G. CHAMFER

H. BEADING

I. COVE AND BEAD

J. OGEE

K. KEY SLOT

L. ROUND EDGE

M. SLOTTING

N. PANEL RAISER

Fig. 3-4. This assortment of router bits comprises a set that can do more with a router than just shape edges or form dadoes and rabbets. You might start with straight bits and decorative bits, which are good apprenticeship tools, then add rabbeting and dovetail bits later.

Fig. 3-5. The bit on the left, with integral pilot, is made of high-speed steel. The second one, with a ball-bearing pilot, has a tool steel body with brazed-on tungsten carbide blades that keep a keen cutting edge up to 25 times longer than the all-steel unit.

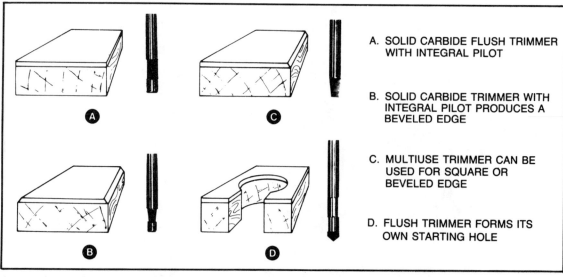

A. SOLID CARBIDE FLUSH TRIMMER WITH INTEGRAL PILOT

B. SOLID CARBIDE TRIMMER WITH INTEGRAL PILOT PRODUCES A BEVELED EDGE

C. MULTIUSE TRIMMER CAN BE USED FOR SQUARE OR BEVELED EDGE

D. FLUSH TRIMMER FORMS ITS OWN STARTING HOLE

Fig. 3-6. Cutters like these, which hold up nicely under the abrasive action of plastic laminates, are often solid carbide. Note that one has a penetrating point so it can pierce like a drill bit when internal cutouts are needed. All are designed to trim a cover material flush with the edge of the core it is mounted on.

polycrystalline diamonds (man-made diamond crystals) bonded by special means onto a carbide base material. This design holds keen cutting edges up to 400 times longer than carbide, so it's cost effective for production work. Would you care to spend $1,000 for, say, a 1/2-inch diameter bit?

BIT DESIGNS

In addition to router bits being grouped in terms of the material they are made of, they enter categories like one-piece units with integral pilots; assemblies that consist of a shank, cutting blade, and screw-on pilot; and those equipped with removable ball-bearing pilots (Fig. 3-7).

The *pilot* on a bit is what is used to guide it through a cut. The router is moved so the pilot bears against the edge of the workpiece throughout the pass. On one-piece bits, the pilot is turning just as fast as the cutting blades and creates considerable friction that often results in discolored work edges. When the operator applies too much pressure to keep the pilot in contact, or pauses somewhere during the pass, the pilot can actually indent the work edge, especially on soft wood. Because the cutting blades follow the travel of the pilot, the occur-rence causes a flaw. A dull cutter exaggerates the potential for errors because more feed pressure is required to keep the router moving. Good practice calls for sharp cutters, a steady feed speed, and only enough pressure against the work edge to keep the pilot in contact.

Ball-bearing pilots (Fig. 3-8) rotate only as fast as you move the router. Thus the trouble-causing friction factor isn't present, which means burn-free edges and less effort on your part to move the tool. There is also the option, often overlooked, of using different diameter bearings. This contributes a degree of control over how wide a cut the bit will make.

Bit assemblies, which consist of the components shown in Fig. 3-9, look exactly like a one-piece bit when the parts are put together (Fig. 3-10). The advantage is that a single interchangeable arbor can be used with a variety of cutting blades. Blades are available in HSS or in carbide-tipped designs. Some of the arbors are made to take solid steel pilots so the assembled unit works like a bit with an integral pilot, others are designed for ball-bearing pilots. In each case, several pilots of different diameter are supplied. Units in this area can be purchased as sets that include the arbor assembly and an assortment of cutters, or you can buy the arbor

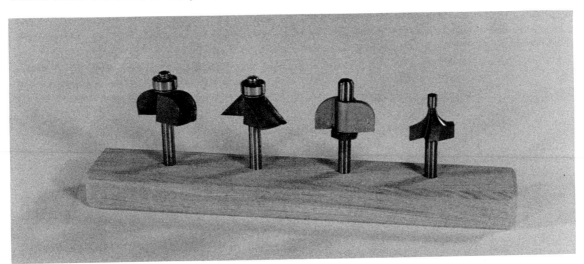

Fig. 3-7. Basic bit designs. From the right, one-piece HSS unit with integral pilot; assembly consisting of arbor, cutter and pilot; and two bits with tungsten carbide blades and ball-bearing pilots.

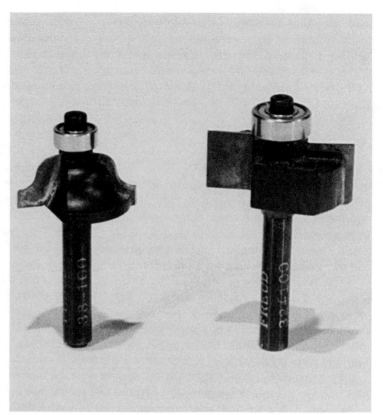

Fig. 3-8. Regardless of the rpm of the cutter, ball-bearing pilots rotate in tune with feed speed, which is how fast you move the router to make a cut. Thus, the friction that is caused by an integral pilot, which turns just as fast as the cutter, is eliminated.

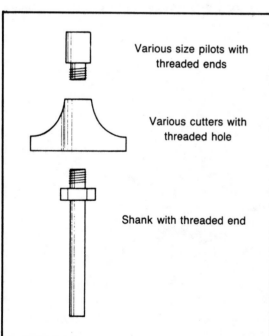

Various size pilots with threaded ends

Various cutters with threaded hole

Shank with threaded end

Fig. 3-9. Typical bit assemblies consist of a shank, or arbor, interchangeable cutters, and pilots. They are available in sets that include various cutters or as components purchased individually, giving you the opportunity to acquire cutters of your choice.

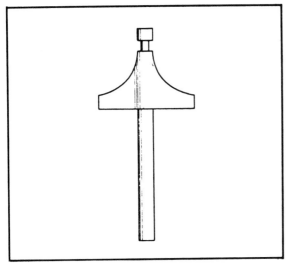

Fig. 3-10. The pilots that are available for router bit assemblies can be solid steel, like this one, in which case the assembled unit works like a bit with integral pilot, or it may be a ball-bearing type. Also, the interchangeable blades can be purchased in HSS or tungsten carbide.

and then choose the cutters you want to use with it.

When using a piloted bit, always make certain that the pilot has sufficient bearing surface against the work edge (Fig. 3-11). This is important for safety as well as for good results. When the depth of cut you need doesn't allow sufficient bearing surface for the pilot, you can compensate by tack-nailing or clamping a piece of stock to the underside of the workpiece.

In order to get professional results when using a piloted bit, be sure the work edge is smooth and free of flaws. The pilot will faithfully follow any roughness, bump, or crevice and guide the cutter to duplicate it. It's also important to be certain that the pilot, integral or otherwise, be smooth and free of any wood residue.

PILOTLESS BITS

An assortment of pilotless bits is shown in Fig.

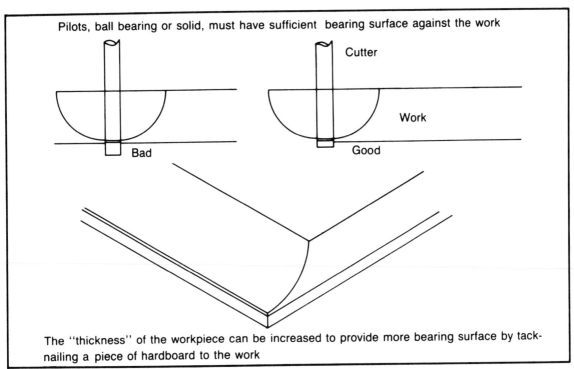

Fig. 3-11. When using a piloted bit, it's important for quality work and safety for the pilot to have sufficient bearing surface against the work edge. The thickness of stock that is too thin for the cut you want plus bearing surface can be increased by using a temporary "riser."

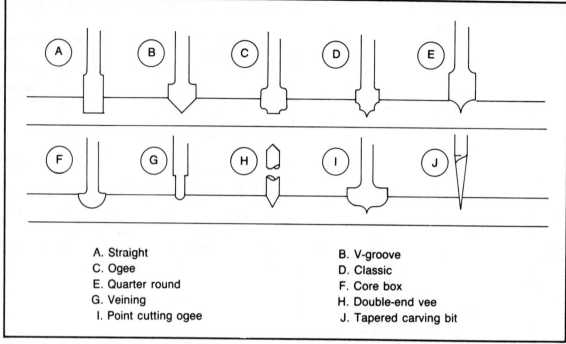

A. Straight
C. Ogee
E. Quarter round
G. Veining
I. Point cutting ogee

B. V-groove
D. Classic
F. Core box
H. Double-end vee
J. Tapered carving bit

Fig. 3-12. Generally, when pilotless bits are used, the router's movement must be controlled with an edge guide or some other improvised means. Bits of this type are often used to form decorative surface cuts.

3-12. Many of these, and others that are not illustrated, can be classified as decorative bits. Some, like straight bits, can be used for fancy grooving, but they are essential for practical applications such as shaping joinery forms like dadoes and rabbets as well. Regardless of the bit's general classification, it's what you are *doing* with a bit that defines it as a decorative or utility cutter. The V-groove bit, which is often used for simple or intersecting surface cuts, can be used to do some chamfering. Bits like the quarter round, ogee, and the core box bit (in the pilotless area) might be classified, as surface-cutting bits, but they can be used to form a decorative detail on an edge so long as the router is properly guided.

What is characteristic of cutters of no-pilot design is that the operation must be organized so the router itself is guided. This can be accomplished by many methods. The simplest and most often used is a commercial edge guide or a straight strip of wood clamped to the work against which the subbase of the router bears as the cut is made.

MAKEUP

Figure 3-13 shows the business end of a router bit and identifies its parts. The cutting circle is the actual working area of the bit. The shank diameter may be the same, but many times it is smaller. A bit with a 1/2-inch cutting circle can have a 1/4-inch shank. When the shank diameter is greater than 1/4-inch, you can assume that the bit should be used in a heavy-duty router.

Shanks on quality bits are fully hardened and precision ground to a tolerance of 0.002. High hook angles plus adequate chip clearance areas (sometimes called *gullets*) provide for cleaner, cooler cutting. Radial relief provides clearance so only the cutting edges of the bits make constant contact with the work. Without it, the bit does as much rubbing as cutting. Bits

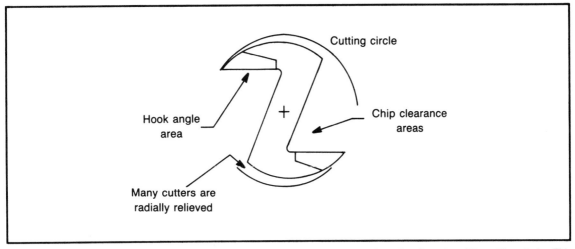

Fig. 3-13. The distance from back edge to back edge on a quality bit is less than the diameter of its cutting circle. This provides radial relief so the bit works with minimum "rubbing."

with carbide inserts must be designed with a wall thickness that adequately backs up the brazed-on blade. The best ball-bearing pilots are double shielded to protect the bearings from dust.

Generally, single-flute bits are stronger than double-flute bits (Fig. 3-14), but assuming some factors like tool rpm and feed speed, they make half as many cuts per inch of work as a double-flute version. Most times the end of the bit is relieved so it can, when necessary, enter the work at a 90-degree angle (plunging).

Stagger tooth bits, like the carbide-tipped example in Fig. 3-15, are designed for balance and strength. They are used extensively by manufacturers of products whose components might be of composition materials like chipboard, particleboard, and plywood.

Other "straight" bits, some of which are just appearing and which are probably of greater interest to industry than the home craftsmen, include:

☐ Bits with concave (O-flutes) that, be-

Fig. 3-14. Single-flute bits have more bulk behind the cutting edge and are generally stronger than double-flute bits so they can be used with faster feed rates, a factor appreciated more by industry than home woodworkers.

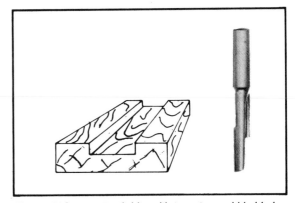

Fig. 3-15. Stagger tooth bits with tungsten carbide blades stand up to the abrasive action that is present when working on materials like particleboard, hardboard, and plywood.

cause of additional strength, can be fed faster through solid wood.

☐ Chip-breaker bits that cut fast through abrasive, dense materials.

☐ Down-cutting or up-cutting spiral bits that push waste to below the work or up to its surface. Spiral bits cut constantly unlike, say, a single-flute bit that makes one cut per revolution.

☐ Shear-cut bits look like straight flute bits but have inclined cutting edges. The manufacturer says that they are very free-cutting and require less horsepower for efficient results.

SIZES

When buying bits, you have a choice not only in configuration but in the size of the cut the bit will produce. Other factors are total length, cutting length, and shank length.

Figures 3-16 and 3-17, which were copied from a Freud catalog, show typical offerings in the area of straight bits and dovetail bits. This also applies to decorative bits. For example, and again quoting from one manufacturer's catalog, the radius of cove bits can start at 3/16 inch and go to 1/2 inch while the large diameter begins with 3/4 inch and ranges to 1 3/8 inches. There must be some compatibility. The smaller the radius of the bit, the smaller its large diameter. A 3/16-inch radius bit will have a large diameter of 3/4 inch, while a 1/2-inch radius bit goes with a large diameter of 1 3/8 inches. Size considerations of other bits, like ogee, beading, and rounding over bits, can be described in similar fashion. In the case of chamfer bits, there may be a choice in the degree of the cut angle, 15, 25, and 45 degrees being fairly common.

Cutting Diameter	Cutting Length	Overall Length	Shank Length
1/8	3/8	1 3/4	1 1/4
3/16	1/2	2	1 1/4
1/4	2	1 1/4	
1/4	3/4	2 1/4	1 1/4
1/4	1	2 1/2	1 1/4
9/32	1	3	1 1/4
5/16	1	2 1/2	1 1/4
5/16	1 1/4	2 3/4	1 1/4
3/8	1	2 1/2	1 1/4
3/8	1 1 1/4	2 3/4	1 1/4
7/16	1	2 1/2	1 1/4
1/2	3/4	2 1/4	1 1/4
1/2	1	2 1/8	1 1/4
9/16	3/4	2 1/8	1 1/4
5/8	3/4	1 1/8	1 1/4
3/4	3/4	2 1/8	1 1/4
1	3/4	2 1/8	1 1/4

Dimensions in Inches

Fig. 3-16. The number of router bits increases because of the various sizes that are available in a single bit design. The cutting diameter is not the only factor to consider.

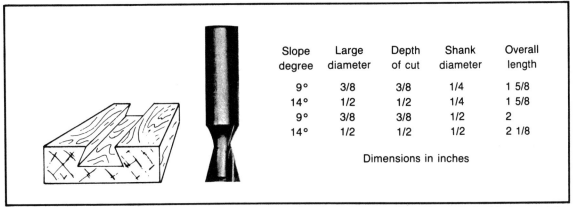

Slope degree	Large diameter	Depth of cut	Shank diameter	Overall length
9°	3/8	3/8	1/4	1 5/8
14°	1/2	1/2	1/4	1 5/8
9°	3/8	3/8	1/2	2
14°	1/2	1/2	1/2	2 1/8

Dimensions in inches

Fig. 3-17. Various sizes are available in most bit designs, including dovetail cutters. Many times, similar bit characteristics are available in 1/4- and 1/2-inch shank diameter units.

BUYING BITS IN SETS

There are advantages to buying bits in sets like the examples shown in Figs. 3-18 and 3-19, and there is a disadvantage. Getting a dozen or so bits at once sets you up pretty nicely for general router operations. The cost of a set is much less than the total price of the same bits purchased individually. Sets come in wood or plastic containers so the bits can be safely stored. A disadvantage is that you may get more bits than your work scope justifies or designs you might ordinarily do without.

There are bits that must be purchased in sets because each bit does a job that is necessary for a satisfactory final result. The Sears Crown Molding Kit shown in Fig. 3-20 is one example. Finding molding in a particular wood species is difficult if not impossible. With an assortment of bits in a set you can custom-make moldings using wood from your wall paneling or

Fig. 3-18. Fifteen bits in a set offered by Freud are either solid carbide or have tungsten carbide blades. Pilots on those tools that require them are ball bearing. The bits are displayed in a storage block, but they are supplied in a handsome wood case.

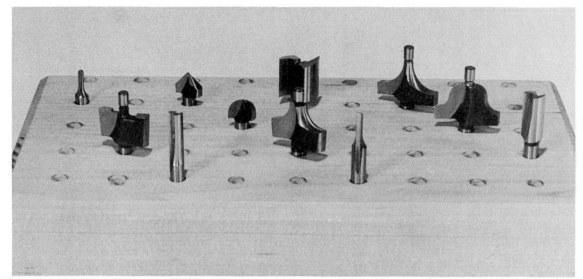

Fig. 3-19. Eleven-piece set of quality HSS bits together with a husky, plastic storage case is offered by Black & Decker. Selected assortment allows router users to perform many standard router operations.

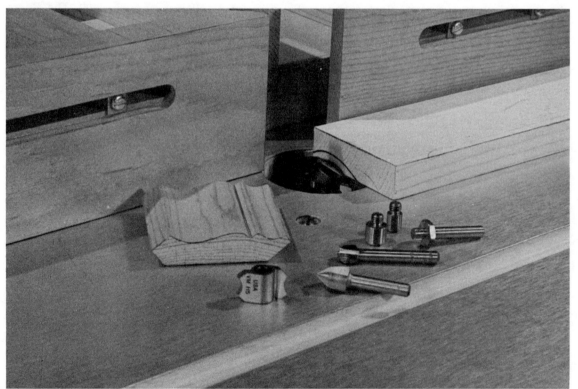

Fig. 3-20. The Sears Crown Molding Kit includes all the cutters required to produce various molding designs. Thus, the woodworker can select a wood species that matches what has been used in a project. The bits must be used in a router/shaper stand.

furniture project. The kit contains bits for V-grooves, end coves, beading and chamfering, cove box, plus an adapter (arbor) and several pilots. Each bit is shaped to form part of a pattern so a sequence of passes, like those in Fig. 3-21, results in a profile that duplicates a standard molding or an exclusive one that you create. The bits *must* be used in a router that is mounted in a router/shaper table. The shank diameter on bits and adapter is 1/4 inch.

Making cope cuts, forming stiles and rails, and producing a particular edge on panels are all cuts that are required in the construction of framed paneled doors and have always been associated with a stationary shaper. Now several manufacturers are offering husky router bits so that anyone with a heavy-duty router can accomplish the same chores in a professional manner. The only catch is that the tool must be used in a router/shaper table, one that you buy or one that you make.

Each of the five cutters in the Freud set shown in Fig. 3-22 does a specific job. The cope and stile cutters are a matched set that is an asset for forming cuts that mate precisely. The set includes a glue joint bit for edge-to-edge joints when the panel is made of solid wood and a door lip bit that is used for a hinged door that overlaps a frame as shown in Fig. 3-23.

Zac Products, Inc., offers "The Door Shop," which consists of the cutters shown in Fig. 3-24. Figure 3-25 is a quick look at how these cutters are used. Note that some of the cutters do double-duty and that where they cut depends on the cutter's height above the table. This permits some variation and also allows working on stock of various thicknesses.

It's important to remember that bits in this area must not be treated lightly. The size of some of them alone should be enough to inspire respect and caution. More about paneled door making in Chapter 12 "The Router as a Shaper."

SPECIAL BITS

I use the word "special" casually for bits that might be needed infrequently and for those that are made for a specific chore. Anyone involved in a considerable amount of work with plastic laminates would not be without carbide-tipped plunge bits and laminate trimmers. Since they are necessary for this work, they can hardly be considered "special." On the other hand, they might be viewed so by the dedicated woodworker who is confronted with a one-time counter-covering job.

The same thought is not so extreme when slotting cutters are involved. The countertop fabricator feels they are necessary for easily forming grooves in countertop edges that will be covered with a press-in metal molding, while the woodworker can make use of them in off-beat fashion in some joint designs. Workers making many projects like picture frames and plaques consider the key slot cutter essential, while others not so involved might make do with a different hanging method.

The router bits shown in Figs. 3-26 through Fig. 3-32, can be considered special or routine. All are interesting, and anyone owning a portable router should be aware of them.

GETTING MORE FROM A BIT

In terms of shapes that can be formed with a single cutter, many bits are multipurpose. When making a full cut, the shape produced is the reverse of the cutter's profile. But with adjustable actions, such as cutter projection (depth of cut) and the width of the cut that can be regulated with guides, you can achieve partial cuts that, in effect, are variations of the full design (Fig. 3-33).

Other examples of bit technique are shown in Figs. 3-34 and 3-35. In one, the cut made on one edge is repeated on the opposite edge. The other illustration shows a cross section of the result when one cut is repeated on all edges of the material.

These few ideas are offered merely to spur you into thinking imaginatively. Using every bit exactly as it was designed places limits on router versatility. In my shop I keep full-size profiles of

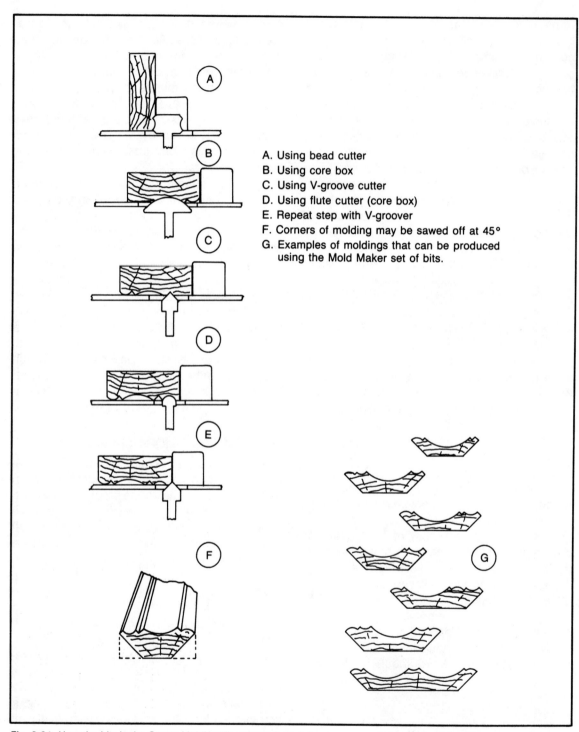

A. Using bead cutter
B. Using core box
C. Using V-groove cutter
D. Using flute cutter (core box)
E. Repeat step with V-groover
F. Corners of molding may be sawed off at 45°
G. Examples of moldings that can be produced using the Mold Maker set of bits.

Fig. 3-21. How the bits in the Crown Molding Kit are used, and the sequence of steps followed when using the bits. You can duplicate classic molding forms or create your own designs.

Fig. 3-22. All the cutters that are needed to produce professional raised panel doors are included in this five-piece set of carbide-tipped cutters from Freud. A door lip cutter and a glue joint bit are included.

Fig. 3-23. The door lip cutter in the Freud set is used to shape edges on doors that overlap a frame. The shaped edge consists of a rabbet with a beveled shoulder, a quarter-round configuration, and a shoulder.

Fig. 3-24. The cutters in the Door Shop set offered by Zac Products, Inc., include ogee, slot-cutting, and panel-raiser bits. All have tungsten carbide blades and must be used in a heavy-duty, 1/2-inch capacity router that is mounted in a router/shaper stand.

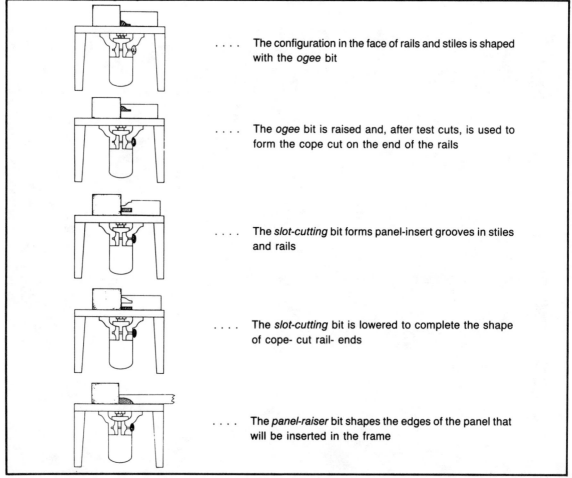

. . . . The configuration in the face of rails and stiles is shaped with the *ogee* bit

. . . . The *ogee* bit is raised and, after test cuts, is used to form the cope cut on the end of the rails

. . . . The *slot-cutting* bit forms panel-insert grooves in stiles and rails

. . . . The *slot-cutting* bit is lowered to complete the shape of cope- cut rail- ends

. . . . The *panel-raiser* bit shapes the edges of the panel that will be inserted in the frame

Fig. 3-25. The cutters in the Door shop set provide flexibility because cutting setups can be organized in relation to the thickness of the stock.

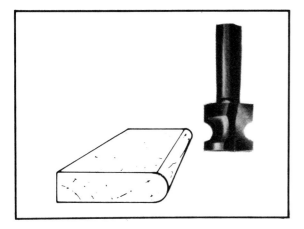

Fig. 3-26. Half-round bits are often called bull nose bits, probably because large ones can be used to form the shape (bull nose) that is often found on the front edge of stair treads. The radius on bits of this type can range from 3/32 to 5/8 inch.

Fig. 3-27. Edge-forming bits are often used to form a slight, round edge on project components like tabletops. The double unit can be used to form twin beads or a single one. Results are affected by cutter projection.

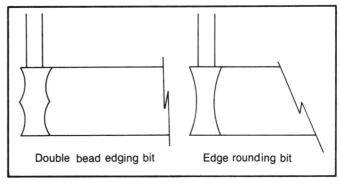

Double bead edging bit   Edge rounding bit

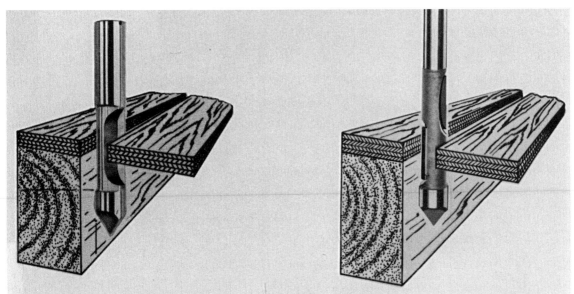

Fig. 3-28. With pilot panel bits you can plunge through a workpiece at any point. A common application is making a cutout for a sink. Other uses include trimming plastic laminates and wood veneers and making cutouts in wall paneling for switch boxes and the like. The one on the right is a "stagger tooth" design.

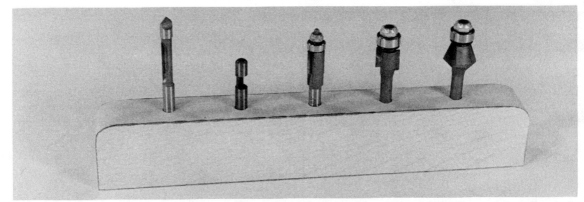

Fig. 3-29. Examples of bits that are specially designed for trimming plastic laminates. The one on the left is a pilot panel bit. The short one is solid carbide. The remaining ball-bearing piloted ones have carbide cutting blades. The bit on the right forms a 22-degree beveled edge, which is often the way the edge of a laminate-covered countertop is finished.

all cutters on tracing paper. Then, over an actual-size drawing of the edge I will work on, I can preview what can be done or test the practicality of what I envison.

CARE OF BITS

An essential part of portable router craftsman-ship is maintaining bits in pristine condition. Part of this is establishing a safe storage environment. Cutting edges on bits, especially those on carbide-tipped units, are easily nicked, and this results in an unwelcome volunteer detail on the cutter's profile. We'll all agree that storing bits like so many beans in a drawer is not the way to go.

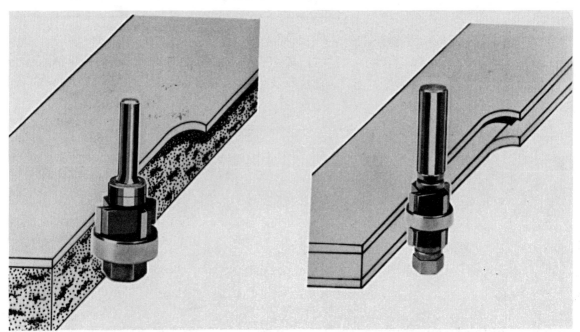

Fig. 3-30. Flush trimmers work precisely because the diameter of the pilot and the cutter are the same. The example on the right has a pilot between two cutters. Thus, the bit trims top and bottom cover material simultaneously.

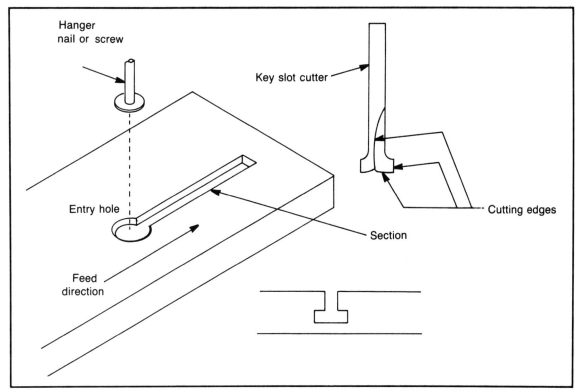

Fig. 3-31. The key slot cutter makes a limited-depth plunge cut that is then extended to form a T-slot. It's a very practical bit for forming the hanger shape that is commonly used on the back of plaques, frames, and other wall-hung projects.

Fig. 3-32. Slotting cutters are usually assemblies that include an arbor, cutter, and pilot. Arbors are available in 1/4- and 1/2-inch shank diameters; cutters for various slot widths are interchangeable. The bit is popular for cutting slots in counter edges that will be covered with a press-in, metal molding. Cutting grooves for splines and feathers in joinery work is another application.

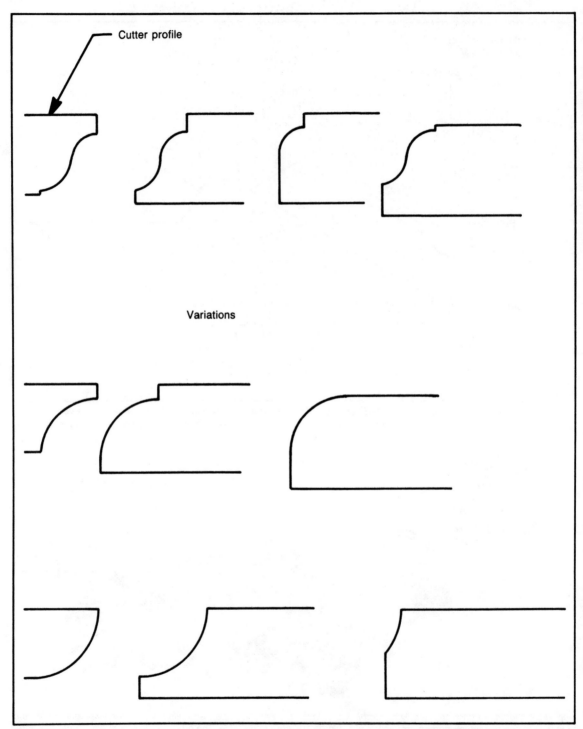

Fig. 3-33. How much of a cutter's profile contacts the workpiece determines the shape that results. Variations are possible by how you control the width of the cut and its depth.

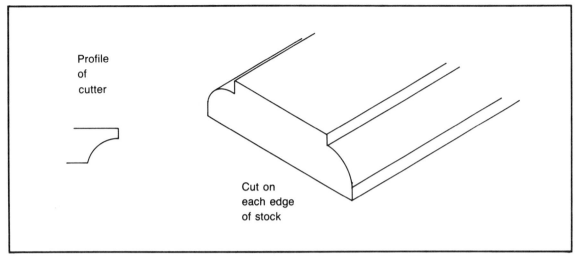

Profile
of
cutter

Cut on
each edge
of stock

Fig. 3-34. Similar cuts made on each edge of workpieces result in batten-type strips. When working on narrow stock, it's crucial that the work be firmly secured with clamps or other means.

An easy and practical storage system consists of a 1 1/2-inch thick block of wood which has been drilled to receive the shanks of the bits. Don't just drill equally-spaced holes and then see how to arrange the cutters. Instead, plan the hole spacing to accommodate the various cutting diameters of the bits. Also, allow sufficient finger room between the bits to avoid the possibility of a cut when you remove one.

Original containers can be used to store bits, especially those supplied in sets and which are packaged in neat plastic or wood chests. Even so, to avoid the possibility that the cutters might move about and bang against each other, stuff the open areas in the containers with lint-free cloth before putting the cutters away.

Clean the bits after each use. Resin tars and pitch are adhesive materials and can accumulate on a bit to the point where chip clearance is reduced and friction is increased. Both factors contribute to poor quality cuts and extra strain on the router and you. Pilots and ball-bearing guides require as much attention as cutting edges. Special wood-pitch removers and other solvents are available for cleaning router bits and other woodworking tools. Be sure to read the safety instructions on the containers of such materials before using them.

Often I find that just a gentle scrubbing with an old toothbrush and warm water and detergent is enough to do the job and is better than working with a solvent. The bit must be thoroughly dried before it is put away. When necessary, I use a hair dryer or a heat gun.

Whatever the cleaning method, coat the bits with a light oil or a spray lubricant before storing them. It's also a good idea to use the same lubricant in the holes of storage blocks.

Fig. 3-35. Cross section of stock with all edges shaped. When a long workpiece is edge-shaped this way, it can be cross-cut into narrow strips to produce many similar pieces. The technique is often used when, for example, many slat-type pieces with shaped ends are needed.

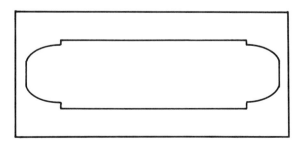

SHARPENING

Router bits, even carbide-tipped ones, do get dull and require sharpening and will get to the point where they need renewing or should be discarded. I'm a firm believer that there are certain functions in tool use that are best left to experts. Sharpening woodcutting tools, especially router bits with their special characteristics, is one of them.

Particular HSS bits, like those with straight flutes, V-cutters, and the like, can be touched up with India or aluminum oxide slip stones. Work on the inside the cutting faces while main-

taining correct rake angles. The same kind of work can be done on carbide-tipped bits with a 400- or 600-grit diamond hone. Advance the thought to grinding instead of light touch-up work, and it is feasible for the work to be done with power, say with a suitable arbor-mounted stone in a drill press.

A thought for anyone wanting to get serious about bit sharpening is to check out a router cutter-grinding attachment (Fig. 3-36). As shown in Fig. 3-37, the attachment is used on the inside flat surfaces of cutting tools.

The amateur shouldn't attempt grinding or

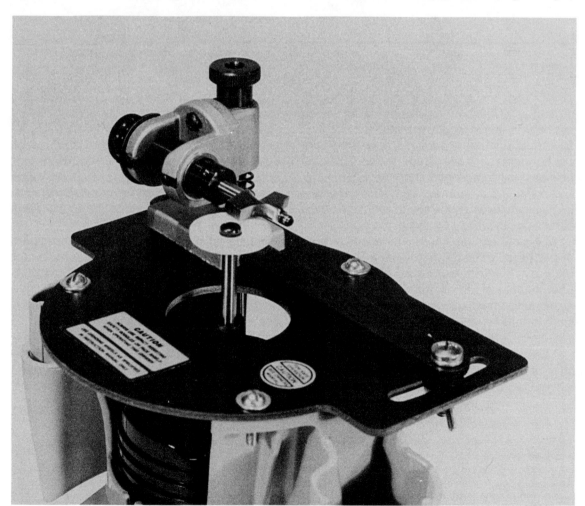

Fig. 3-36. If you do want to try grinding router bits, it's probably wise to acquire an accessory like this Sears Cutter Grinding Attachment. Special grinding wheels are available for steel bits and for carbide-tipped bits.

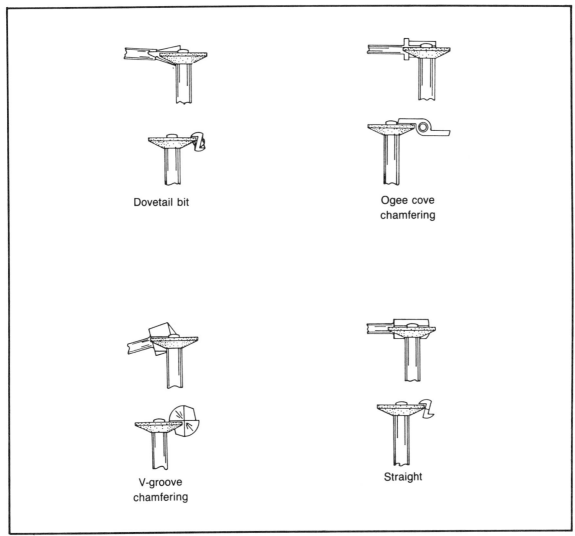

Dovetail bit

Ogee cove
chamfering

V-groove
chamfering

Straight

Fig. 3-37. How the Sears grinding attachment is used for sharpening various bits. Be sure to study and closely follow the instructions that are supplied with the attachment. Impact-resistant safety goggles are a must!

even touch-up work on the perimeter of bits. Imperfect work can reduce cutting diameter, affect clearance, and change rake angles, all of which contribute to inferior bit performance.

Many manufacturers offer sharpening services for HSS and carbide-tipped bits and can also, when necessary, replace carbide blades. Some will even shape a bit to your specifications. Chances are that there are local experts so you don't have to work by mail. Overall, in the interests of quality work with minimum hassle, accept the contribution that an expert sharpener can make.

Chapter 4

Router Maintenance and Basic Adjustments

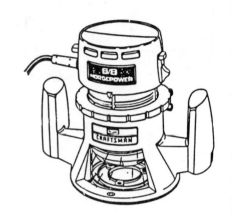

ALL POWER TOOLS EVENTUALLY MANIFEST SYMPtoms of wear that users should be prepared to diagnose—the portable router is not exempted. In fact, when you consider the speed at which the average router operates and the length of time it takes to get through many routine operations, it's surprising that the bearings in the tool don't start to make a fuss even sooner than they normally do. How you care for the tool, how much respect you have for its capabilities, and especially, its limitations have much to do with its useful life before an overhaul is justified.

Warning signs that might indicate bearings are starting to go include excessive vibration in the tool itself and cuts that are not as smooth as they should be. Before sending the tool off for possible repair, examine the router bits you have been using to be sure they are in prime condition. A bit with chipped cutting edges, or one that is not running concentrically, or one that has been incorrectly ground can cause abnormal vibration and rough cuts. Check the cutter

for straightness. It's not likely that a bit will bend, but it's a possibility.

If the cutter passes the examination with high marks, then it's time to suspect the bearings. Unplug the tool and remove any mounted bit, the collet locknut, and the collet. Hand-turn the spindle (motor shaft) and attempt to sense any roughness or irregularity. It's also a good idea to try to move the spindle in various radial directions. If you can to any degree, it's likely that the bearings have had their day and that the tool should be sent to a factory repair shop for inspection and any necessary repair.

Collets can wear, and when they do, a bit will "run-out," which simply means that the bit will rotate erratically. You can check a collet (with tool unplugged) by inserting a length of drill rod or the longest bit you have and finger-tightening the locknut. If you feel movement when you apply some left and right pressure against the test item, replace the collet.

Remember that incorrect operational procedures can cause excessive vibration that might lead you into thinking the router is failing. Typical operator faults include trying to make in a single pass cuts that are too deep or too wide for the router to handle and trying to speed up an operation by force-feeding the tool.

Keep the router clean. Use a brush or a blower to remove waste from around the collet area and motor or any nook or cranny where it's likely to collect. Check the owner's manual for information about replacing motor brushes. Examine electric cords and plugs occasionally to be sure they are in good condition.

DEPTH AND WIDTH OF CUT

Depth of cut has to do with the bit's penetration; *width of cut* has to do with the distance across a cut (Fig. 4-1). Depth of cut is controlled by how far the bit projects below the subbase of the tool. Width of cut is controlled by pilots or with guides. How deep and how wide you can cut in a single pass depends partially on the cutter, but mostly on the horsepower of the tool. Heavy-duty routers, those in 2 to 3-horsepower area, are considerably more tolerant under conditions imposed by deep/wide cuts than light-duty tools,

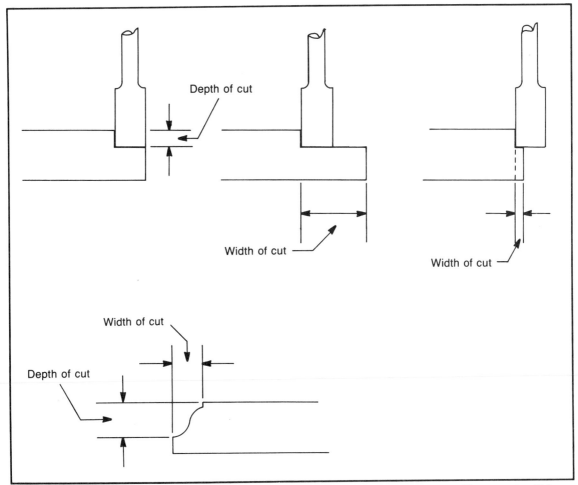

Fig. 4-1. The depth of cuts and the width of cuts are two basic, operational router adjustments. The extent to which you can make them in a single pass depends primarily on the horsepower of the tool. It's never a good idea to try to work faster by forcing the tool beyond its capacity.

Fig. 4-2. Collets are available in different sizes. The collet on the left is designed to accept adapter sleeves. This type of accessory might not be suitable for use in all collets.

but all routers have limitations. You'll know when you are abusing the tool and asking for trouble in the cut, because the tool will slow up excessively, overheat, and complain with abnormal noises. It's always best to survey the situation any time you must apply excessive feed pressure to keep the router moving.

Efficient router use calls for the right combination of feed pressure and depth and width of cut in line with the horsepower of the tool and the material being worked on. But there are no secrets. Router expertise naturally comes from obeying the rules and allowing the tool to work *with* you.

COLLETS

Collets come in different sizes to accommodate bits of various shank diameters (Fig. 4-2). Light-duty routers are usually limited to a 1/4-inch collet, while larger ones that normally use a 1/2-inch collet can operate with smaller ones. Typical collet sizes include 1/4, 3/8, and 1/2 inch. Being able to handle bit shank diameters of various sizes increase the versatility of any router.

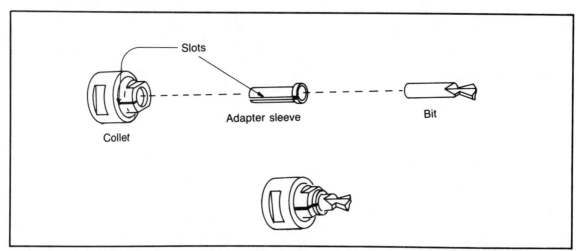

Fig. 4-3. Adapter sleeves make it possible to use bits of various shank diameters in a single collet. Be sure the slot in the sleeve lines up with the slot in the collet (bottom).

The design of some manufacturers accommodates different shank diameters with adapter sleeves that slip into the standard collet (Fig. 4-3). Sleeves are provided with the tool or are available as accessories. The design of the sleeves can vary, and they might not be interchangeable among tools, so be sure to check instructions for correct installation.

Treat collets and locknuts as carefully as you would any precision instrument. Check them occasionally for wear and keep them clean and polished. If you have several, coat the idle ones with a spray lubricant and store them safely.

SECURING BITS

Many routers require two wrenches, used as shown in Fig. 4-4, to secure bits. One wrench is used to keep the motor spindle from turning, the other tightens the locknut. How to go about mounting a bit or changing from one to another has much to do with personal preference. Wrench-turning room, when the router base is

Fig. 4-4. Many routers are designed so two wrenches are required to secure bits in the collet. Others that are equipped with built-in spindle locks get by with a single wrench. Either way, the motor spindle is kept from turning while the collet locknut is tightened.

in place, is pretty tight, so some operators remove it until the bit is secure. The router can be placed on its side or, if designed to permit it, stood upside down.

An assist in bit-changing procedures is provided by routers that have a spindle lock. A device of some design is used to keep the spindle from turning so that only one wrench, used on the collet locknut, is required.

Insert bits fully into the collet and then retract them not more than 1/8 inch before tightening the locknut. Don't attempt to increase depth of cut by minimizing the length of shank the collet will grip. Also, don't test your strength when tightening the nut. Overtightening can cause problems when you wish to remove the bit and can damage the collet. Tighten only as much as is necessary to keep the bit from slipping in the collet when you are cutting.

DEPTH OF CUT ADJUSTMENTS

The base of the router is a sleeve that incorporates a system for vertical adjustment of the motor. Being able to raise or lower the motor in the base is what accounts for the distance the bit projects beneath the base, which is the depth of cut.

A common system has mating spiral grooves on the motor and on the inside surface of the base, or the motor has spiral grooves that mate with just a pin in the base. Either way, the motor is raised or lowered by turning it like a screw. In addition, there is a depth adjusting ring, usually marked in graduations, on the top perimeter of the base. Typically, the ring is used as follows. Rest the router on a piece of wood and adjust the motor until the installed bit just touches the wood. With the base secured, turn the adjusting ring until its zero mark is opposite the index mark that will be on the motor housing. Then, with the base loosened, tilt the router and adjust the vertical position of the motor until the index mark on the motor housing reaches the desired setting on the ring, which will be the cut depth you decide on. The procedure might sound complicated, but it's pretty straightforward when you are actually doing it. You can always adjust the cutter's projection by simply measuring with a flex tape or ruler.

Some routers employ a rack-and-pinion system to adjust the motor's height in the base (Fig. 4-5). It's a neat design that might even include a rotating scale so you can read settings. In the interests of accuracy, however, it always pays to actually measure the cutter's projection regardless of how the system works.

Depth-of-cut adjustments are made with the motor loose in the base. Always remember to use the base locking mechanism before you start working (Fig. 4-6).

Depth-of-cut systems on plunge routers are a little different. Arrangements can consist of a stop rod, a scale, and possibly, a rotatable stop block that makes it possible to preset for three cut depths (Fig. 4-7). The first step is to release

the stop rod so its bottom end contacts the stop block. The motor, which is spring-loaded so it is normally in an "up" position, is pushed down and locked by whatever means the router employs so that the installed bit touches the surface of the workpiece. This establishes the zero setting. The next step is to adjust the stop rod and lock it when its pointer is on the scale graduation that indicates the depth of cut. Thereafter, the bit projection will be to the predetermined depth each time you press down the motor. By adjusting the three screws that are in the turret-type stop block to different heights, you can preset for three different depths of cut.

The option of presetting depths of cut is a great feature of plunge routers but not mandatory for their use. All you have to do anytime you choose to work without the feature is lock the stop rod in an elevated position.

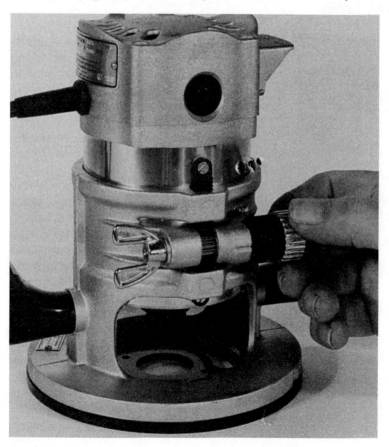

Fig. 4-5. The motor in this Black & Decker router is raised or lowered in the base by means of a rack-and-pinion mechanism. The wing nut at the left is used to secure the motor at the height needed to achieve the depth of cut.

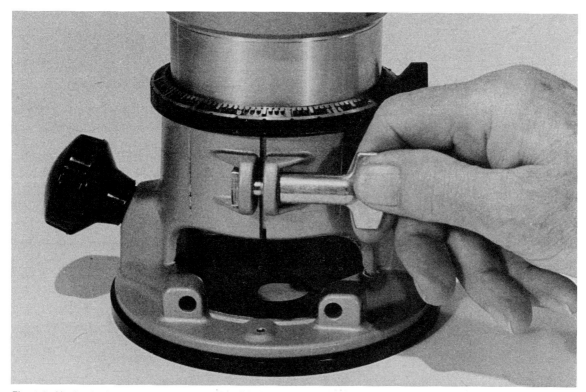

Fig. 4-6. All depth-of-cut adjustments on conventional routers are made with the motor free to move vertically in the base. Be sure to use the locking mechanism after you are satisfied that the cutter projection is correct.

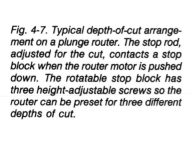

Fig. 4-7. Typical depth-of-cut arrangement on a plunge router. The stop rod, adjusted for the cut, contacts a stop block when the router motor is pushed down. The rotatable stop block has three height-adjustable screws so the router can be preset for three different depths of cut.

Chapter 5

Basic Tool Handling

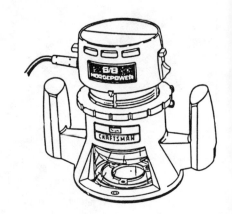

THE PORTABLE ROUTER IS A TOOL THAT WILL DO, or attempt to do, whatever you ask of it. Recognizing that the tool and the operator must work together as a team, with the operator planning the strategy, is the first and major step toward working efficiently with a router or any tool. Like any team assembled for the first time, coach and players should get to know each other and learn to cooperate by going through some practice sessions.

If having a portable router is a novel experience, the first step is getting to know the "feel" of the tool. It's assumed that you have studied the owner's manual and know the particular characteristics of the machine and have followed instructions for adjusting the motor in the base, securing a bit, and so on. Now, while holding the tool firmly, turn it on for a second or two and then turn it off. Do this several times so you can experience the characteristic starting torque and be prepared for it. Be aware that when you shut down the tool, the bit continues to turn for a while. Whether you continue to

hand-hold the tool or set it on its side while holding it firmly until the bit stops is unimportant. Chances are that on particular occasions you will opt for one of the methods. It's simply important to remember that the bit is turning and you must avoid having it touch you or any other object.

For practice cutting, have a few reasonably sized pieces of soft wood, like pine, on hand. Be sure the edges you will work on are smooth and straight. For starters, plan to make a shallow cut with a decorative, piloted bit.

BIT ROTATION AND FEED DIRECTION

A bird's eye view of the router reveals that the motor, and thus the bit, rotate in a clockwise direction (Fig. 5-1). The ideal course (feed direction) for the tool when making a cut opposes the motor's torque and keeps the cutting edges of the bit moving *into* the work. On a straight cut, the feed direction is from left to right. Moving the router in the opposite direction gives the cutter a chance to move like a wheel along the work

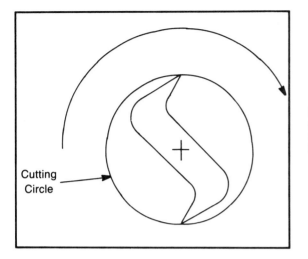

Cutting
Circle

Fig. 5-1. The router should be moved so the cutting edges on the bit are constantly moving into the work. On straight cuts, the ideal feed direction is from left to right. When viewed from above, the cutter rotates clockwise.

edge, and the operation requires considerably more control. It's also likely that the cut will be rougher than it should be.

Follow the sequence of passes shown in Fig. 5-2 when it is necessary to shape all edges of the work. Cuts that are made across end grain almost inevitably result in some splintering or feathering where the cutter leaves the work. The passes that are made parallel to the grain of the wood remove these imperfections. Also notice in Fig. 5-2, that while feed direction is a normal left to right on the outside edges, the edges of an internal cutout are shaped by moving the router in a clockwise direction.

The same techniques apply when shaping curved or circular edges (Fig. 5-3). Move the tool

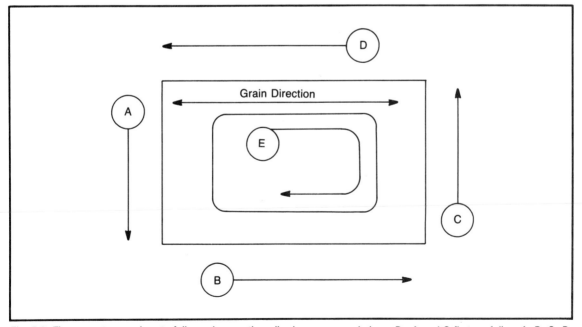

Fig. 5-2. The correct procedure to follow when routing all edges on a workpiece. Do A and C first, or follow A, B, C, D in sequence. Follow E for inside cuts.

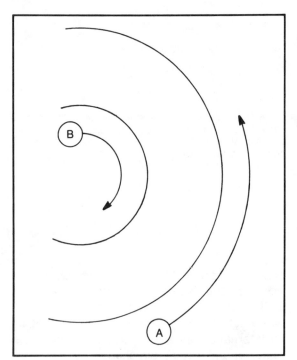

Fig. 5-3. Ideal feed directions when shaping edges of circular work and curved pieces. For outside curves (A), move counterclockwise. For inside curves (B), move clockwise.

the rate at which the work moves past a cutter is mechanically controlled for compatibility with the rpm of the cutter. Factors considered by tool setup engineers are denseness of the material, design and size of the cutter, depth and width of cut, and so on. Regardless of paper work technology, it's results that count. The ideal solution might come to light by means of trial and error.

Somewhere between forcing the router to do more than it can and being too cautious is the ideal feed speed for the work on hand. It's a judgment that becomes easier to make wisely as you progress with router work. If you feed too fast, the motor will complain. If you feed too slowly, you won't accomplish as much as you can and might hold contact between bit and wood in a given area long enough to generate excessive heat, which can burn the wood and even draw temper from the bit. Ideally, you will move the router calmly without excessive pressure while keeping the cutter working.

Important factors include horsepower of the tool, condition of the bit, size of the bit, depth and width of cut, hardness or softness of the material, and grain direction. It's interesting that as you get deeper into portable routing these considerations become part of a sixth sense that helps you get through all situations with minimum fuss and with good results.

Start all cuts with the router firmly in position but with the bit away from the work edge. Make initial contact slowly, *after* the tool has been switched on and has attained full speed. The direction of feed depends to a good degree on the job being done and the size of the work. So long as you remember that, whenever possible, the cutter should be moving *into* the work, you can push the router, or pull it, or take a frontal position and "walk" with it (Fig. 5-4). Turn the tool off after the cut is complete. Always be aware of that spinning bit, especially when you are moving the router toward your body.

Because only part of the base is on the work when you are making edge cuts, pay special attention to keeping the router level throughout the

counterclockwise (left to right) on outside edges; clockwise when shaping inside curves or circular cutouts.

There are times when the feed direction rule might be broken. This will happen, for example, when doing freehand routing to recess a background. There will also be situations where it is practical and expedient to use several feed directions. Sometimes the router must be moved obliquely across wood grain. The latter situation and some others still permit a reasonable feed direction, but the cutter will encounter strange grain patterns. The important factor, always, is to control the tool to maintain constant contact between cutter and work at a feed speed that permits the cutter to work as it was designed to do.

Feed speed, which again is how fast the router is moved through the cut, is variable. In a factory where quantities of similar parts are routinely spewed out, setups are established so

Fig. 5-4. *The operator's convenience is a prime factor when determining whether to push or pull the router or to stand in front of it and walk along with it. The latter method works best when working on long boards.*

pass. Any tilt will cause the bit to dig in and mar the work; it might even jerk the router so you lose your grip. When I can, I place a support piece under that part of the base that isn't on the work. Any straight piece of wood that matches the works thickness will do (Fig. 5-5). The idea can also serve when shaping curved edges. Often the waste piece that remains after the project component has been sawed to shape can be used as shown in Fig. 5-6. The support pieces make it a lot easier to keep the router level.

KEEPING WORK SECURE

The material you are working on must stay put during the router operation. This is not a problem when you are routing details on a large, assembled project (Fig. 5-7) or when you are shaping edges on a large plywood panel, for example. Special precautions should be taken when the workpiece is small and light enough to move about as the router is applied.

One system that works for individual pieces

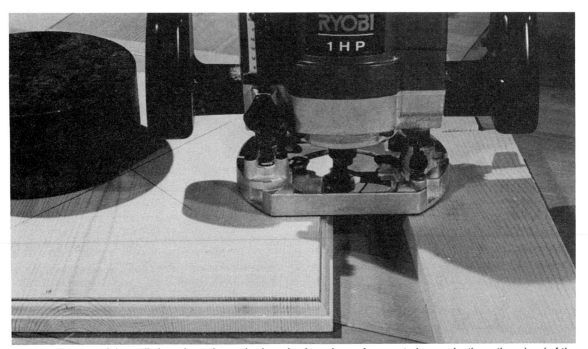

Fig. 5-5. *Only part of the tool's base is on the work when shaping edges. A support piece under the outboard end of the subbase helps to keep the router level.*

Fig. 5-6. The support piece idea is also practical when working on curved components. The waste that remains when the part is sawed to shape serves nicely. Place the extra support so it won't be contacted by the bit as you make the pass.

Fig. 5-7. It's often possible to route decorative details on projects after they have been assembled.

and which is especially useful when many similar parts are needed is shown in Fig. 5-8. The clamp strips, which are tack-nailed to a bench top or to something like a sheet of plywood, are situated to accommodate the size and shape of the work. Clamp strips placed against outside edges allow shaping edges of cutouts. The reverse is also true. When shaping the outside edges on solid material, the clamp strips must be thin enough to allow a cutter's pilot or an edge guide to get by.

Tack-nailing, which simply means using the smallest nails or brads that will secure a workpiece to a solid surface, is often used to keep work still. The only objection is the holes that remain when the brads are removed, but they are tiny and can be easily filled. Often tack-nailing can be done in waste areas or an area that will be concealed by another component so even that problem is eliminated.

Another idea is shown in Fig. 5-9. A heavy steel weight that is part of my workshop equipment is often enough to keep a workpiece in place while the routing is done.

Pieces too small to tack-nail or secure by other means can be held down with hot-melt glue that is dispensed with a special glue gun like the one in Fig. 5-10. The glue sets quickly and hasn't much penetration, so the project will not be difficult to release if the glue is applied in a minimum number of small dots or tiny beads. When ready, lift the project from the surface it's bonded to by carefully using a thin, sharp chisel or knife. Also use the chisel to remove whatever glue still adheres to the workpiece. Follow with routine sanding before applying a finish coat.

SLIM MOLDINGS

The portable router can be used to shape slim moldings, but the best and safest method is to form the shape on material that is large enough to be held securely and then to saw off the part you need (Fig. 5-11). Repeat the procedure when you need many similar pieces, but be sure to sand the sawed edge smooth before you apply the router. When you need many short pieces of molding, it's best to shape the edge of a long board and cut the strip you saw off into specific lengths.

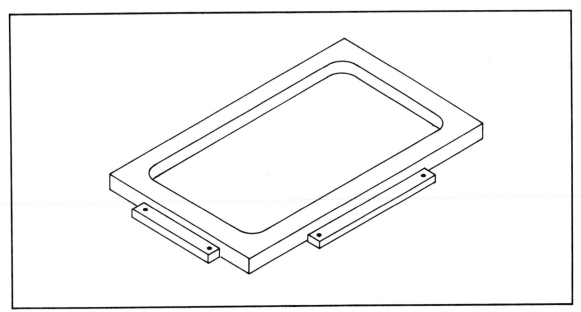

Fig. 5-8. Clamp strips are tack-nailed on 3 or 4 sides of the work and can be used to keep work from moving as the router is applied. Ideas like this are tailor-made to suit the project when conventional C-clamps and similar holders won't do.

Fig. 5-9. A heavy steel weight often serves as a "hold-down" for work being routed.

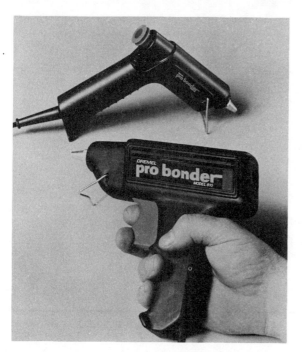

Fig. 5-10. Hot-melt glue applied with a special glue gun can temporarily secure small workpieces. The project will not be difficult to release if you apply the glue in a miserly fashion.

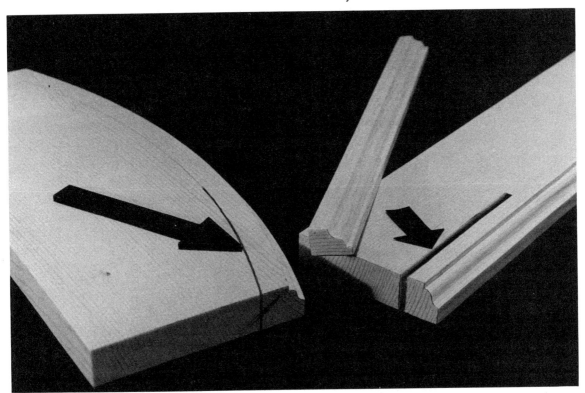

Fig. 5-11. *The safe and sane way to produce slim moldings.* Shape the edge of a wide board, which will be easy to secure, then saw off the part you need. Arrows indicate saw kerfs.

THE FINISH YOU GET

All router cuts should be smooth, but the texture of the cut depends to some degree on the material used (Fig. 5-12). There should be no problem with solid wood or cabinet-grade plywoods, especially if they have solid lumber cores. Don't expect to get super results on anything like shop-grade fir plywood that, for one thing, often has voids.

Results on other man-made materials, like various types of particleboard, hardboard, and flakeboard, will vary depending on the density of the product. Sometimes routing must be followed with a filler, then sanding before a satisfactory surface for a finish is achieved.

Dense plastics—a material like Corian (Fig. 5-13)—can be routed in fine style, but tungsten carbide cutters should be used. In fact, it's recommended that carbide cutters be used with most man-made products that use various adhesives as binders to keep wood chips or flakes or whatever together or which, like plywood, use glue to laminate layers of wood material.

A SAMPLE CUT LIBRARY

In my shop, and I'm sure that other router-users do the same thing, I have a "library" of sample cuts like those shown in Fig. 5-14. After establishing and proving a setup for a particular cutter and stock thickness, cut off a short section of the shaped project and store it for use as a gauge when the same operation must be duplicated. The system considerably reduces setup time on future projects and ensures that the correct cutter/wood relationship be established with minimum fuss. You will find that the idea helps whether you are handholding the router or using it in a router/shaper table setup.

Fig. 5-12. The machining qualities of various materials do differ, so even optimum cuts might require further attention before a finish can be applied.

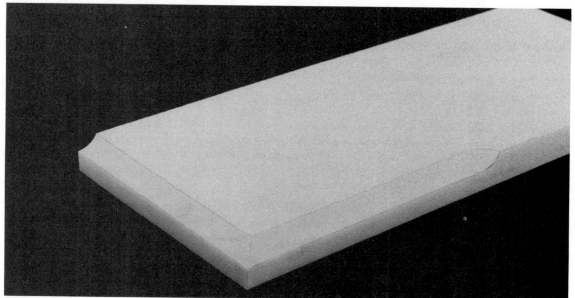

Fig. 5-13. Plastic materials like Corian machine very nicely, but tungsten carbide cutters should be used. A heavy-duty router is also a good idea.

Fig. 5-14. Sample cuts can be used as gauges to duplicate setups with minimum fuss. It's not a bad idea either to have a set of samples that show the full profile of each bit you own.

Fig. 5-15. Special subbases can be made of hardboard. Apply several coats of sealer, with a light sanding between them, and then a final one. Apply paste wax and rub to a polish so the auxiliary base moves easily.

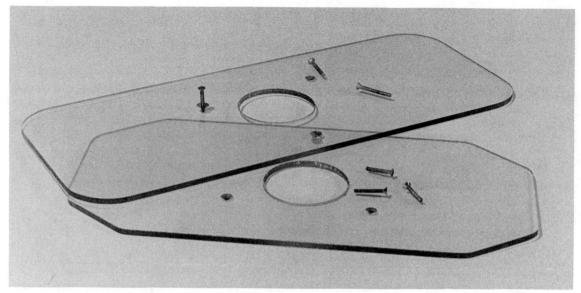

Fig. 5-16. Use a plastic material like Lexan for see-through subbases. The material is shatterproof and scratch resistant, but it can be worked with ordinary woodworking tools.

INCREASING ROUTER SPAN

You will find, in some situations, that the diameter of the router base is not enough to span across support areas. This occurs often when doing recessing jobs. The solution is to remove the tool's subbase and substitute specially made ones like those in Figs. 5-15 and 5-16. The overall size and shape of the auxiliary subbase is influenced by the job on hand. The location of the attachment holes and the center of the hole through which the bit will pass are determined by using the original subbase as a pattern.

Auxiliary subbases of this type, not necessarily with the shapes that are shown, are often made to accommodate bits with a cutting circle that is larger than the center hole in the original subbase. Two materials that serve well in this capacity are tempered hardboard and a shatterproof, scratch-resistant plastic like Lexan.

Chapter 6

Straight Cuts

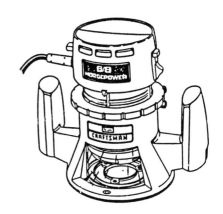

STRAIGHT CUTS ARE MADE ALONG THE WORK'S edge or somewhere in the field. They might be parallel to edges, with the grain or against it, across end grain, at right angles to an edge, or directed obliquely across the work. *Through* cuts start and end at edges. A *stopped* cut starts at an edge but is complete before reaching the opposite edge. A *blind* cut starts and stops between edges. Straight cuts can be made freehand by directing the router along a marked line, but it's a tricky system at best. Whenever possible, guide the router by a piloted bit, an edge guide, or by some improvisation that can be as simple as a straight strip of wood clamped in place (Fig. 6-1).

PILOTED BITS

The most straightforward method of guiding a router along an edge is to use a bit with an integral or ball-bearing pilot. You'll get good results if the edge is smooth and free of irregularities and if you keep the router flat on the work and with the pilot bearing against the edge throughout the pass. Some lateral pressure is required for the pilot to do its job, but don't overdo it. More pressure than is needed, especially with a one-piece bit, will result in blemishes like burn marks and indents. This is less likely to happen with a ball-bearing pilot, but it's still good practice to apply the minimum amount of pressure for the job.

It's often wise to reach the final result by making repeat passes, increasing the depth of cut a bit each time, the final pass being just a shaving cut. You'll soon be able to judge when this technique is needed and how to get the job done in a *minimum* number of passes. Factors involved are horsepower of the tool, the size of the cut, and the material. A wood species like pine cuts a lot easier than something like oak or maple.

EDGE GUIDES

Edge guides (Figs. 6-2 and 6-3) are available for

Fig. 6-1. A common method of making straight cuts is to guide the router along a strip of wood that is held with clamps. Be sure the bearing edge of the guide is smooth and straight and that it is stiff enough to avoid being deflected by router pressure.

Fig. 6-2. The router edge guide is used for cuts on an edge and, as shown here, for cuts that are parallel to the edge. Maintain full contact between guide and work throughout the pass.

all routers. When one is not supplied with the tool, it should be a first-choice accessory along with a few bits. Buy one that is designed specifically for use with the router you own.

The attachment can be used for cuts on edges that are made with pilotless bits and for cuts like dadoes and grooves that are parallel to an edge. More sophisticated edge guides can be used as shown in Fig. 6-4. After the first cut (in this case a dado) is made, the guide is set to establish the distance between cuts.

Straightedge guides, which can be straight strips of wood tack-nailed or clamped in place or an on-hand tool like the clamp shown in Fig. 6-5, are often used in place of commercially made edge guides. The system is necessary when the cut is too far from an edge for a ready-made guide to work and when cuts are not par-

allel to the work edge. When establishing the position of the straightedge, be sure it is parallel to the line of cut and that you have allowed for the distance between the cutting edge of the bit and the outside edge of the subbase.

It's a good idea to make a note of the bit size and the offset distance you establish for a particular cut so you'll have to fuss less when you're faced with duplicating the operation. Many professional router users make gauges for future use by noting the bit diameter on strips of wood that have been cut to correct length.

An edge guide idea that is practical for production work is shown in Fig. 6-6. A wood straightedge of suitable length is attached to the subbase with screws that pass through existing holes or even through special holes that you drill. Another way is to make a special subbase with

Fig. 6-3. The guide ensures equal edge distance on all cuts so long as the work edges are smooth and straight. Note that the work is held in a vise, which is a good way to go when work size permits it.

Fig. 6-4. Some edge guides can be organized to control the distance between cuts. Be careful on operations like this to keep router and guide moving smoothly as a team.

Fig. 6-5. A clamp of this type, which has no projections above its bar, functions ideally as a straight-edge. In all cases, the guide must be positioned to allow for the distance between the cutting edge of the bit and the outside edge of the subbase.

Fig. 6-6. Production workers often attach a guide of this type permanently to a homemade subbase or to an extra commercial one.

a permanently attached straightedge. Once made, you can use the tool to duplicate cuts exactly at any time. Be sure that the distance between the cutting edge of the bit and the bearing edge of the straightedge is exact (Fig. 6-7).

HOMEMADE GUIDES

T square-type guides, detailed in Figs. 6-8 and 6-9, are easy to make and will help you achieve accuracy with many router cuts. An advantage is that they are always on hand and often relieve

Fig. 6-7. The distance between the bearing edge of the guide and the perimeter of the bit must equal the edge distance of the cut.

Fig. 6-8. Examples of homemade guides; one for square cuts, the other for cuts at a 45-degree angle. Assemble the parts with screws or with glue and nails.

you of the chore of having to improvise with a strip of wood and clamps. The sizes that are suggested work out nicely for average size boards and can usually be secured with a single clamp. If you make larger ones, use wider material for both the head and the blade. Keep the guide secure by using a clamp at its head and a second one at the free end of the blade.

Constructing a guide isn't complicated but obviously must be made accurately. For example, the angle between the blade and head of the square guide must be 90 degrees (Fig. 6-10). When making one that will serve for angular cuts, use a protractor to set the blade correctly when assembling the pieces. Figures 6-11 and 6-12 show two of the guides in use.

MAKING CLAMP GUIDES

Clamp guides, which are very convenient for guiding the router through straight cuts, can be made in several ways. Two types that are standard equipment in my shop, and which you can duplicate, are displayed in Fig. 6-13. Figure 6-14

offers the construction information for one with a fixed length that is suitable for boards not much more than standard width. An alternate design that suits the clamp for various widths beyond the limits of the fixed version is also shown. What makes the capacity of the extended length design variable is a rear block that can be moved to and fro along a slot cut into the fixture's arm (Fig. 6-15). What makes it possible for the clamp to grip securely across the work is the press screw that is mounted in the block at the front end of the clamp (Fig. 6-16).

When organizing the adjustable clamp for use, retract the press screw and lock the rear stop block so the distance between them is an inch or so more than the width of the workpiece. Then, after positioning the guide arm for the cut that is needed, tighten the press screw.

MAKING A FRAME GUIDE

The unit that is displayed in Fig. 6-17, and whose construction details are shown in Fig. 6-18, is called a frame guide. It has two parallel straight-

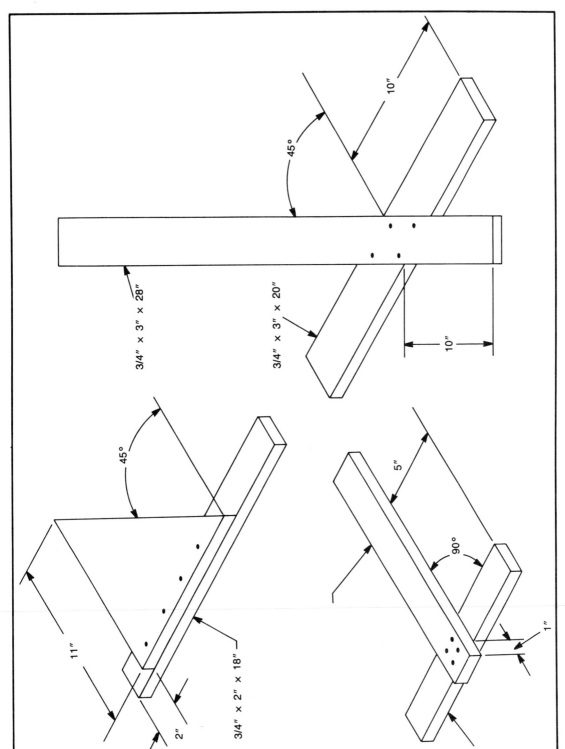

Fig. 6-9. Construction details of guides that you can make.

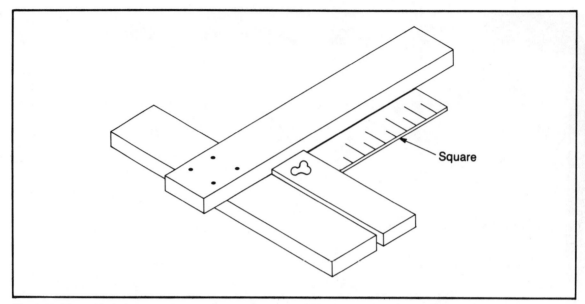

Fig. 6-10. The guides are simple tools, but don't be casual when making them. Set the angle between blade and head with a square or, when necessary, with a protractor. Both parts of the tools must have smooth, straight edges.

Fig. 6-11. Use a clamp to secure the guide for each of the cuts you make. Mark the work beforehand so the guide can be set for the spacing you need. A cut through the head can also serve if the cut locations are marked.

Fig. 6-12. Follow the same procedure for cuts made at an angle. If you make guides with very long blades, use a clamp at each end of the tool.

Fig. 6-13. Homemade clamp guides are fine for straight cuts because they can be locked securely without the fuss of C-clamps.

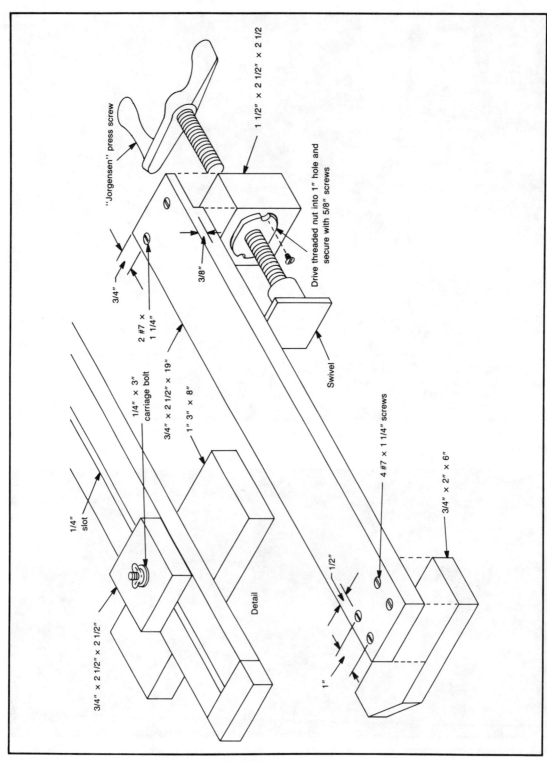

"Jorgensen" press screw

1 1/2" × 2 1/2" × 2 1/2"

Drive threaded nut into 1" hole and secure with 5/8" screws

3/4"

3/8"

2 #7 × 1 1/4"

Swivel

1/4" slot

1/4" × 3" carriage bolt

3/4" × 2 1/2" × 19"

1" 3" × 8"

3/4" × 2 1/2" × 2 1/2"

Detail

4 #7 × 1 1/4" screws

1/2"

1"

3/4" × 2" × 6"

Fig. 6-14. How to make clamp guides. One has a fixed length; the other, which can be almost any length, has an adjustable gripping span. Follow design in detail to make clamp longer and adjustable. (It can be long enough to span 48-inch panel.)

Fig. 6-15. The lock bolt for the adjustable stop slides in a slot that is centered in the clamp guide's bar. Face the underside of the top block with sandpaper so it will grip more securely. You can do this, too, on the area of the stop that contacts the bar.

edges that are spaced to accommodate the diameter of the router's subbase. Many times a jig like this is made with fixed blocks at the front and rear. I prefer a fixed front block and an adjustable rear one so the unit can easily conform to the width of the work. It's often possible to use the adjustable version without clamp security (Fig. 6-19), but don't assume it's so for all work. If only as a safeguard, use at least one clamp at the fixed block end of the jig.

The frame jig can also be used for angular cuts. In such a case, place the adjustable block at the extreme end of the arms and use clamps to secure the jig at the necessary angle. When

Fig. 6-16. The "Jorgensen" press screw is installed this way. Straight grain fir or other wood species like maple or birch are good materials for clamp guides.

Fig. 6-17. The frame guide has two parallel straightedges that are spaced to accommodate the diameter of the router's subbase. Some are made with a fixed head at each end. This one is adjustable.

you make the jig, be sure that the distance between the arms is just right for the tool. You should be able to move the router without having to force it, but at the same time, there should be no room for the tool to move laterally.

THROUGH CUTS AND BLIND CUTS

A through cut can be one that penetrates the work or, in router applications, one that travels edge to edge across the stock as typified by the dado and rabbet cuts shown in Fig. 6-20. The rabbet cut is always on an edge of the stock. The U-shaped cut, which is called a *dado* when made across the grain and a *groove* when it is in line with the grain, can be made anywhere in the field. These particular shapes will be discussed further in Chapter 9. It's best to guide the router along a straightedge and to work with a straight bit whose diameter matches the width of cut you need. When this isn't possible, the straightedge is repositioned so a second pass opens the cut to the necessary width.

Figure 6-21 shows blind cuts. Here, cuts start and end in the field; the edges of the work

are left intact. To make these cuts accurately, stop blocks, which can be secured by some means to the straightedge or to the work itself, are used to position the router at the extremes of the cut. With a conventional router, the tool is tilted and then lowered so the bit penetrates and the router is flat on the work. Then the tool is moved along the straightedge until it contacts the second stop block. This is a typical area of portable routing where the plunge router has advantages. The tool can be set in place, solidly on the work, before the bit is made to penetrate by pushing down the motor.

SURFACE CUTS

Surface cuts are those embellishments that add interest and texture to otherwise flat panels. The examples shown in Figs. 6-22 and 6-23 aren't even the first taste of a gourmet's meal. You do need particular bits to accomplish this sort of thing, but with a few of them, results are limited only by your desire to create.

Except under certain circumstances, decorative surface cuts are accomplished with

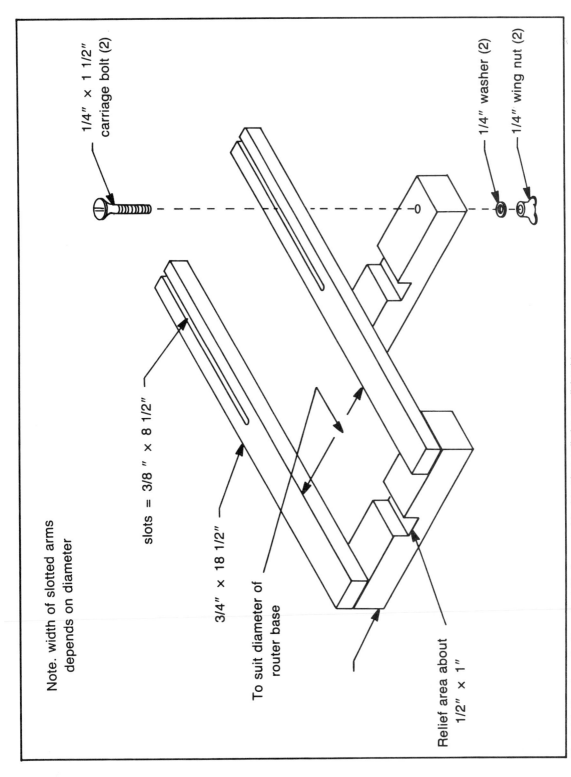

Note. width of slotted arms depends on diameter

1/4″ × 1 1/2″ carriage bolt (2)

1/4″ washer (2)

1/4″ wing nut (2)

slots = 3/8 ″ × 8 1/2″

3/4″ × 18 1/2″

To suit diameter of router base

Relief area about 1/2″ × 1″

Fig. 6-18. How to make the adjustable frame guide. It's often called a parallel guide.

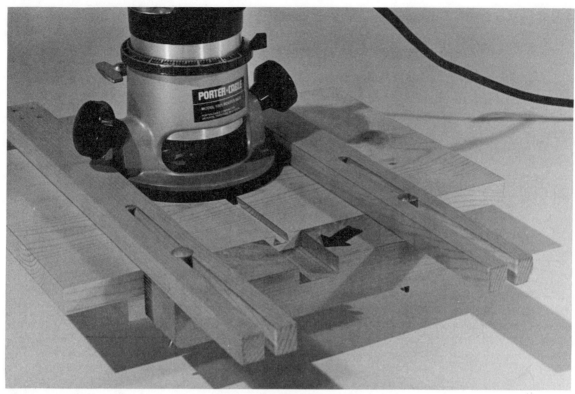

Fig. 6-19. Relief areas keep the heads on the frame guide from being messed up. Be sure to space the bars so the router can move easily but without side-to-side tolerance.

Fig. 6-20. The dado (U-shaped) and the rabbet (L-shaped) shown here are examples of through cuts. The router is moved completely across the work.

Fig. 6-21. *The blind cut starts and ends away from edges. Stop blocks are used to control the position of the cut and its length. Cuts like this can be made with any router, but a plunge router is more convenient and accurate.*

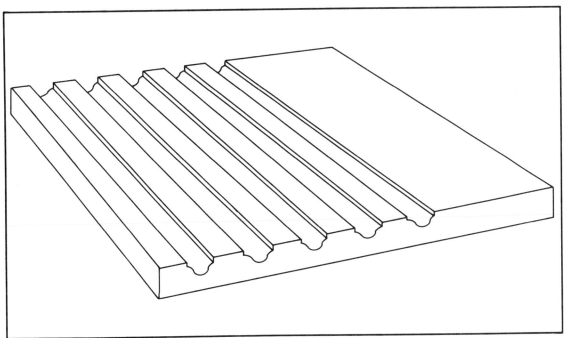

Fig. 6-22. *Surface cuts can be as simple as this: formed in equally spaced, parallel lines. This is also a good way to make molding. The board is cut into individual pieces after the shaping is finished.*

Fig. 6-23. Intersecting cuts add another dimension to surface cutting. Be sure to work with a keen bit to minimize, if not eliminate, feathering that might occur where the cuts cross each other.

pilotless bits of the type shown in Fig. 6-24. Many, what you might call "mod" router users, do much work of this type freehand. For starters, though, while still creating impressive geometri-cal patterns, it's best to make parallel cuts or in-tersecting cuts by guiding the router along a straightedge (Fig. 6-25).

The results you get will be determined by

Fig. 6-24. Surface cutting is usually done with pilotless bits. The depth of the cut, regardless of the cutter you use, has much to do with the effects you create.

Fig. 6-25. Surface cuts turn out best when the router is guided by a straightedge. Mark the workpiece beforehand so you'll know where to situate the guide for each cut. The bit in use here is a V-cutter.

factors such as the shape of the bit, the depth of the cut, the spacing of the cuts, whether the cuts cross at 90 degrees or some other angle, and so on. It is crucial to work with keen bits be- cause cuts are made across the grain and even against the grain. You want the work to be ready for final finishing without tedious touch-up attention.

Chapter 7

Curves
and Circles

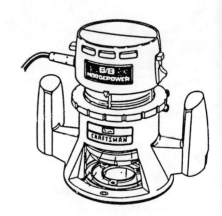

EDGES ON WORKPIECE THAT HAVE UNIFORM OR IR-
regular curves can be shaped by using a
piloted bit and moving the router in routine fashion (Fig. 7-1). As always, a crucial factor for optimum results is that the edge be smooth and
free of irregularities.

The same considerations apply when shaping edges on circular pieces. You can work with
the same edge guide that is normally used for
straight edges (Fig. 7-2). Some of the guides
have a V configuration in the bearing edge so
the unit can be used without special adjustment.
Others are designed for use in a reverse mode
that brings into place a bearing edge that con-
forms more readily to circular edges. Accessories for an edge guide might include arc
components that are attached to the straight
edge when needed (Fig. 7-3). In any case, while
circular edges can be shaped by working only
with a piloted bit, you will work more accurately
if you utilize any mechanical help that an edge
guide might provide.

The bit will encounter various grain patterns
when it is moving along a circular edge and even
when following irregular curves. It will cut with
the grain, against the grain, and even quarter
the grain, so it's logical to expect that the
smoothness of the cut will not be consistent. If
you have followed the rules and used a keen bit,
however, any extra work should not involve more
than a light touch with fine sandpaper on some
areas.

PATTERNS

Patterns can be used to guide the router through
surface cuts that are not straight. In the examples shown in Figs. 7-4 and 7-5, the technique is the same as the one used for straight
cuts. The guide, in these cases a specially designed pattern, is attached to the work by
tack-nailing or with clamps. The location of the
guide must allow for the distance between the
cutting edge of the bit and the outside edge of
the subbase, which is the same provision re-

Fig. 7-1. Uniform or irregular curves can be edge shaped by working with a piloted bit and moving the router in a routine counterclockwise direction. Notice how the scrap piece that remains after the part has been sawed to shape is used to help keep the router on a level plane.

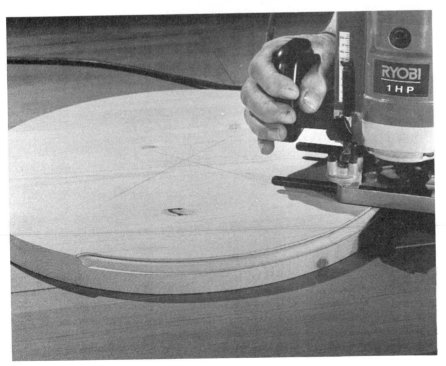

Fig. 7-2. Some edge guides are designed so they can contribute some extra control when shaping edges of circular pieces. They can also be used on some uniform curves but not on edge shapes, like scallops, that have tight concave and convex lines.

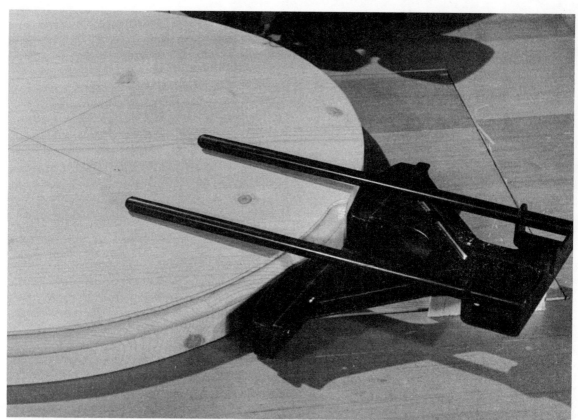

Fig. 7-3. How an edge guide that is usable on curved or circular edges should be organized depends on its design. This one has extra, arc-shaped components that are screw attached to the basic straight line fence.

Fig. 7-4. It is often necessary to guide the router through a cut by using a pattern. The pattern, like this one, can be used something like a straightedge. The subbase rides against the pattern. The location of the pattern allows for the distance between the cutting circle of the bit and the edge of the subbase.

Fig. 7-5. The pattern can be any shape you wish so long as its contours can be followed by the router's subbase. A single pattern can be repositioned for a combination of cuts that result in the overall effect you want. This calls for a little preplanning, something you can do first on paper.

quired when using a straight edge.

This aspect of portable routing is discussed in greater detail in Chapter 8.

PIVOT GUIDES

Circular surface cuts, which might be simple grooves done with a straight bit or decorative ones with a pilotless bit, can be done easily and accurately by equipping the router so the circular feed path is mechanically controlled. Picture a strip of wood with a nail at one end to act as a pivot and a pencil at the other end so you can draw a circle, and then substitute a router bit for the pencil.

A very simple arrangement is shown in Fig. 7-6. A length of drill rod, drilled at one end for a nail, is secured in the router base with one of the screws normally used for an edge guide. This is a type of offset arrangement where the radius of the circle is determined by the distance between the pivot nail and the bit, not the work-

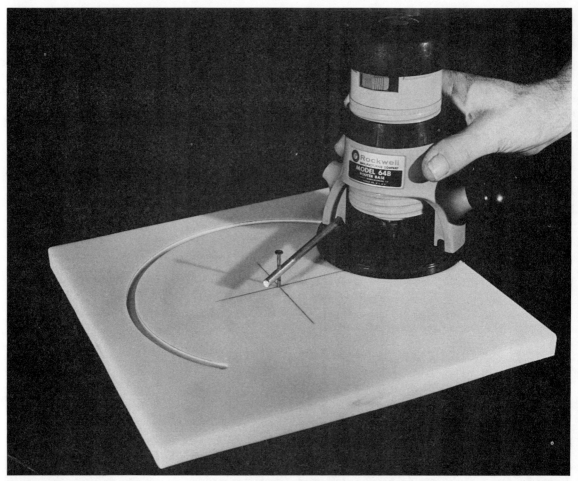

Fig. 7-6. This is about as basic a pivot guidance system as anyone can devise. The drill rod is the control, but the radius of the circle is the distance from the pivot nail to the cutting edge of the bit. This material is Corian, a dense plastic that is best cut with bits that have tungsten carbide blades.

ing length of the rod.

Some edge guides are designed to accommodate trammel points so they can be used for pivot cutting, but capacities are within particular limits. It's possible, with some units, to increase capacity by substituting longer rods for the original ones. Because not all edge guides can be used for this particular application, it might be necessary to devise a jig that can guide the router as accurately as any commercial unit.

One example that I use in my shop is shown in Fig. 7-7. The special 1/4-inch plywood base, which is shaped like a paddle, substitutes for the regular subbase. Small holes with optional spacing are drilled in the arm of the paddle on a line that passes through the center of the opening for the bit. Make the holes so they will provide a snug fit for a small nail or brad. The length of the jig is optional, but one that will allow circular cutting up to about 24 inches in diameter seems right for average work.

Another type of pivot guide (or circle guide) that you can make is shown in Fig. 7-8. This one is more convenient to use because the router merely sits in the retaining ring whose inside diameter matches the diameter of the subbase.

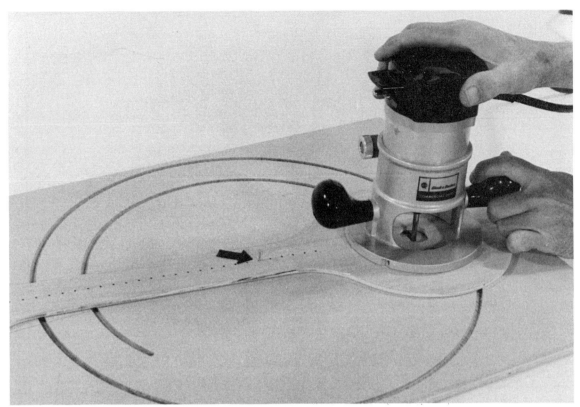

Fig. 7-7. This homemade pivot guide is actually an auxiliary subbase, but if you choose, it can be attached to the router without removing the regular subbase. The arrow indicates the pivot nail that is at the center of the circular cut.

Fig. 7-8. This type of homemade pivot guide features a retaining ring that is sized to suit the diameter of the router's subbase. The ring can be permanently attached for a single router, or you can make several of them for routers whose subbase diameters might vary and attach them, as needed, with short screws.

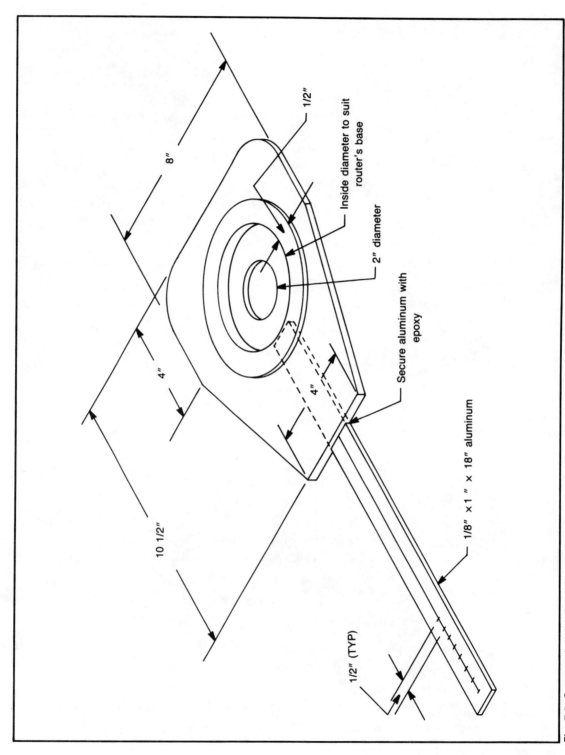

8"

1/2"

Inside diameter to suit router's base

2" diameter

4"

4"

Secure aluminum with epoxy

10 1/2"

1/8" × 1 " × 18" aluminum

1/2" (TYP)

Fig. 7-9. Construction details of the pivot guide that employs a retaining ring to situate the router.

Fig. 7-10. Pivot guide jigs can also be used to control the router through circular, decorative cuts. The jigs can be used with conventional routers or plunge-cutting types.

You can design the jig for use with several routers that might have different diameter subbases by making several retaining rings that can be attached to the jig's platform with short screws. Construction details for this pivot jig design are shown in Fig. 7-9.

There can be times when a commercial jig or one that you have made will not have the capacity for a particular job. In such a case you can get by this way: Cut a piece of 1/4-inch hardboard or plywood about 4 inches wide and to any length you need. Draw a centerline on the material and then, on the line, bore a hole at one end for the bit to pass through. Drive a small nail

to serve as a pivot at a point that will provide the radius you need. The temporary jig can be attached to, or used in place of, the subbase.

Pivot guides can also be used for decorative surface cuts (Fig. 7-10). Factors that can contribute to the results include depth of cut, changing circle diameter for repeat cuts, making stopped cuts, and making cuts with different bits.

Pivot guides can be excellent controls when you need perfectly round discs or have to form large holes. In such applications, the bit must pass through the work, which calls for certain procedures covered in Chapter 11.

Chapter 8

Working with Template Guides

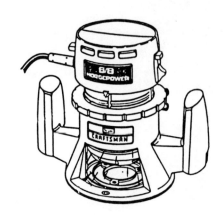

ALL ROUTER OPERATIONS ARE FASCINATING, BUT on a scale of one to ten, template routing has to rank near or at the top. The technique can be used for production work or to solve a one-time, difficult woodworking problem. The idea can be used for incising and for cutting through material. Often it can be used for work that is ordinarily consigned to a jigsaw, saber saw, or band saw.

When the router is equipped with a special guide, it can follow a template to produce projects like those shown in Fig. 8-1 in quantity. At the other end of the scale, template routing makes it easy, for example, to form the precise grooves that are needed for sliding doors and for tambour doors (Figs. 8-2 and 8-3).

Once you get into template routing, you'll discover a host of enjoyable and practical uses for it. If all this makes the technique sound complicated or difficult, forget it. Actually, the most difficult step in this phase of router work is making the template.

Template routing is often called pattern routing and vice versa. I guess there isn't much wrong with using the words "template" and "pattern" interchangeably, but there is a basic difference between the techniques. When a pattern is used, it is the same size as the part to be duplicated. Cutting is usually done with piloted straight bits or with a panel bit. The pilot rides the edge of the pattern while the bit's blades cut the work in line with the pattern's edge. You might say that the core material for a countertop is the pattern for a plastic laminate cover.

A template is followed by means of a guide that is installed in the base of the router. The guide has a sleeve through which the bit passes. The sleeve, which follows the template, must have wall thickness. This means that the bit is cutting away from the template slightly, so the template is sized a bit larger or smaller, depending on the cut, than the project in order to compensate.

Fig. 8-1. Special guides that are installed in the router's base, together with homemade templates, allow you to make projects like this in quantity.

Fig. 8-2. The grooves that are needed for components like tambour doors must be perfectly matched in top and bottom case members. Template guides makes it easy to do the work perfectly.

Fig. 8-3. A template, which is sized and positioned to suit the grooves that are needed, is followed by the sleeve that is part of the template guide. In essence, the sleeve does the same job as the pilot on a bit.

Fig. 8-4. Template guides are not interchangeable among tools made by different manufacturers. Be sure to buy those that are suitable for the router, or routers, that you own. These are attached to the router's base with screws.

TEMPLATE GUIDES

After all the applause for template routing, it's interesting to discover that the accessory required for the router is not an amazing conception but a rather simple, low-cost item. Designs do differ, however, so it is important to buy those that can be mounted in the router you own. Some, like the examples in Fig. 8-4, are attached with screws, while others are assemblies that consist of a threaded body and a knurled, ring-type locknut (Fig. 8-5). All router subbases have a recess so that the only part of the guide to project below the base is the sleeve (Fig. 8-6). This is the part of the guide that bears against the edge of a template. In a sense, it's a pilot; it moves along the template's edge, and so does the cutter.

All guides, regardless of how they are se-

Fig. 8-5. Another type is an assembly that is composed of a threaded base that slips through the hole in the subbase. A ring-type locknut secures it. These accessories should be maintained in pristine condition.

Fig. 8-6. Regardless of its design, the template guide fits into the router's subbase so the only part that protrudes is the sleeve through which the bit passes. Before installing one, be sure that the recess that receives it is free of debris.

cured in the subbase, have common characteristics. One of the most important factors is the inside diameter of the sleeve. If you work with a 1/4-inch diameter bit, then the inside diameter of the sleeve should be compatible and allow the bit to turn without excessive friction. This applies whether you choose to work with a 3/8-inch or 1/2-inch bit. Another variable factor is the length of the sleeve (Fig. 8-7). In use, there must be clearance between the bottom of the sleeve and the workpiece. If, for example, the sleeve projects 1/4 inch below the bottom of the sub-base, then the thickness of the template must be greater than 1/4 inch. Guides are made with

Fig. 8-7. The size differences among template guides has to do with the length and the diameter of the sleeve. Normally, the shank diameter of the bit should match the inside diameter of the sleeve. Sleeves are made so there is enough clearance for the bit to spin without excessive friction.

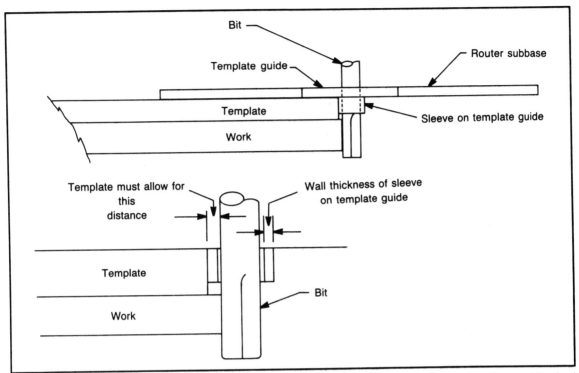

Fig. 8-8. *Illustrated here are important factors to remember when making a template. Essentially, the template must be sized to compensate for the distance from the outside edge of the sleeve to the cutting edge of the bit.*

sleeves of different length, but the assortment that is available is not likely to cover all situations. One solution is to use a material for the template that is thick enough to go along with the sleeve length of the guide you wish to use. Another is to shorten, by grinding, the sleeve of a guide so it will work with the thickness of the stock you decide to use for the template.

Figure 8-8 shows the major operational factor to consider when preparing to cut with a template guide. Because the bit rotates in the guide's sleeve, and the sleeve walls have cross-sectional thickness, the template is sized to compensate for the distance from the cutting edge of the bit to the outside edge of the sleeve. If, for example, you are using a guide to form a disc, the diameter of the template will be less than the diameter of the part you need. If you are forming a hole, the inside diameter of the template will be greater than the diameter of the hole you need.

Another point to remember is that the intricacy of the template is limited by the diameter of the guide's sleeve. For example, if the sleeve's diameter is 1/2 inch, it won't be able to get into a corner that has a 1/8-inch radius. Also, because all cutters have a circular cutting path, they can't form a square corner.

TEMPLATES

Some ready-made templates are available. Jigs that let you cut dovetail joints (Fig. 8-9) are supplied with special finger templates. Others that are available include various sizes and styles of letters and numbers, and those that guide you through forming recesses (mortises) for door hinges. Commercial ones are fine, and it's wise to include some in your workshop equipment, but the real fun of template routing comes with making your own. You can create something exclusive for a design or a project, solve a woodworking problem, or conceive a method that makes a routine shop chore easier and more accurate.

Templates can be secured to the workpiece in several ways—by clamping, tack-nailing, or adhering them temporarily with hot-melt glue. Which method depends on factors like the size and shape of the template, whether holes left by tack-nailing are objectionable, and so on. The most convenient method is the best method.

The material you use for templates is optional. Commercial houses that might use a particular template interminably might use aluminum or even steel. Hardboard, preferably tempered, is a good choice for the home shop. Plywood is alright, but edges might become marred after a lot of use. Much depends on frequency of use and anticipated service life. For one-time use, almost any available scrap piece of wood might do—like the example in Fig. 8-10 that served nicely for the decorative cuts on the drawer fronts shown in Fig. 8-11.

Be as careful with the edges on templates as you are with edges that provide bearing for a piloted bit. The guide's sleeve will faithfully follow any roughness or irregularity and duplicate it in the work. The thickness of the template is optional so long as it is compatible with the guide's sleeve length and allows the depth of cut you need. You'll find that 1/4-inch thickness works out pretty nicely for most of the work you will do.

DOING THE CUTTING

How to start the cut depends on what you envision as the final result. If the background of the project will be recessed, then the cut can start anywhere with the router moved until it is halted by the contact between guide sleeve and template edge. This also applies if the design will be recessed. In a sense, the template serves as a "stop."

The method must differ if the template serves mainly as an outline guide (Fig. 8-12). In this case, the sleeve should be in contact with the template and the bit should be turning be-

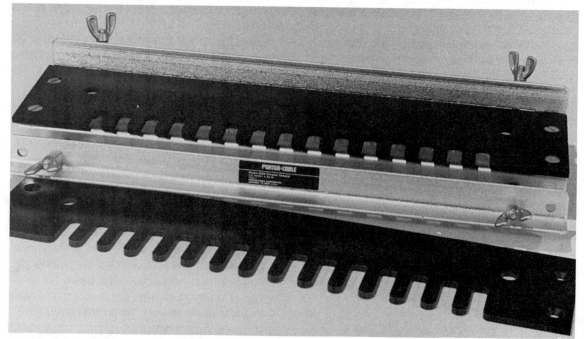

Fig. 8-9. Dovetail jigs are supplied with finger templates. The router is moved so the sleeve on the template guide follows the configuration of the fingers.

Fig. 8-10. An example of a "quickee" template. Layout and cutting can't be done casually even though you can use almost any piece of scrap wood to make such a one-time-use item. It's probably wise to store any template you make. You never know what the future holds.

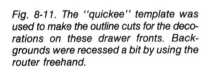

Fig. 8-11. The "quickee" template was used to make the outline cuts for the decorations on these drawer fronts. Backgrounds were recessed a bit by using the router freehand.

Fig. 8-12. A typical template that is used as an outline guide. The width of the cut depends on the bit you work with. Often cuts like this are made with veining bits, which produce a round bottom groove.

fore it contacts the work. The common solution is to have the tool running while you hold it on the work, titled just enough to avoid cutter-to-work contact. Then, very slowly, bring the router into working position. There are times when you might be able to start with the router level and the sleeve in correct position but without cutter contact. Then it's a matter of lowering the router until it sits solidly on the template. These methods don't apply if you are using a plunge router. The tool can be firmly in position with the

guide sleeve against the template's edge before the bit is lowered into the work.

Once the cut is started, be sure to maintain the necessary contact between sleeve and template throughout the pass (Fig. 8-13). On cuts of this nature, where the bit encounters all sorts of grain patterns and directions, you must be prepared to oppose the router's inclination to take an easier route rather than follow the template. At the end of the cut, lift the router vertically or, as many workers do, turn the tool off while maintaining the end-of-cut position and remove the tool after the bit stops. The whole idea is to avoid marring the work by tilting the router or moving it away from the template.

Outline cuts are often filled with a material that contrasts with the wood. This can be a wood filler or something like the plastic aluminum I used on the horse design in Figs. 8-14 and 8-15. It's usually best to apply more filler than is needed. Excess can be sanded flush after the material dries by working with a pad sander or sandpaper wrapped around a block of wood.

TEMPLATES THE EASY WAY

It might not be justifiable to call the setup that is shown in Fig. 8-16 a template; temporary guidance system might be more in order. The point is that elaborate templates that require time and effort to make are not always necessary, especially if what you are doing might never be repeated. While the arrangement might be an improvisation, the results will not lack professionalism. The tack-nailed arrangement of bits and pieces that were shown in Fig. 8-16 proved as efficient as necessary to produce the incised cut shown in Fig. 8-17.

All the cuts in Fig. 8-18 were produced by guiding the router with on-hand straight pieces and discs and squares of wood. For arcs and quarter circles and scallop designs, a disc can

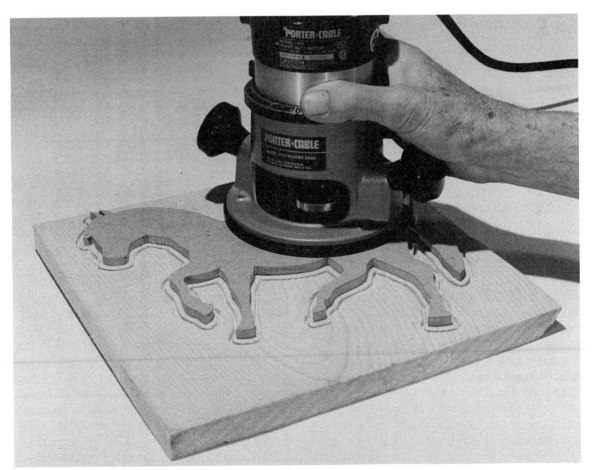

Fig. 8-13. The router must be moved to make the cut while the guide's sleeve is in constant contact with the edge of the template. Be firm; the bit might choose to follow grain direction instead of the template.

Fig. 8-14. Outline cuts can be filled with a contrasting material. Plastic aluminum was used here, but there are many types of wood fillers that can do very nicely.

be cut to suit on a band saw or jigsaw or with a handsaw. Figure 8-19 is a simple example of how a single guide (or in this case a template) can be used to produce various designs. The second cut was made after the guide's position was changed. Many variations are possible. The cuts can be made in parallel or opposing fashion, or they can cross each other at right angles or obliquely. You do want to give some thought to final results. Often the guide can be used to trace lines on paper so you can preview what various arrangements will produce.

Figures 8-20 and 8-21 show what might be the extremes of template design. When it was necessary to make cutouts in the top of a workbench, which was a one-time operation, I tacknailed an arrangement of straightedges to the bench top to outline the opening I needed. Another shop project involved a set of chairs that were designed with solid wood sides. It was necessary to provide a reuseable template so all the parts (12 were needed) would be exact duplicates.

The procedure required to cut through a workpiece is the same regardless of how the router is being guided. When the material is thin,

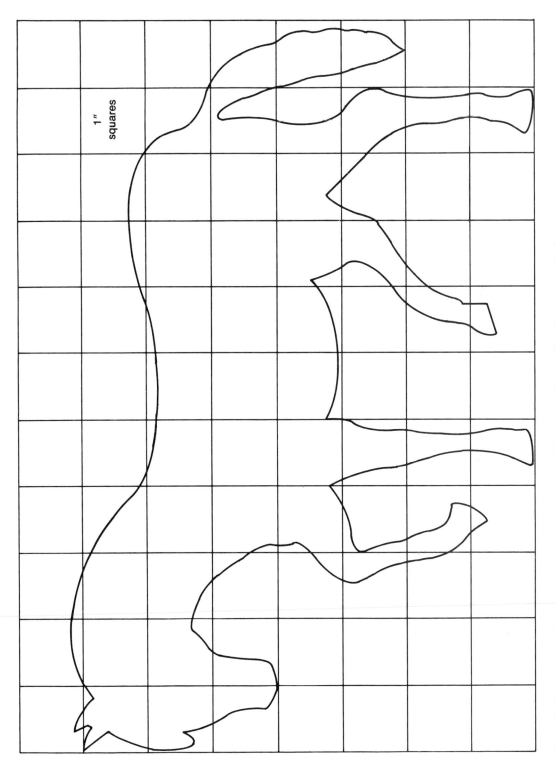

1"
squares

Fig. 8-15. The horse template can be made as large as you wish by using the traditional squares method.

113

Fig. 8-16. These are just bits and pieces of hardboard, but when organized and tack-nailed to the work, they serve as well as any one-piece template.

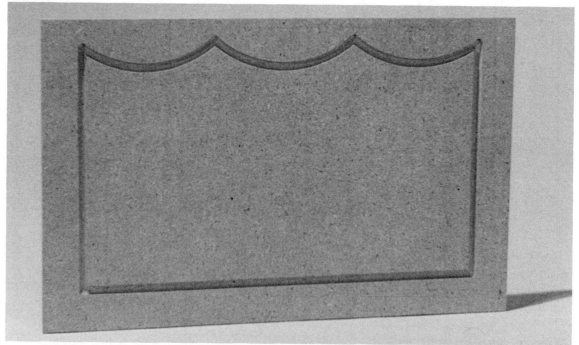

Fig. 8-17. Improvising templates by using separate pieces of wood doesn't downgrade the results you get. The idea might not be so exciting when you need to repeat the operation many times.

Fig. 8-18. All of these surface cuts were made with improvised, separate templates.

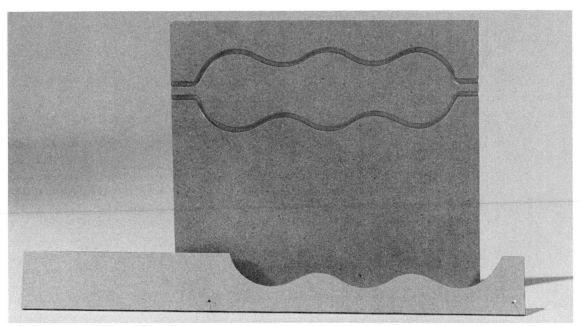

Fig. 8-19. A single template can be used to create interesting patterns. Results are best when you plan in advance how to situate the template for sequential cuts.

Fig. 8-20. A series of straightedges were used here as templates to outline the shape of a cutout needed in a workbench. Notice the support piece under the open end of the router base; this helps keep the tool level while cutting.

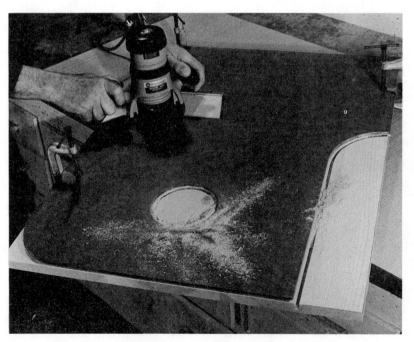

Fig. 8-21. There are many times when improvising a template by using separate pieces just won't do. The part you need might have an intricate profile, or you might need many duplicates. This hardboard template was used to produce 12 side pieces for a set of chairs.

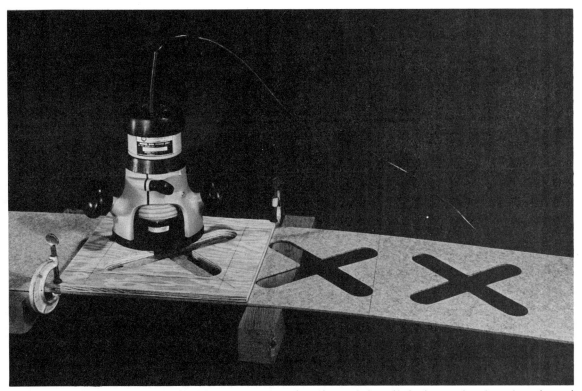

Fig. 8-22. Templates are also used when it is necessary to cut through a workpiece. Notice how work and template, clamped together, are elevated so the bottom of the bit is in open air.

say 1/4-inch plywood or hardboard, it would be a poor router indeed that could not do the job in a single pass (Fig. 8-22). When the material is thick, which is a relative term, the number of passes required, with depth of cut increased for each one, depends primarily on the horsepower of the tool. Judging whether to use one or two or even three passes relates to how the tool behaves. Smaller routers can rival big routers in terms of getting through particular stock thicknesses. It just takes longer to get there.

A FEW PRODUCTION IDEAS

Most commercial houses design special holding fixtures for components that are required in quantity to make it easier to do repeat design work. There's no reason why, under similar circumstances, you can't do the same. The exam-ple shown in Fig. 8-23 is a trough with side pieces separated by the width of the workpiece. The hinged cover, which is actually the template, is swung down after the cut-to-size workpiece is secured in the trough. Repeating the cut along the length of a workpiece is just a matter of repositioning the work for each operation. Marking the work beforehand for the cut spacing you want makes it easy to be accurate each time you move the work.

Figure 8-24 shows the details of another version of a trough jig. The concept is the same but the lid/template is registered correctly over the work by means of the locating pins. The height of the locating pins should be less than the thickness of the material used for the lid. Jigs of this type can be used for incising surface designs, recessing, and for cutting through.

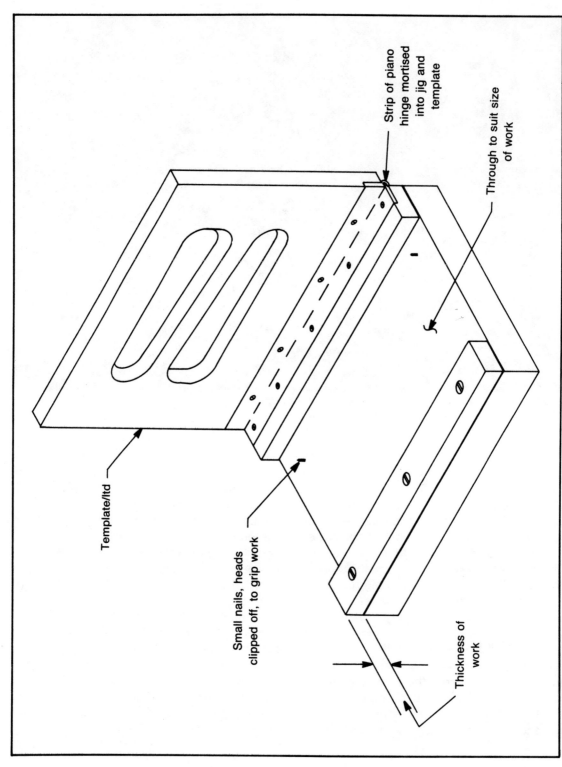

Strip of piano hinge mortised into jig and template

Through to suit size of work

Template/ltd

Small nails, heads clipped off, to grip work

Thickness of work

Fig. 8-23. Trough-type jigs make it easier to turn out pieces in quantity.

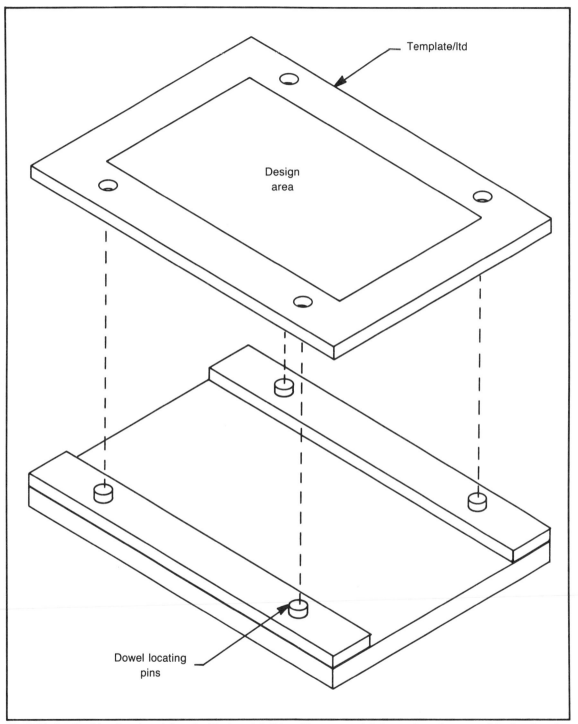

Template/ltd

Design
area

Dowel locating
pins

Fig. 8-24. Another idea for a trough-type jig. The template/lid positions accurately for each use because of the locating pins. Jigs like this are fine for production work or if they solve a special problem. It doesn't pay to make them for just one or two pieces.

Chapter 9

The Router as a Joinery Tool

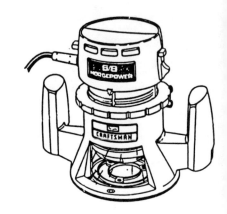

BY THIS TIME YOU CAN APPRECIATE THAT THE portable router is usable for more than skin-deep applications like shaping a fancy edge on a tabletop. Such work contributes visual impact and can often be the difference between a so-so project and a professional-looking unit. But it's in the often-concealed areas of furniture where you find the hallmarks of quality construction—the connections between components that make the difference between a chair or chest that soon wobbles and one that becomes an heirloom.

Any woodworking joint can be formed with hand tools or with stationary power tools used individually or in combination. A bit and brace, various chisels, and saws are needed to form a mortise and tenon joint by hand. With stationary power tools you would need a drill press for the mortise and a table saw or radial arm saw for the tenon. The unpretentious portable router does it all on its own—efficiently, often without having to change the bit, and with reasonable speed. Unless you're a purist with a love of dove-

tail saws and chisels and such, the router is the only way to get precision-fitted, classic dovetail joints in minimum time and with minimum fuss. This observation applies to all the sample joints shown in Fig. 9-1.

It's not all roses, though. The tool does what you ask it to, right or wrong, so careful tool handling is necessary. Most times a guide is required. This might be the pilot on a bit, a simple straightedge, a commercial accessory like a dovetail jig, or jigs that you make. Don't feel that the more advanced joints like the mortise and tenon or dovetail are the only ways to go, even though the portable router makes them more feasible. It's wise to determine the easiest-to-do joint in terms of what the project will be. You go all out for long-lived, esthetically pleasing furniture, but the same attention and design values for shelves in a garage that will hold garden tools and paint cans isn't justified.

RABBETS

A rabbet is a rabbet regardless of whether it is

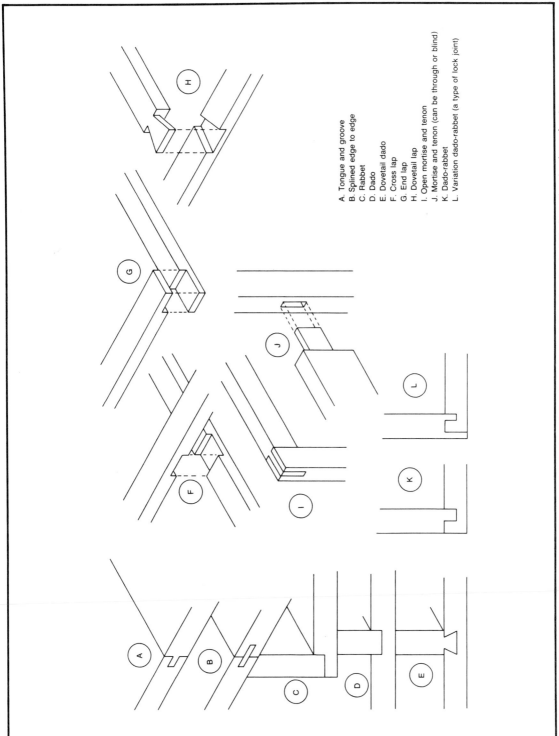

A. Tongue and groove
B. Splined edge to edge
C. Rabbet
D. Dado
E. Dovetail dado
F. Cross lap
G. End lap
H. Dovetail lap
I. Open mortise and tenon
J. Mortise and tenon (can be through or blind)
K. Dado-rabbet
L. Variation dado-rabbet (a type of lock joint)

Fig. 9-1. Typical joints that can be formed with a portable router. Notice how many of them involve just U-shaped or L-shaped cuts.

made across the end grain or parallel to an edge (Fig. 9-2). The width of the L-shaped cut usually matches the thickness of the mating piece. The depth of the cut is somewhat arbitrary, ranging from one-half to two-thirds the thickness of the component in which it is made. An extreme case is one involving plywood, where the cut is so deep that only the edge of the surface veneer is visible when the joint is assembled (Fig. 9-3). This is alright as far as appearance is concerned because it conceals unattractive plies in the material, but there will be weakness at the base of the shoulder (where width of cut and depth of cut meet). There is no problem if the project is designed to oppose the lateral forces that might cause a rupture at the weak point. Otherwise, glue blocks or other reinforcements should be introduced to increase the strength of the joint.

A common technique that results in smooth, trim corners after the project is assembled is shown in Fig. 9-4. Cut the rabbet a fraction wider than necessary so that after the glue used in the joint is dry, the excess can be sanded off so the edge will be perfectly flush with adjacent surfaces.

Rabbet cuts can be formed with a piloted bit, but the maximum width of cut available would be less than one half the cutting circle because you have to take into account the diameter of the pilot. For example, a rabbeting bit with a 1 1/4-inch diameter might have a cutting edge (width of cut) of 1/2 inch, and a one-pass depth of cut of 3/8 inch. This is fine for production work when the component that must fit the L-shaped cut is 1/2 inch thick. But how do you work with the variables that are present in one-time or infrequently confronted situations?

The solution is shown in Fig. 9-5. You work with a straight bit with a cutting circle that comes as close as possible to the rabbet's width of cut, and you guide the router along a straightedge. If the width of the cut you need is greater than

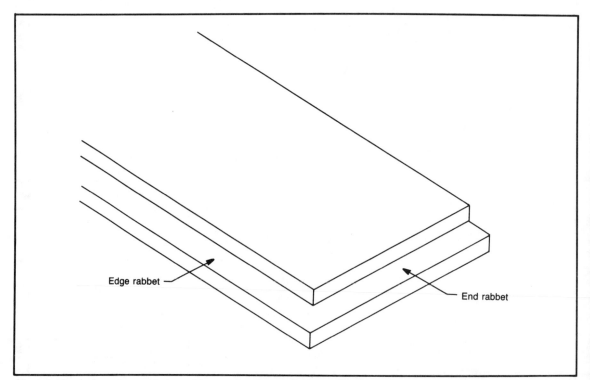

Fig. 9-2. The L-shaped cut called a *rabbet* can be cut across the end grain or along an edge. The shape is formed with a straight bit. Use repeat passes when necessary to widen the cut.

Fig. 9-3. Rabbet cuts are often deep enough so only the surface veneer of plywood and similar materials is visible. Joints like this should be reinforced with glue blocks when possible.

the diameter of the bit, then you reposition the straightedge and make another pass. The advantage of a pilotless, straight bit for this kind of work is that you can decide the width of the cut by the location of the straightedge. Any cut width from zero to the real diameter of the bit is available in a single pass.

It's characteristic of the rabbet joint that some of the end grain of the part in which the L-shaped cut is made will be exposed. This can

be objectionable. When constructing a case-type project, make the rabbet cut in side members so exposed end grain will be topside and less visible.

Components of case goods and cabinets are often rabbeted along back edges so a panel can be inset as a back seal (Fig. 9-6). When the rabbeting is done before assembly, the panel can have square corners. The corners of the panel must be rounded to mate with the corner radius left by the bit when rabbeting is done after assembly. If the project is something like a kitchen cabinet that will be wall-hung, cut the rabbet anywhere from 1/4 inch to 1/2 inch deeper than necessary so the back edges of the cabinet can be trimmed to conform to any irregularities in the wall.

A rabbet is often used in utility drawers as the joint between drawer front and sides (Fig. 9-7). How wide you cut the rabbet determines whether the drawer front will be flush or have a lip. This is not the strongest joint for the purpose, especially if only glue is used, so reinforcements such as nails, screws, or dowel pegs are usually added. These should be driven through the side of the drawer into the shoulder of the rabbet.

Fig. 9-4. Making the rabbet a bit wider than the thickness of the mating component is a good idea. The excess is sanded off after the joint is assembled.

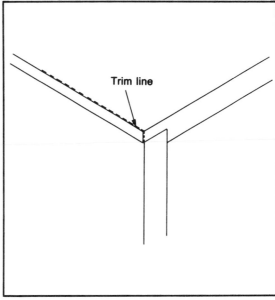

Trim line

Fig. 9-5. Rabbeting bits are available but are limited in how wide they can cut. Straight, pilotless bits, with the router guided by a straightedge, let you cut rabbets of any width.

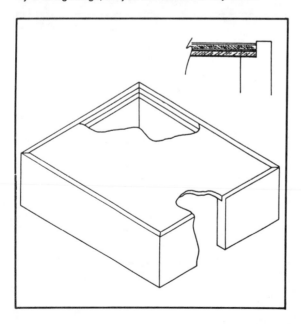

Fig. 9-6. Back edge of cabinets are often rabbeted so a panel can be inset as a back seal. The rabbeting can be done after assembly or on individual components before parts are put together.

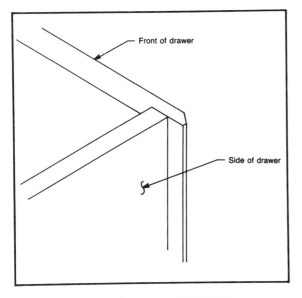

Front of drawer

Side of drawer

Fig. 9-7. Rabbets are often used on utility drawers as the joint between front and side pieces. The connection should be reinforced with nails, screws, or dowel pegs driven through the side into the shoulder of the rabbet.

DADOES AND GROOVES

Dadoes and grooves (Fig. 9-8) are U-shaped cuts formed in one component to accept the squared end of another part. A typical application is a bookcase where the ends of the shelves are set into dadoes formed in the vertical members. The width of the cut matches the thickness of the insert piece, but being precise to the point

where the insert must be forced into place can cause problems. It's best that the width of the dado allow the insert to slip into place, but without gaps. The depth of the cut is usually about one-half the stock's thickness. It can be more, but going too deep will create a weakness in the area.

The advantage of the U-shaped cuts be-

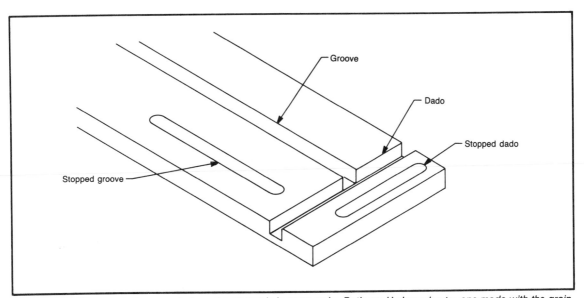

Groove

Dado

Stopped dado

Stopped groove

Fig. 9-8. The difference between a dado and a groove is in name only. Both are U-shaped cuts; one made with the grain, the other across the grain.

comes obvious when they are stacked against a butt joint. The shape of the joint forms a ledge for the insert, and there is more surface area for glue. But there is a disadvantage. The U-shape, which is not very attractive, is visible at front edges when the cut runs across the component. When this is bothersome, one of the ideas shown in Fig. 9-9 can be used to conceal the joint or, as they say, "to fool the eye."

Another solution is to make stopped or blind cuts and to shape the insert in one of the ways shown in Fig. 9-10. The only difference between this cutting technique and forming the cut completely across the stock is that blocks are used so the router can be started and stopped at specific points (Fig. 9-11). A plunge router has advantages for this type of operation because the tool can be firmly positioned before the bit is made to penetrate the work. The procedure with a conventional router calls for tilting the tool

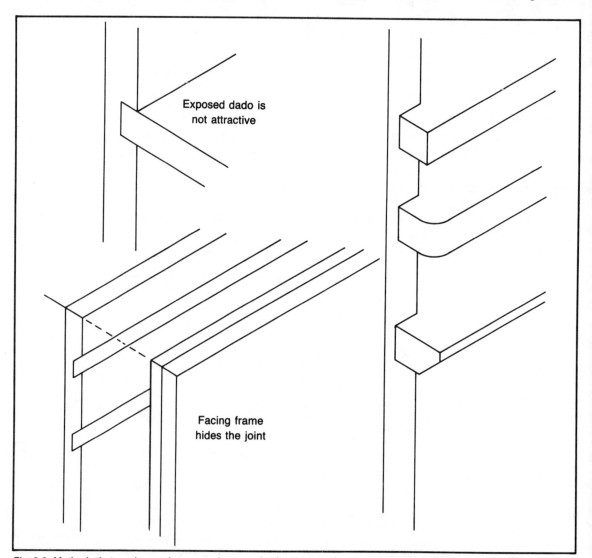

Exposed dado is
not attractive

Facing frame
hides the joint

Fig. 9-9. Methods that can be used to conceal or to make the U-shaped cut less viable. These extra steps are not necessary on utility projects, like shelves in a garage or tool shed.

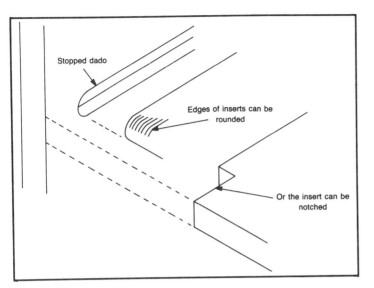

Fig. 9-10. The ends of insert pieces can be shaped in one of the ways shown here when a blind or stopped dado is used.

Fig. 9-11. The length of stopped or blind dadoes (or rabbets) is controlled by using stop blocks to determine where the cut starts and ends. It's on jobs like this that the plunge router displays its merits.

to start with and then slanting it down so the bit can get going.

Unless the cut you need is reasonably close to an edge so the router can be used with an edge guide, dadoing and grooving are done using straightedges. These can simply be strips of wood that are clamped or tack-nailed in place. You can also use one of the ideas that were described in Chapter 6 dealing with straight cutting.

Grooves are often needed in edges of fabricated panels like plywood or particleboard, so trim can be added to conceal unattractive core material. Often the trim, which is not uncommon on table edges and countertops, is ready-made metal molding with an integral, serrated "tongue" that is forced into the groove (Fig. 9-12). Professionals use slotting cutters for this kind of work, but it's possible, when you lack the tools, to get by with a small, regular straight bit. It's crucial that the width of the groove be exactly right for the tongue on the molding.

Figure 9-13 shows other ways to take care of unsightly edges. As you can see, the added strip can be simple or can be designed to contribute to the overall appearance of the project. Strips can be preshaped, but when solid wood edging is used, it's best to do router work after the new pieces are in place. Often a contrasting material is used for the edge strips; for example, strips of walnut or cherry on the perimeter of a birch or maple table.

HALF-LAP JOINTS

Examples of common half-lap joints are shown in Figs. 9-14 and 9-15. When the parts to be joined have equal width and thickness, the width of the cut is the same as the stock's width, while the depth of the cut is one-half the material's thickness. This applies whether the joint will be at a midway point or at an end, in which case the joint is technically an "end" lap.

It's always best, whether two pieces or a dozen pieces are involved, to hold the piece together with clamps or some other means, so cutting is done across them all at the same time. Use a straightedge as a router guide and cut with the largest diameter straight bit you have. Use repeat passes to widen the cut when necessary. End laps should be done the same way. Assuming a four-piece frame, assemble the parts as a unit so you can cut across them as if the assembly were a single board.

MORTISE AND TENON JOINTS

The mortise and tenon joint, whose parts are il-

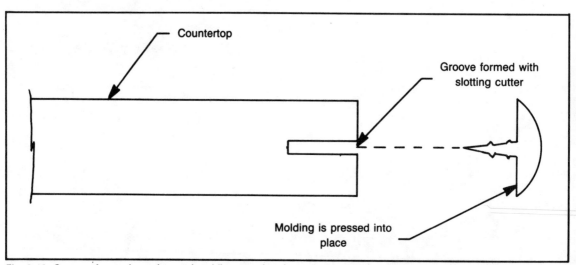

Countertop

Groove formed with slotting cutter

Molding is pressed into place

Fig. 9-12. Grooves for ready-made metal molding are often formed with slotting cutters, but you can get by with a small straight bit when necessary.

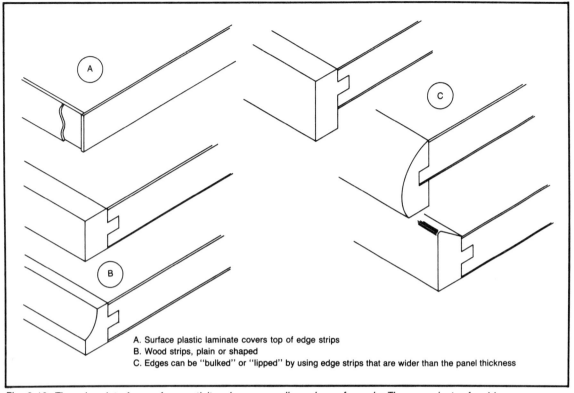

A. Surface plastic laminate covers top of edge strips
B. Wood strips, plain or shaped
C. Edges can be "bulked" or "lipped" by using edge strips that are wider than the panel thickness

Fig. 9-13. There is a lot of room for creativity when concealing edges of panels. These are just a few ideas.

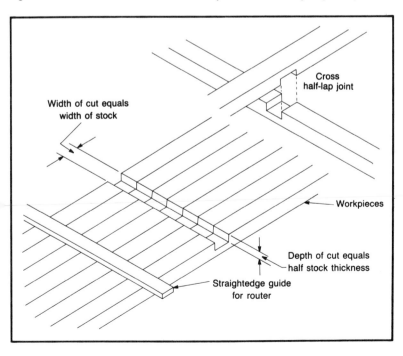

Cross
half-lap joint

Width of cut equals
width of stock

Workpieces

Depth of cut equals
half stock thickness

Straightedge guide
for router

Fig. 9-14. View the cuts needed for crossing half-lap joints as dadoes.

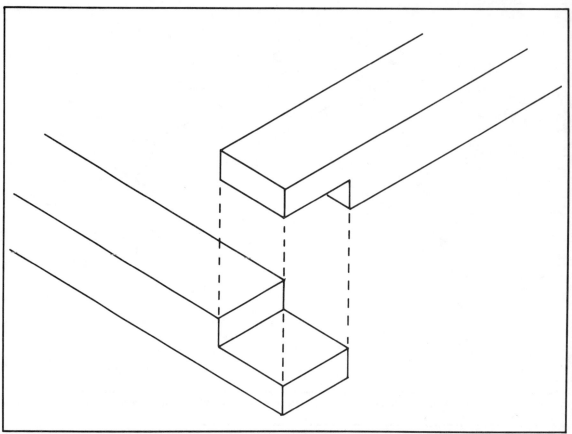

Fig. 9-15. Cuts required for end laps are just rabbets. The rabbets are equal when the components have the same width and thickness.

lustrated in Fig. 9-16, ranks with the dovetail joint in terms of heirloom-quality construction. Often a doweled joint is used as a convenient substitute. This is acceptable, but the design isn't more than a butt joint reinforced with pegs. The mating surfaces of the components present end grain to surface grain, which doesn't provide for the strongest glue bond. It's better to arrange for the glue bond to occur long-grain-to-long-grain, which is what a tenon in a mortise does. With a mortise and tenon you get maximum glue bond on interior contact surfaces, plus the interlocking feature provided by the joint's design.

There are many variations of the mortise and tenon joint, some of which are illustrated in Figs. 9-17 and 9-18. The concept is an integral projection on one component that is sized for a

cavity, usually rectangular, that is formed in the mating piece. The projection is the tenon, the cavity is the mortise. The mortise may be of limited depth (blind) or it can pass through the material. This determines how long the tenon must be. When the tenon is used with a through mortise, cut it a fraction longer than necessary. Then the amount that projects can be sanded flush to adjacent surfaces after the glue dries. If the mortise is blind, cut the tenon a fraction shorter than the depth of the mortise; this provides a bit of room for excess glue.

In my shop, the mortise is always cut first. Then the tenons are formed so they slip-fit into the cavity. The tenon must not wobble when you insert it, but on the other hand, it shouldn't be necessary to use excessive force to seat it.

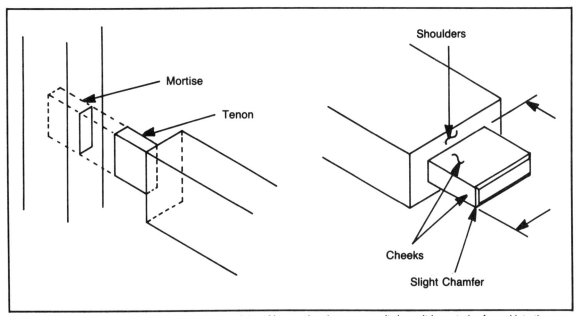

Fig. 9-16. Nomenclature of the mortise and tenon joint. Always size the tenon so it doesn't have to be forced into the mortise. The tenon can be "through" or "blind."

Tenons that are too tight can cause mating pieces to split, even force excess glue to travel through the pores of the wood. The thickness of the tenon, and so the width of the mortise, should not be greater than one-third to one-half the thickness of the mortised component.

JIGS TO MAKE

The jigs that I use in my shop that practically eliminate the possibility of human error when forming mortise and tenon joints are a vise clamp (Fig. 9-19) and a special, adjustable router base (Fig. 9-20). One of the problems associated with forming mortises is that they are most often formed in the narrow edge of stock. This poses the problem of keeping the router level as you make the cut. Traditionally, the solution is to clamp an extra piece on each side of the work to provide more support surface for the tool. The vice clamp provides this automatically without the need of additional clamps (Fig. 9-21). The work is gripped by the jaws of the vise clamp that, in turn, is secured in the bench vise. When the same cut is required in several pieces, butt the parts together on a flat surface and hold them with a clamp so you can mark across all of them at the same time.

Figure 9-22 shows the special router subbase ready for mounting, while Fig. 9-23 shows it in action together with the vise clamp. Once the adjustable guides in the subbase are set, you'll know that all the cuts you make will be on the same centerline. Because the guides are individually adjustable, the tool can be positioned for mortise cuts that are off center as well as on center. The setup provides plenty of bearing surface for the router, and the guides ride snug against the jaws of the vise clamp to assure that the bit travels in a straight line. Cuts with a conventional router are started, as usual for this type of work, with the tool tilted and then slanted down so the bit can penetrate. With a plunge router, the bit is made to enter while the tool is firmly in position. Make repeat passes, when necessary, to deepen the cut.

FORMING TENONS

Forming tenons is like making back-to-back rab-

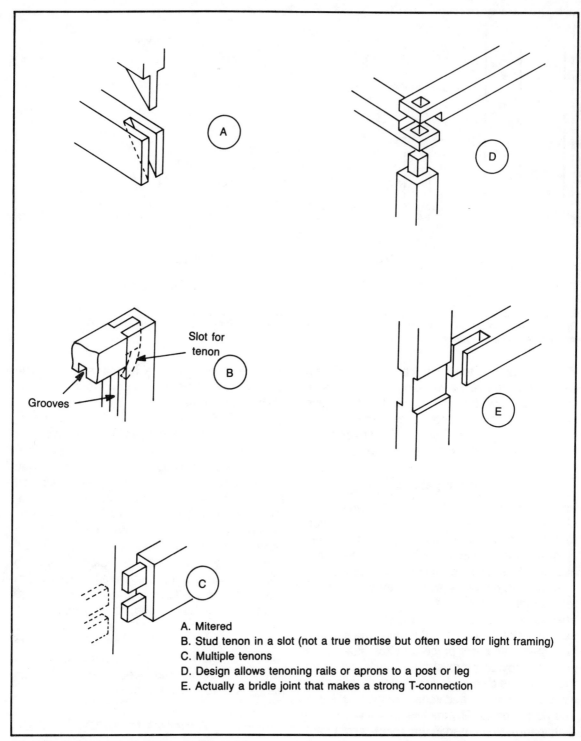

A. Mitered
B. Stud tenon in a slot (not a true mortise but often used for light framing)
C. Multiple tenons
D. Design allows tenoning rails or aprons to a post or leg
E. Actually a bridle joint that makes a strong T-connection

Fig. 9-17. Various types of mortise and tenon joints.

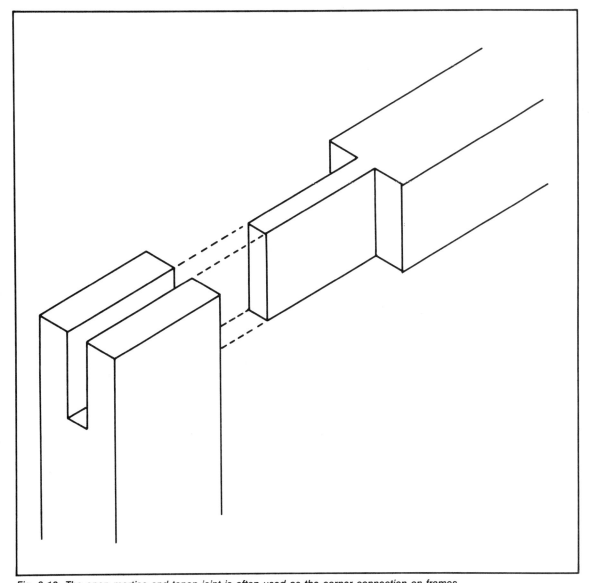

Fig. 9-18. The open mortise and tenon joint is often used as the corner connection on frames.

bet cuts. Similar ones are often needed on several of the project's components; for example, rails and stretchers for a chair. The tenons can be formed after the parts have been cut to width and length, but there is a better way. Select a piece of stock that is wide enough to accommodate the number of parts you need and cut it to correct length. If you need four parts 2 inches wide, then the stock should be about 9

inches wide. The extra width is for the saw cuts that will be made to separate the stock into individual pieces.

The next step is demonstrated in Figs. 9-24 and 9-25. Work with the largest straight bit you have. The depth of the cut, which is made on both sides of the work, should leave a projection of correct tenon thickness. In this case, on 1 1/2-inch material the cut-depth is 1/2 inch, so

133

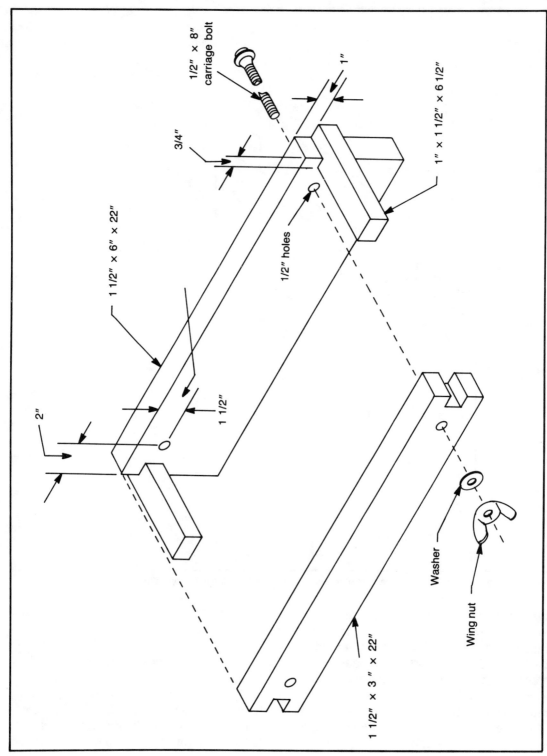

1/2" × 8"
carriage bolt

1" × 1 1/2" × 6 1/2"

1"

3/4"

1/2" holes

1 1/2" × 6" × 22"

1 1/2"

2"

Washer

Wing nut

1 1/2" × 3 " × 22"

Fig. 9-19. Construction details of the vise clamp. Drill the holes for the carriage bolts after the parts have been formed and assembled. Be sure the top edges of the jaws are flat and flush with each other.

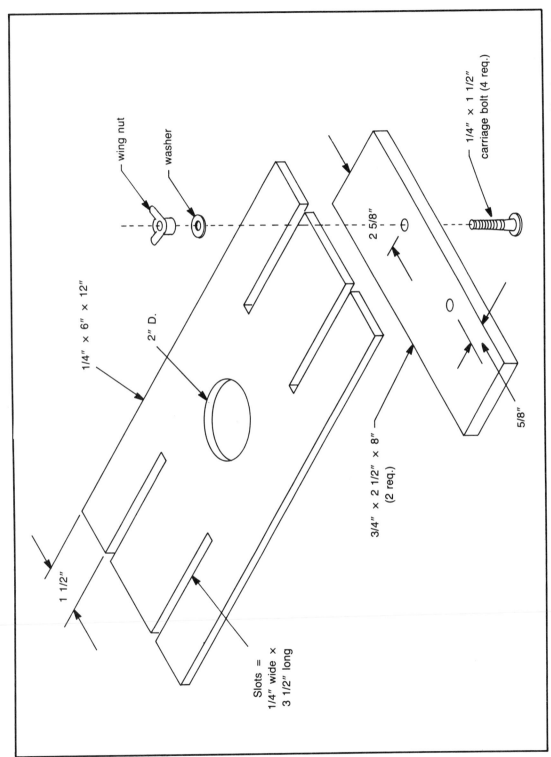

wing nut

washer

1/4" × 6" × 12"

2" D.

1 1/2"

Slots =
1/4" wide ×
3 1/2" long

3/4" × 2 1/2" × 8"
(2 req.)

2 5/8"

5/8"

1/4" × 1 1/2"
carriage bolt (4 req.)

Fig. 9-20. How to make the special router subbase for use when mortising, forming dovetails, edge grooves, and similar chores. Use the router's own subbase as a pattern for locating the center opening and holes for attachment screws.

Fig. 9-21. Workpieces are gripped between the jaws of the vise clamp. The setup provides plenty of support area for the router.

Fig. 9-22. The assembled, special subbase. The self-adhesive measuring tapes are optional, but they do provide a quick means of setting the guides.

Fig. 9-23. Once the guides on the subbase are set, you can be sure that all the cuts you make will be on the same centerline. Cuts can be made to marked lines, or you can work with stop blocks.

Fig. 9-24. The first step when similar tenons are required on multiple pieces. The shape is formed on material that is wide enough to be sawed into the number of parts you need. Notice the use of the outboard support block.

Fig. 9-25. Make repeat passes when necessary. Mark the work accurately beforehand so you'll know where to position the straightedge for each of the cuts.

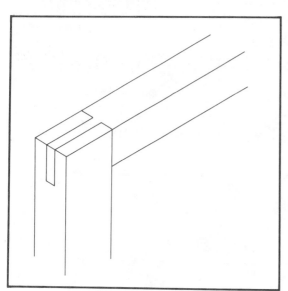

Fig. 9-26. If you are producing open mortise and tenon joints, the tenon part of the work is done after the sawing operation.

the tenon thickness will be 1/2 inch. Be sure to mark the work correctly on both surfaces so the straightedge can be positioned accurately for the back-to-back cuts.

When the routing is complete, the stock is sawed into correct width components. If the tenon is for an open mortise and tenon joint (Fig. 9-26), then the job is done. If a true tenon with four shoulders is required, then the additional step shown in Fig. 9-27 must be taken. This is like the first phase of the job. The individual pieces are clamped together or secured in a vise; routing is done as if the assembly were a solid block. Be sure that the pieces are in perfect alignment before using the router.

Mortises that are formed with a router bit will have round ends, so the tenon must be shaped accordingly (Fig. 9-28). The tenons can be used as is if you square the ends of the mortises with a chisel.

Mortising can be done in miter cuts that will be reinforced with a spline by using the same vise clamp and special base setup (Fig. 9-29). Two factors are crucial in order for the joint to mate perfectly. The miter cut must be perfect, and the cut end must be set perfectly flush with the jaws of the vise clamp. Figure 9-30 shows how the spline, in this case a strip of hardboard, is used in the joint. The spline should be sized for a slip-fit; its length should be a fraction less than the combined depth of the mortises.

Figure 9-31 shows another practical use for

Fig. 9-27. To produce a true tenon, the individual pieces are clamped together and the final routing is done as if they were a solid block. Move the router slowly and be sure to keep it perfectly level.

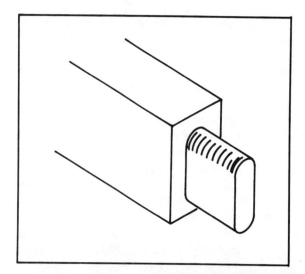

Fig. 9-28. Tenons can be shaped to suit the round end of mortises that are formed with a router bit, or you can square the ends of the mortises with a small chisel so the tenons can be used as is.

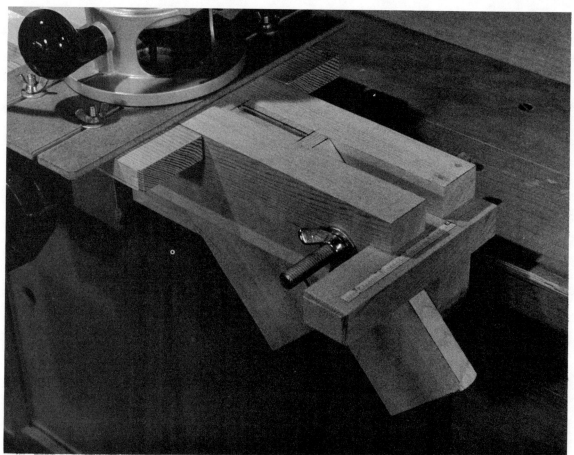

Fig. 9-29. The vise clamp and the special subbase can also be used when you choose to form mortises in miter cuts. The miter cut must be perfect to begin with.

Fig. 9-30. Like a tenon, the spline used in the miter joint should have rounded edges to suit the shape of the mortise.

Fig. 9-31. Holding slim pieces of wood securely for edge shaping is another use for the vise clamp.

the vise clamp—securing a narrow strip for an edge cut. When necessary, the work can be elevated on blocks that are placed at each end of the vise clamp.

A COMMERCIAL JIG

The jig shown in Fig. 9-32 was once known as "Morten the Jig," a cute name for a very practical idea. It's now a Porter Cable product, simply called a mortise and tenon template, but the changeover hasn't made it less useful. The jig is intriguing because it allows the user to be flexible. Single, double, even triple mortise and tenon joints can be accomplished with impressive accuracy and, once you have become ac-

quainted with the system, in reasonable time (see Figs. 9-33 to 9-35). The heart of the accessory is the template and the way it can be registered on the frame assembly for particular cuts. Little, if any, measuring is required. Detailed instructions are provided with the jig package. Do not ignore the instructions. To get the most from a tool like this, it's best to go through a test period by trying procedures on scrap stock.

BECOMING A DOVETAIL EXPERT

Dovetails are hallmarks of quality construction. This eminence can be appreciated when you understand how superior a dovetail joint is when used as the connection between the front of a

Fig. 9-32. The frame assembly of the mortise and tenon jig has locating pins so the template can be located accurately for specific operations. Notice that the bit, which is supplied, has a ball-bearing guide located above the cutting edges.

Fig. 9-33. The jig is secured to the workpiece, which is gripped in a vise. Here a double mortise is being completed. Allow the router to come to a full stop before lifting it from the work.

Fig. 9-34. The router is moved so the guide on the bit starts to follow the template at the open end. Cutting must be done carefully to avoid damaging the first tenons that are formed.

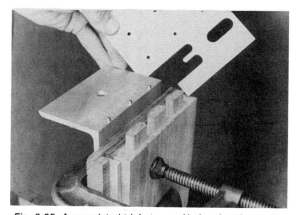

Fig. 9-35. A completed triple tenon. Notice the pins on the frame assembly that are used to register the template. To become expert with jigs like this you must obey all the instructions.

drawer and its side members. Each time you open a drawer the major stress on the assembly is where front and sides are joined. The pull on the drawer front is opposed by the other parts of the drawer and the weight of its contents. When you consider the number of times a kitchen drawer is opened during the life of the unit, you realize what the front-to-side connection must withstand.

The dovetail joint is an interlocking design. Pins, or tongues if you wish, have tapered sides that mesh with matching sockets. The connection opposes forces that tend to pull it apart, and it will do this even if the glue should fail.

Dovetail joints can be formed by hand with dovetail saws, coping saws, chisels, and such. They can also be formed by improvising procedures on a drill press, a table or radial arm saw, or even on a stationary shaper. The portable router, especially since the advent of modern techniques and jigs, allows anyone to quickly do professional work without sacrificing individuality and with minimum apprenticeship.

DADOES AND GROOVES BY DOVETAIL

Too often dovetail thinking is limited to case goods, drawers, and such, and the host of other possible applications are overlooked. A few of these are shown in Figs. 9-36 through 9-39. Dovetail grooves, together with matching dovetail tongues, are excellent substitutes for regular dadoes and grooves when the strength required in the joint is crucial, or when you have a yen to do something a bit different from the norm. The idea can also be used for sliding connections, in which case either the groove or the tongue must be "eased" enough to provide smooth movement. Areas where the sliding design can be used include guidance systems for drawers, adjustable shelves or partitions, pullout shelves, sliding vertical supports that can be part of book or record racks, and projects like the box with sliding cover shown in Fig. 9-37.

Any straight-line dovetail can be formed in line with or across the grain of workpieces by using a straightedge or one of the ideas demon-

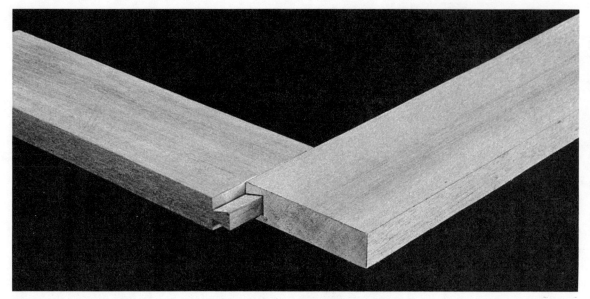

Fig. 9-36. Dovetailed grooves and tongues provide strong, interlocking connections.

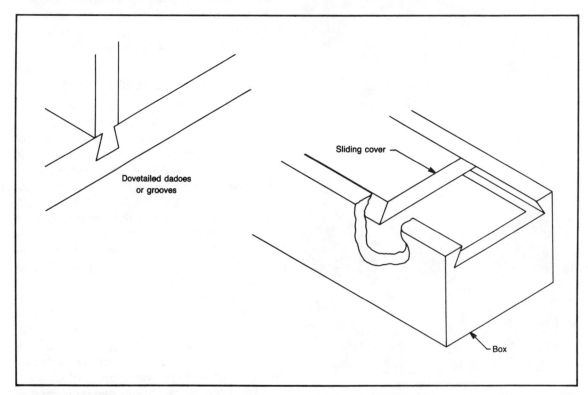

Fig. 9-37. Dovetail-shaped grooves can be formed with or across the grain. Matching tongues can be glued in place for a permanent assembly, or one of the components can be "eased" a bit for a sliding assembly. Sliding dovetails are often used on box projects.

144

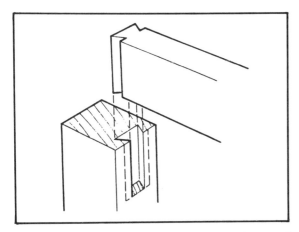

Fig. 9-38. This type of dovetail joint is often used in place of a mortise and tenon joint when, for example, making leg and rail assemblies.

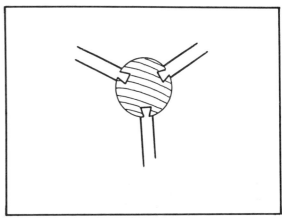

Fig. 9-39. A similar application is often used to join legs to a pedestal. Dovetail cuts in round components can be formed accurately by using the fluting jig (discussed in Chapter 10).

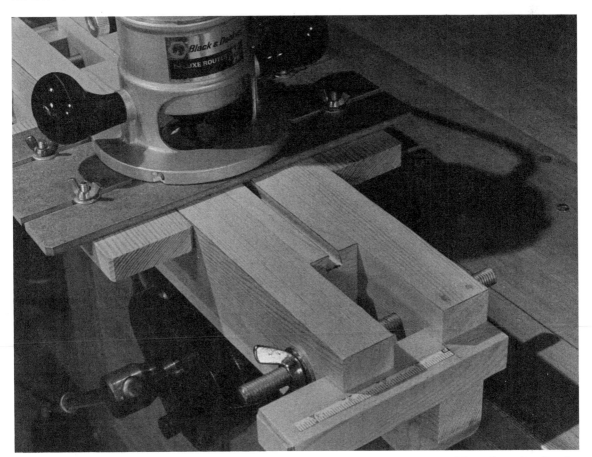

Fig. 9-40. Forming a dovetail in the edge of narrow work can be done accurately and with minimum fuss when the vise clamp and the special router subbase are used.

strated in Chapter 6. When the cut is required in the edge of workpieces, then the right setup is similar to what you would use when forming a mortise. The work would be sandwiched between extra pieces of wood to provide adequate support surface for the router; the router would be moved along with an edge guide.

When the length of the workpiece allows it, the vise clamp and special router base setup can be used. The dovetail groove is formed as shown in Fig. 9-40. The tongue needs a little more attention (Fig. 9-41). The work is placed between scrap pieces because cuts are required on both its edges. Notice that only one of the adjustable base guides is used. When one side of the cut is finished, the router makes a second pass af-

ter it has been turned so the guide bears against the opposite edge of the jig. There is no need to readjust the guide.

Figure 9-42 shows more details of forming dovetail grooves in edges. Notice that the same technique can be used to produce tongue and groove joints, an example of which is shown in Fig. 9-43.

READY-MADE DOVETAIL JIGS

There are quite a few commercial dovetail jigs on the market, and any router-user who doesn't own one or two is missing a good bet. All the fuss and bother of layout and hand work, or the improvisations that are necessary when other

Fig. 9-41. The same setup can be used to form the dovetail tongue. The work is sandwiched between scrap pieces. The cuts are made without having to change the position of the guide on the subbase.

146

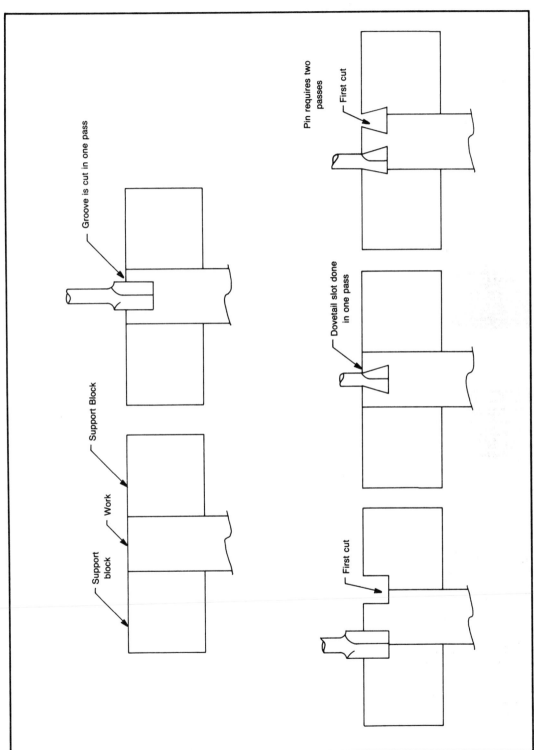

Fig. 9-42. How dovetail grooves and tongues (or if you wish, slots and pins) are formed. When work is too long for the vise clamp, you can still use the special subbase. Just clamp the work between support blocks. Here the tongue requires two passes; the router bit cuts into support blocks. This also applies to groove-type dovetails.

147

Fig. 9-43. Sample of a tongue and groove joint that was formed following the same procedure for dovetailing.

tools are used, is eliminated when a dovetail jig is used to guide the router. All the jigs allow producing the two dovetail connections that are shown in Fig. 9-44, which are fairly standard designs in drawer and case constructions. The difference between them is more visual than anything else. The joint lines of the through dovetail are visible side and front. When the half-blind concept is used on a drawer, for example, the joint lines are visible only when the drawer is pulled out. "Seeing" the joint is not objectionable, however, because they are often deliberately exposed as a sign of dedicated craftsmanship.

Different names are used to identify parts of the dovetail joint, but those shown in Fig. 9-45 are generally acceptable. The configuration that is between sockets is called the *tail.* Confusion can be eliminated if you just think in terms of *pins* and *tails.*

When a jig like the one in Fig. 9-46 is correctly organized, you can produce as many precisely fitting dovetail joints as you like with each one taking only a few minutes to do. But production is not the prime factor. For the woodworker who is usually involved with a single project, it's the ease with which dovetail expertise is acquired that counts. Being able to make joints like the one in Fig. 9-47 in "jig" time is pretty nice.

Using a jig isn't difficult, but you will be in trouble if you plunge right in without studying the manual supplied with the tool and without testing what you learn on some scrap material. When you consider what the results can be, being an apprentice for an hour or two isn't asking much. Important factors include the

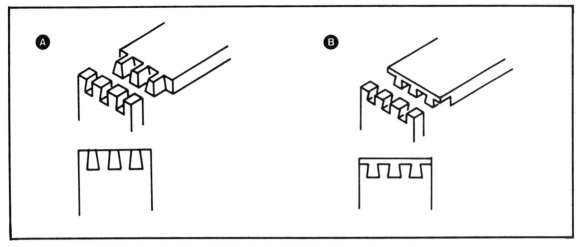

Fig. 9-44. These are the most common dovetail joint designs. A is a through dovetail, B is a half-blind or French dovetail. Some jigs can be used only for the half-blind type; others allow you to do both.

maximum width of stock the fixture can handle, whether you can work with one or several stock thicknesses, the size of the dovetails produced, and the size of the dovetail bit and template guide that should be used.

Most fixtures for half-blind dovetails are equipped with a finger template that is sized for producing 1/2-inch dovetails in stock thicknesses that might range from about 1/2 to 1 inch. It's often possible to purchase an additional template so the fixture can be used for smaller dovetails, usually 1/4 inch. This makes it possible to work on thinner material, from about 5/16 to 5/8 inch, but the work must be done with a template guide and a dovetail bit that are compatible with the finger template.

One of the intriguing features of this type of dovetail jig is that both components of the joint are clamped together in the fixture and the mating configurations (pins and tails) are cut at the same time (Fig. 9-48). When the shaping is complete, the two parts are ready for joining, just like that (Fig. 9-49). You can't go wrong if you follow the instructions for securing the parts in the jig so they have the correct relationship.

Start the cutting by placing the router firmly on the left end of the template but with the cutter clear of the work. Then turn on the machine and move it slowly into the work until the sleeve

on the template guide makes contact with the finger template. Make the pass from left to right while allowing the template guide to control in and out movements. It's crucial to keep the router flat on the template throughout the pass. Turn the router off at the end of the cut, but keep it in working position until the bit stops turning. While keeping it on a horizontal plane, move it away from the template. For perfect results, you must avoid tilting the router at the start, during, and at the end of the cut. Tilting will damage the finger template as well as the workpieces.

Some manuals suggest that the cut be

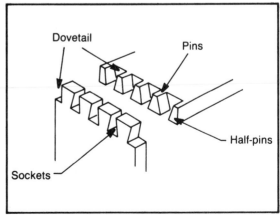

Fig. 9-45. Common names for the parts of dovetails. The shape between sockets is the "tail."

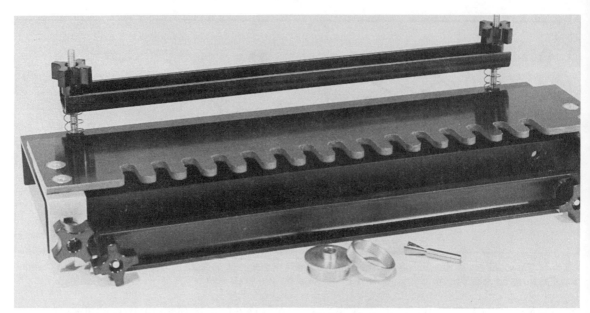

Fig. 9-46. Typical jig that makes it easy to produce equally spaced, half-blind dovetails. It's best to mount the fixture on a sturdy board that, in turn, can be clamped to a workbench.

Fig. 9-47. If you follow instructions so you can use the jig efficiently, you will be able to produce precise dovetail joints in little time.

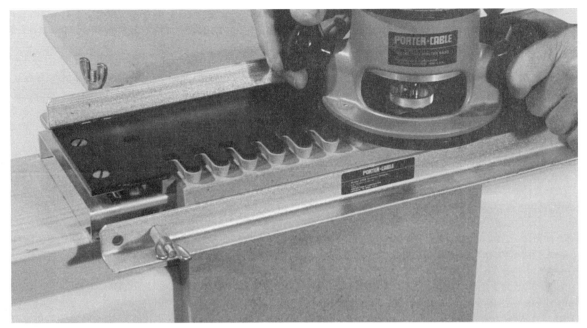

Fig. 9-48. A feature of the jigs is that the components are secured in correct relationship so both parts of the joint are cut at the same time. Keep the sleeve of the template guide firmly against the fingers of the jig's template throughout the pass.

Fig. 9-49. Can you imagine how long it would take to form these dovetail components by hand? And the care required to be as accurate? The only negative factor is that the jig decides spacing and size of the cuts.

started by moving the router in a reasonably straight line along the outside edge of the fingers. Then the shaping is finished by moving the router along the finger template in routine fashion. The thought is that the procedure will minimize the possibility that the part held vertically in the jig will be chipped as the router is moved in and out of the template. It's not an unreasonable idea. At least it's one to consider should you encounter trouble in that area.

It's a good idea when using the jigs for drawer joints to identify the parts of the drawer and inside and outside faces (Fig. 9-50). This will help you place the components in the jig so mating cuts will mesh and parts will appear as you want them to after assembly. The jigs can be used to produce drawers with flush or rabbeted (lipped) edges (Fig. 9-51). For the rabbeted design, the drawer front is prepared as shown in Fig. 9-52 before the dovetail shaping is done.

OTHER TYPES OF DOVETAIL JIGS

Dovetail jigs are fine tools that make it easy to produce dovetail joints you can be proud of, but they do have a drawback. They are designed primarily for half-blind dovetails, and the size and spacing of the cuts are dictated by the finger templates that can be used with the jig. To be more flexible and creative when dovetailing and to be able to decide the size, number, and spacing of the cuts (like those shown in Fig. 9-53), you must check out other dovetail jig concepts. These tools are more expensive, but they are structurally and conceptually impressive and produce advanced dovetailing work quickly. If you will occasionally use a dovetail joint, say in a drawer, then don't look here. If you want to do detailed dovetail joinery, then read on.

Leigh dovetail jigs (Fig. 9-54), which are manufactured in Canada but are widely available in the United States, are made in two sizes. One model can be used with work up to 12 inches wide. Another recently introduced unit can be used with material up to 24 inches in width. This poses little limitation on the sizes of your dovetail projects. Both of the jigs can be used for through or half-blind dovetails (Fig. 9-55), and the number and spacing of the dovetails is decided by the operator, not by a pattern established by a one-piece finger template.

The guidance system of the Leigh jigs consists of individual fingers that have different con-

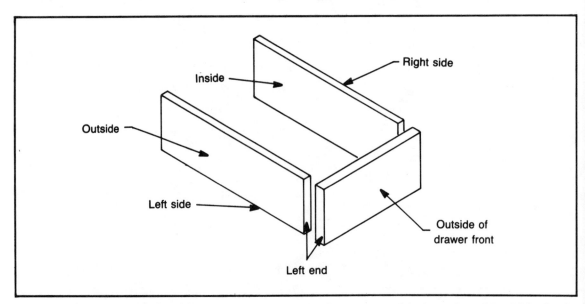

Fig. 9-50. Before doing dovetail work for a drawer, be sure to identify the parts and the faces that will be visible after the project is assembled so you'll know how to place the parts in the jig.

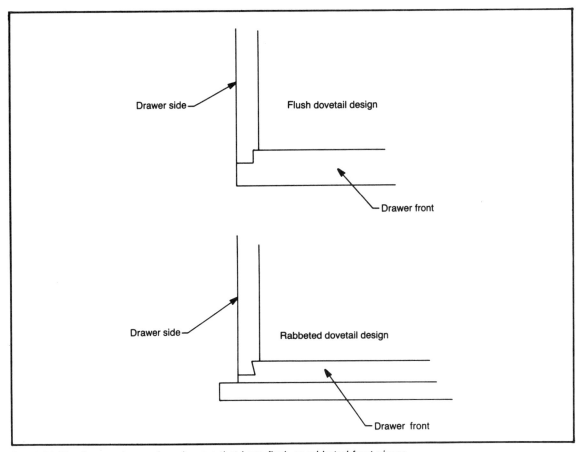

Fig. 9-51. The jigs can be used on drawers that have flush or rabbeted front pieces.

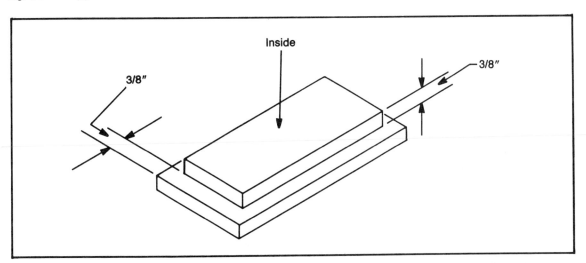

Fig. 9-52. The stock for a rabbeted drawer front must be prepared a certain way. This is just an example. Check the owner's manual for particulars.

Fig. 9-53. To be completely flexible in the area of dovetail joinery you can make cuts with hand tools or with a jig you to size and space the dovetails as you choose.

figurations at each end and that are adjustable in relation to each other because they can be moved along a slide bar. The fingers, after adjustment to suit your purpose, together with the slide bar form an assembly that can be flipped end for end or rotated depending on the work that must be done (Fig. 9-56).

Forming through dovetails on the Leigh jigs is a two-step operation. Shaping the tails is accomplished by guiding a dovetail bit along the straight end of the fingers (Fig. 9-57), while the pins are formed by using the opposite end of the fingers to guide a straight bit (Fig. 9-58). This might sound more complicated than it is. The operation actually goes pretty smoothly because no finger adjustment is needed between the cuts. Placing the finger assembly in correct po-

sition for each of the cuts is made easy by using the scales that are part of the jig design. You do have to be careful with bit projection when changing from one router bit to the other. The work can be facilitated by using two routers, one with the straight bit and the other with the dovetail bit, with each bit set to the correct depth of cut. Whether you work with one router or two, it's best to make all the pin or tail cuts (it doesn't matter which you do first) in all the parts that are involved before changing over to the second operation.

The 24-inch Leigh jig has a greater capacity than the smaller version in thickness of stock that can be handled as well as in maximum stock width. Tails can be cut stock up to 1 inch thick; pins in material up to 3/4 inch. The 12-inch unit

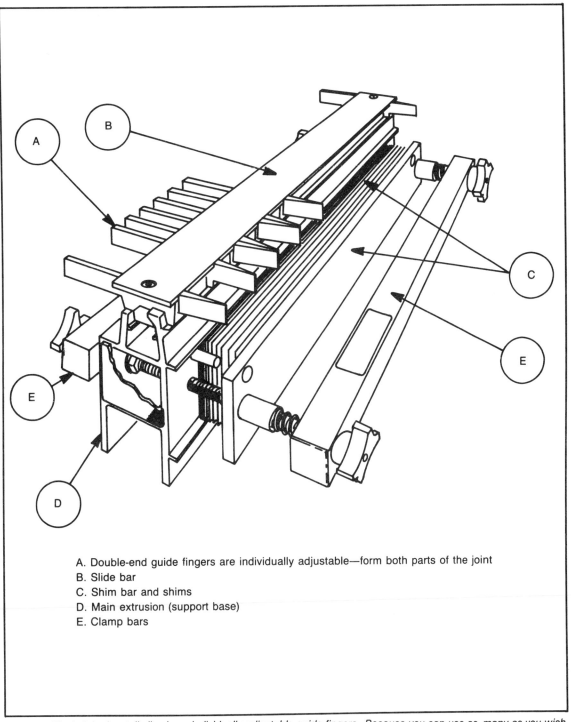

A. Double-end guide fingers are individually adjustable—form both parts of the joint
B. Slide bar
C. Shim bar and shims
D. Main extrusion (support base)
E. Clamp bars

Fig. 9-54. The Leigh dovetails jigs have individually adjustable guide fingers. Because you can use as many as you wish, and spacing is optional, you can form dovetail joints with exclusive patterns.

Fig. 9-55. This is just an example of the flexibility you have when a jig like the Leigh product is available.

can also be used for tails in 1-inch stock, but pin cuts are limited to 1/2-inch material. The instruction booklet that accompanies the jig is very detailed and clear and includes a troubleshooting chart to help you quickly find the solution to any problem. Figures 9-59 through 9-62 show one of the Leigh jigs in action.

Another example of an advanced dovetail jig from the Woodmachine Company is shown in Figs. 9-63 and 9-64. The tool is a husky concept with a cast-iron base, clamps and handles of steel, and templates of 1/4-inch thick aluminum (Fig. 9-65). The 65-pound machine can handle stock up to 1 inch thick and up to 16 inches wide. The dovetail bit, which is supplied with the tool, is guided by a ball bearing. This eliminates the need for a template guide. The basic template is for producing a 1/2-inch machine-type dovetails, but optional templates are available

for flexibility in dovetail design (Figs. 9-66 through 9-68). A special template allows the production of precise finger-lap joints, like those shown in Fig. 9-69.

Like all tools of this nature it is crucial that the user study and diligently follow the operational information to get optimum results. When

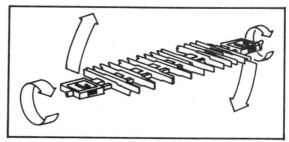

Fig. 9-56. The fingers of the Leigh jigs are locked on a slide bar after you have decided the number and the spacing of the cuts.

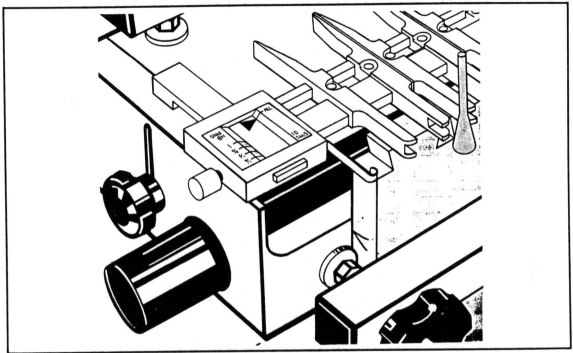

Fig. 9-57. Tails are formed by guiding a dovetail bit along one end of the fingers.

Fig. 9-58. Pins are formed with a straight cutting bit after the finger-slide bar assembly is positioned so the opposite end of the fingers can be used. The scale on the left is used to position the slide bar correctly.

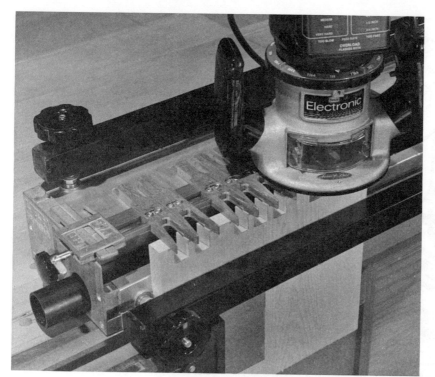

Fig. 9-59. Cutting is done in routine fashion. With all dovetail jigs it's important to keep the router flat on the work throughout the pass. Any tilt will mar the work and can damage jig components.

Fig. 9-60. The opposite end of the fingers are used to make the mating cut. Repositioning the finger-slide bar assembly is made easier by the scales that are located at each end of the tool. Here a dovetail bit is used to form through dovetail tailpieces.

158

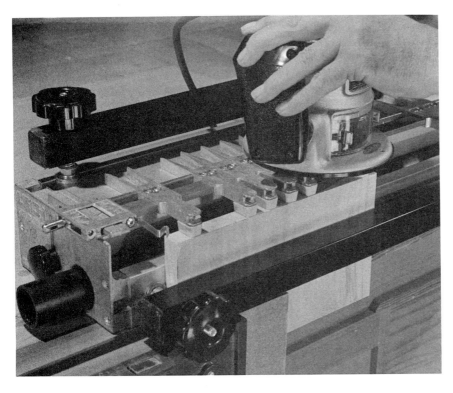

Fig. 9-61. Results are determined by how *you* decide to space and arrange the fingers. Operational procedures do not differ regardless of how you envision the joint. The tube at the left is provided for hookup to a vacuum cleaner.

Fig. 9-62. Pin pieces for half-blind dovetails are shaped with the work in horizontal position. A scrap piece, secured under the front clamp bar, is used as a stop for the part being routed. It's crucial with jigs of this type to test your knowledge of the tool by making test cuts on scrap material.

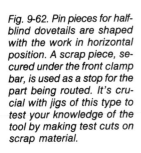

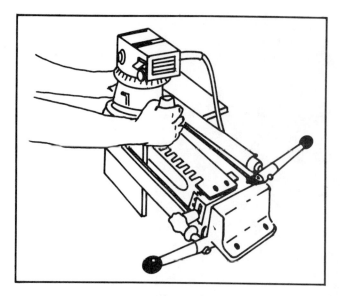

Fig. 9-63. The Woodmachine Company dovetail jig has a close-grained, cast-iron base and clamps and handles that are made of steel. It's not likely to wear out.

errors occur, it's usually because of the desire to get working. That's understandable, but seldom wise.

DROP-LEAF TABLE JOINT

A table with hinged leaves requires little floor space when not in use, but can be "spread" to accommodate quite a few people. Often the edges on the table and leaf are left square, and butt hinges or a continuous (piano) hinge are used as the pivot device. However, the true drop-leaf joint or *rule joint* that is found on many pieces of modern and traditional furniture is the

Fig. 9-64. Actual cutting doesn't differ from other tools in the dovetail category except that the dovetail bit is guided by a ball bearing that follows the fingers on the template. It isn't necessary to have a template guide in the router's subbase.

neater, more professional approach.

As you can see in Fig. 9-70, the secret of the joint is the way the quarter cuts complement each other. When the cuts are made correctly, the drop leaf swings up easily and extends the table surface on a smooth line. The edge of the drop leaf is shaped with a cove bit, while the table's edge is shaped with a rounding-over bit. The bits must have the same radius, and the depth of the cut on each component must be exact.

The hinge that is commonly used is called a *back flap* and is installed so the knuckle fits a shallow groove cut into the wood. You can form the groove with a core box bit or form a suitable mortise for it by using a small chisel. A similar hinge that has one leaf slightly bent is available and can be installed without a groove for the knuckle.

Because of the close tolerances required for optimum results, it's a good idea to test the router setups, even the hinge mounting, on some scrap pieces before working on the project material. Remember that there must be some clearance between the shaped edges so that they won't rub against each other. A trick

that provides adequate clearance is to place a length of wrapping paper between the edges of the table and the leaf when you are assembling them.

SPLINES

Splines are strips of material that are used to strengthen various joints (Fig. 9-71), but they can do more. The use of splines helps to hold parts in alignment during assembly procedures. They are often made of a contrasting material and left exposed as a decorative detail. With a router, the best way to form the grooves for splines is to work with slotting cutters. Because blades for the cutters are available in several thicknesses, there is some liberty in deciding how thick the spline will be.

Plywood, because it has strength in all directions, and hardboard, which is grainless, are good materials to use for splines. When you use lumber to make special ones, be sure the grain of the wood runs *across* the spline. This is wise because wood splits more easily with the grain than across the grain. Splines should slip-fit into the grooves. Having to force them into place will only complicate assembly procedures

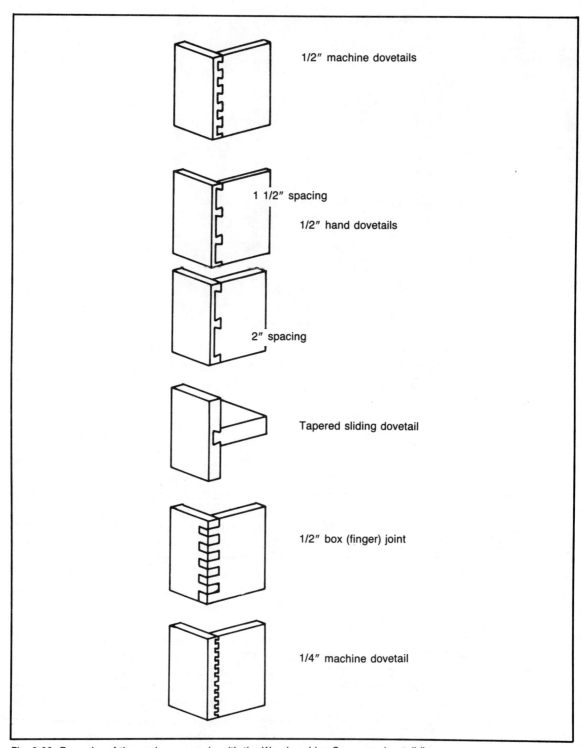

1/2″ machine dovetails

1 1/2″ spacing

1/2″ hand dovetails

2″ spacing

Tapered sliding dovetail

1/2″ box (finger) joint

1/4″ machine dovetail

Fig. 9-66. Examples of the work you can do with the Woodmachine Company dovetail jig.

Fig. 9-67. Standard half-blind dovetails fit as if they were cut with a laser. The machine can cut stock up to 16 inches wide, which is capacity enough even for most case goods.

Fig. 9-68. A feature of the machine, like others of its type, is that you can be creative with size and spacing of cuts.

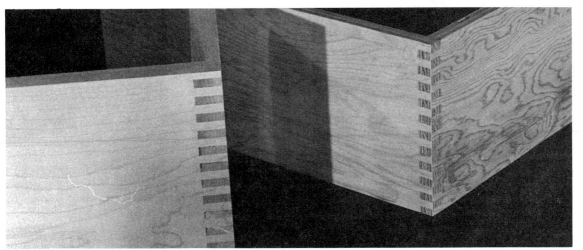

Fig. 9-69. With a special template, the Woodmachine Company jig can be used to produce finger lap joints. Like the dovetail, this joint design is often left exposed. The interlocking fingers and the large glue area make this a very strong connection.

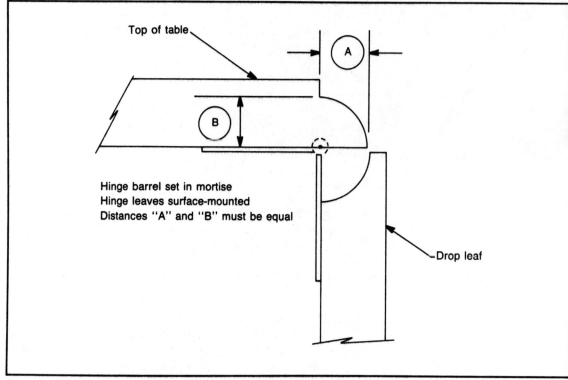

Top of table

A

B

Hinge barrel set in mortise
Hinge leaves surface-mounted
Distances "A" and "B" must be equal

Drop leaf

Fig. 9-70. Details of the drop leaf table joint.

and can even create stresses that might cause components to split.

Another type of spline, actually an inletted piece, is shown on the miter joint in Fig. 9-72. This can be installed after the parts have been glued together. The recess for it is really a blind dado that runs at right angles to the joint line. Make the cut by moving the router along a straightedge clamped at a suitable point across the joint pieces. Stop blocks are not needed because the spline, or inset piece, will be formed to suit the cut. It's okay to work to lines that you mark on the work.

The depth of the recess should be a bit less than the thickness of the spline material. Sand the spline after the glue has had time to set so it will be flush with adjacent surfaces.

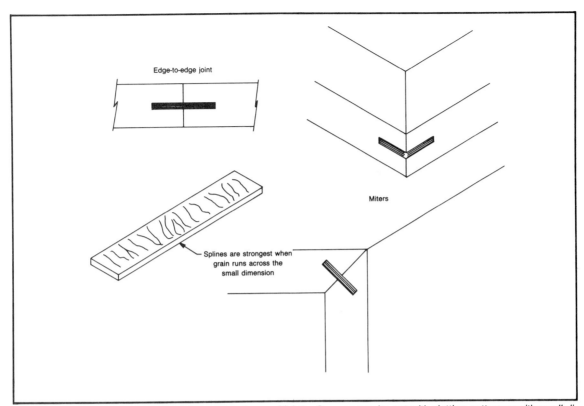

Fig. 9-71. Splines can be used to reinforce many types of joints. Grooves can be cut with slotting cutters or with small diameter straight bits.

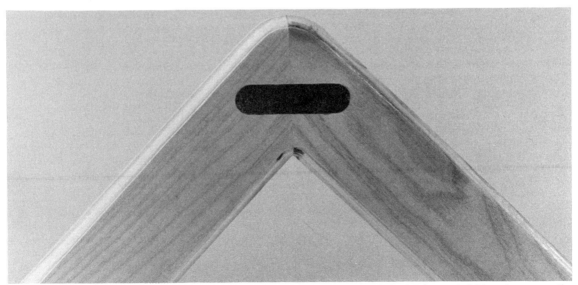

Fig. 9-72. This type of spline is actually a contrasting piece glued into a blind dado that is cut at right angles across the joint. Cut the spline to suit after the recess has been formed.

Chapter 10

Special Jigs

You Can Make

L IKE MANY POWER TOOLS, THE EXTENT TO WHICH a portable router can be used depends on the viewpoint of the user. The tool can be limited to some basic functions, or it can be organized in various ways to serve in capacities even the manufacturer hasn't envisioned. This is where jigs, or fixtures if you wish, come in. The home-made device might serve as an accessory that is not available commercially. It might duplicate to some extent an existing, costly product or one whose frequency of use would not justify its purchase.

To a degree, all homemade jigs are improvi-sations. This shouldn't prompt you into being haphazard when making them. Even if you in-vent a jig that solves a one-time problem, you must be sure that the tool/jig combination—in concept and in construction—is as safe to use as any standard piece of equipment. Any jig you make should become part of your router work-shop. This is easy to accept if the jig will see fre-quent use, but even the one-time problem solver may be needed again.

FLUTING JIG

The fluting jig shown in Fig. 10-1 is an adjustable holding device for spindle-type or square work-pieces on which you can make longitudinal cuts. The jig has a movable *tailstock* and *centers* at each end that adjust vertically so the unit can accommodate workpieces of various lengths and diameters. The sides of the jig provide sup-port for the router.

Figure 10-2 shows how the jig is used. The work is secured between the centers. The router, fitted with a cutter of your choice, is centered over the work and guided through the cut by an edge guide. The special subbase that was shown in Chapter 9 can also be used with the fluting jig. The cut can be of equal depth throughout its length, or, because it's possible to set one center a bit lower than the other, it can be tapered. To make stopped cuts, you just tack-nail a strip of wood across the sides of the jig (Flg. 10-3).

Construction details for the fluting jig are

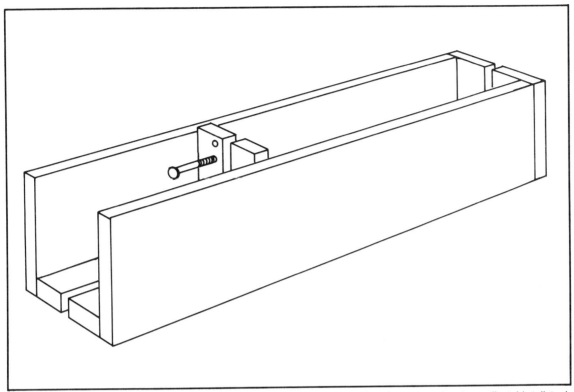

Fig. 10-1. The fluting jig is basically a trough that, like a lathe, has a fixed headstock at one end and an adjustable tailstock at the other end. This makes it possible to accommodate workpieces of various lengths.

Fig. 10-2. The tailstock is situated to secure the work between the *centers* of the jig. The router is placed so the centerline of the bit is over the longitudinal centerline of the work. Cuts can be uniform in depth or tapered, depending on how you decide the vertical position of the centers.

167

Fig. 10-3. The cuts can be across the full length of the work, or they can be limited by tack-nailing a strip of wood across the edges of the jig.

shown in Fig. 10-4. The length of the jig will accommodate legs for chairs and coffee tables, for example, but its length can be extended to work on longer components. The centers are made by grinding points on the end of 1/4- x -2-inch bolts. The holes in the vertical member of the tailstock are for an indexing pin that keeps the work in a fixed position when routing is done. The indexing pin, which is tapped into the end of the workpiece that is positioned in the jig, is made by sharpening the point on a 16d nail (Fig. 10-5).

Use the system shown in Fig. 10-6 to mark workpieces for spacing of cuts. Wrap a strip of paper around the work and cut it so its length

equals the circumference. How you fold the strip determines spacing. For example, once for cuts 180 degrees apart, twice for 45-degree spacing, and so on. The strip can be folded in thirds, or whatever. Then the work is marked on line with the folds in the paper. Position the work in the jig by lining up a mark with the center of the slot that is in the tailstock. Then tap in the indexing nail to hold the work still.

Results depend on the cutter you use. Core box bits, V-cutters, straight bits, and such can be used for simple fluting; pilotless bits for decorative grooves; and so on. If you work with a mortising bit, you can form flats on cylinders. Even jobs like forming stopped dovetails in ped-

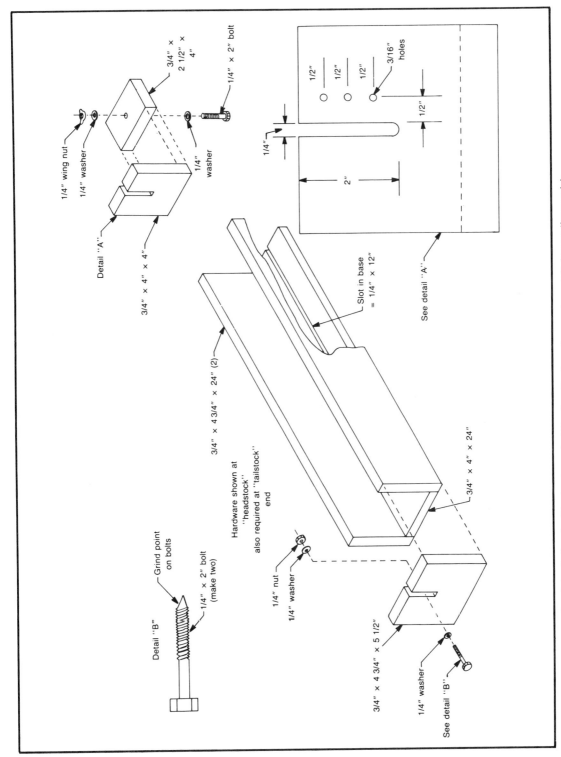

Fig. 10-4. Construction details of the fluting jig. The basic part of the jig—the trough—can be made longer if you wish.

1/4" wing nut

1/4" washer

Detail "A"

3/4" × 4" × 4"

3/4" × 2 1/2" × 4"

1/4" × 2" bolt

1/4" washer

1/2"

1/2"

1/2"

3/16" holes

1/2"

1/4"

2"

See detail "A"

Slot in base = 1/4" × 12"

3/4" × 4 3/4" × 24" (2)

Hardware shown at "headstock" also required at "tailstock" end

Grind point on bolts

Detail "B"

1/4" × 2" bolt (make two)

1/4" nut

1/4" washer

3/4" × 4" × 24"

3/4" × 4 3/4" × 5 1/2"

1/4" washer

See detail "B"

Fig. 10-5. After the work is mounted, the index pin, which is a sharpened 16d nail, is tapped into place so the work will not rotate as the cut is made.

Fig. 10-6. A strip of paper whose length matches the circumference of the workpiece is used to mark the spacing between the cuts. The marks on the work are lined up with the center of the slot that is in the jig's headstock or tailstock.

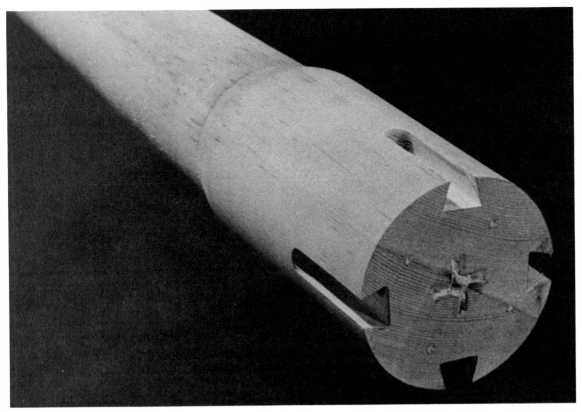

Fig. 10-7. The fluting jig provides an accurate method for forming stopped dovetail slots. Cuts like this are often used on pedestals to accept leg components that have matching dovetail tongues.

estals for leg attachment can be done accurately by using the fluting jig (Fig. 10-7).

The jig is not limited to working on cylinders. Square stock can also be mounted for fluting or for shaping in various ways. The flutes in the example shown in Fig. 10-8 were formed with the router positioned so the bit would cut away from the centerline of the workpiece. Work with a large diameter straight bit or a mortising bit and you can "cut corners" to change the shape of a square into an octagon.

JIGS FOR TAPER CUTS

Legs for chairs, tables, and some other projects are often cut so they taper, either partially or for the full length of the workpiece. A tapering jig is required when this kind of work is done on a sawing machine. This also holds true when a router is used. For a router, the jig is assembled as a trough that suits the size of the work on hand. The work is placed in the trough and elevated at one end with a height block or, preferably, a wedge and secured at the opposite end with a clamp (Fig. 10-9). Mark the lines of the taper beforehand so the work can be elevated at one end, by means of wedges, to suit the cut that is required. You are making a level cut, but it results in a taper simply because the work is secured in a tilted position.

Wedges are suggested as height blocks because they can be adjusted in terms of how high the tapered end of the work must be in the jig. Extra wedges are wise because they can be used between the sides of the workpiece and the jig to provide rigidity as the work progresses. The same jig can be used regardless of whether the

Fig. 10-8. *Square pieces of stock can also be shaped in various ways after they have been mounted in the fluting jig. Off-center cuts result when the router is situated to cut away from the centerline of the workpiece.*

workpiece will be tapered on one or two sides or all four sides.

Another type of taper jig for decorative surface cuts can be organized in a radial pattern (Fig. 10-10). The jig isn't more than a ramp that allows the bit to cut deeper at one end of the pass than at the other. Minimum and maximum cut depths are controlled by the slope of the ramp and the projection of the bit. Jigs like this should be made so the router can be used with a template guide. Therefore, the width of the guide slot in the jig should suit the outside diameter of the sleeve on the template guide (Fig. 10-11). By drilling a series of holes on the centerline of the slot, the one jig can be used on various size workpieces.

To set up for the operation, first draw a cir-cle on the work and then mark the circumference, or the arc as the case may be, so the slot in the jig has points of reference. The pivot point of the jig (a nail) is at the center of the same circle (Fig. 10-12). The jig is set for each cut by aligning the center of the slot with the mark on the circle. The cut is stopped when the forward edge of the subbase comes abreast of the marked circle. The cuts do not have to be the same length. Variations are possible simply by marking different stop points on either the work or the jig (Fig. 10-13).

Results are also affected by the cutter that is used. A round end bit, something like a core box bit, will form grooves like those shown in Fig. 10-14, while a pointed decorative bit or even a V-cutter will add the kind of center detail that is

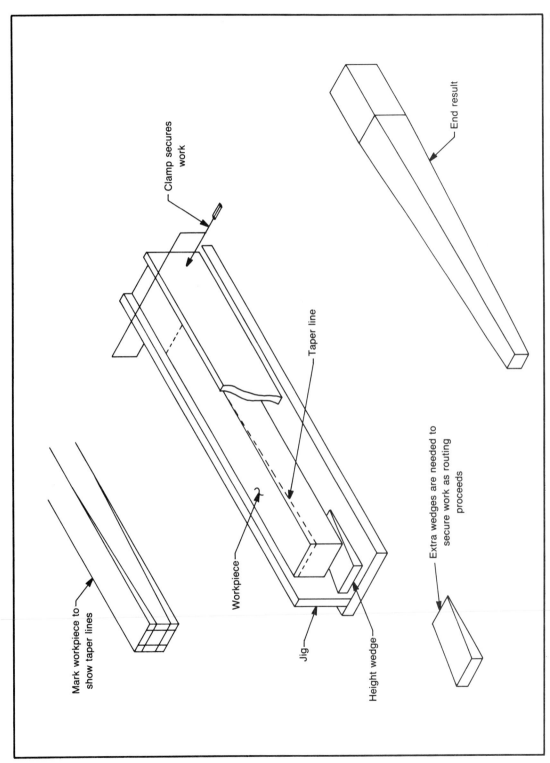

Mark workpiece to show taper lines

Clamp secures work

Taper line

Workpiece

Jig

Height wedge

Extra wedges are needed to secure work as routing proceeds

End result

Fig. 10-9. This taper jig is a trough-type design that is sized to suit the work on hand. The router rides on the top edges of the side pieces. The path of the cutter is horizontal, but the workpiece is tapered because its height at one end of the jig is increased with a height block or with wedges.

173

Fig. 10-10. This type of jig, for tapered surface cuts, is just a ramp. The router rides the slope so the cut becomes gradually deeper as the pass progresses. Jigs like this are made to suit the size of the workpieces involved.

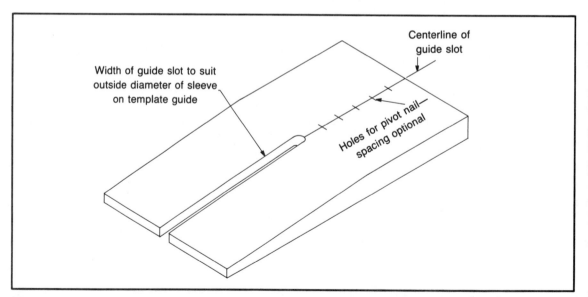

Fig. 10-11. The jig can be made variable for different work-sizes by drilling a series of holes on the centerline of the guide slot. The thickness of the ramp at its small end can't be less than the length of the sleeve on the template guide.

Fig. 10-12. The jig is situated for each cut by lining up the center of the guide slot with location points marked on the circumference of a circle. The pivot point (arrow) is just a small nail.

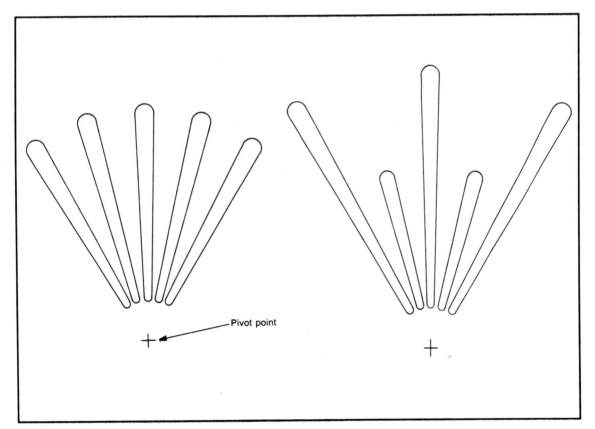

Pivot point

Fig. 10-13. The cuts can be uniform in length or they can vary. It's just a question of marking the work or the jig so the router can be stopped at particular points.

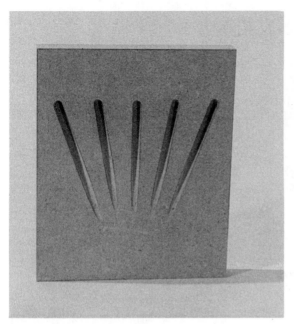

Fig. 10-14. The bit you use affects the cuts you get. These tapered grooves were formed with a small core box bit.

shown in Fig. 10-15. When the design you wish to create is too small for a full-size router, use a Moto-Tool or even a trimming router.

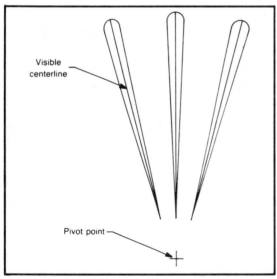

Visible
centerline

Pivot point

Fig. 10-15. Results resemble this when a bit like a V-groove cutter is used. The point on the bit leaves a visible centerline that adds to visual impact.

A PERIPHERAL ROUTING JIG

Routing into the edges of circular pieces and others with regular or irregular curves can be done easily and accurately if you make a peripheral routing jig like the one shown in Fig. 10-16. Figure 10-17 demonstrates a typical application. The jig, which secures a router or laminate trimmer motor, is clamped to a workbench. The work is elevated on a block so it will be at the correct height and moved past the cutter while being guided by the post in the base of the jig. The post also assures a uniform depth of cut.

Construction details for a typical peripheral jig are shown in Fig. 10-18. It's best to make the holding block from a solid piece of stock. The tool hole must suit the diameter of the router motor and can be formed in various ways. Make a template and use a router equipped with a template guide and straight bit to do the cutting. If you have the equipment, the hole can be formed on a drill press with a hole saw or fly cutter. It can also be formed by hand with a coping saw. After the block is formed, drill pilot holes for the sheet metal screws and then saw the piece on the centerline of the tool hole. The saw kerf should be about 1/8 inch wide so that when the screws are tightened, the upper part of the holder bears down on the motor to hold it securely.

Figure 10-19 shows decorative surface grooving being done on a curved component. It's important to keep the work flat on the height block and firmly against the guide post throughout the pass. Achieve depth of cut by how you position the motor in the tool holder, not by excessive projection of the bit.

The operation can be reversed (Fig. 10-20). The work can be held securely with a clamp while the jig is moved to make the cut. It's important to work on a clean, flat surface so the jig can move smoothly.

THE SWIVEL JIG

The swivel jig (Fig. 10-21) consists of a sturdy, raised platform that supports a rotatable indexing plate with an attached toolholder that is

Fig. 10-16. The peripheral routing jig is basically a holding device that grips a router motor securely in a horizontal position. The guide post (arrow) is a headless 1/4-inch bolt that threads into a T-nut that is let into the base of the jig.

Fig. 10-17. With the jig secured to a workbench or similar structure, the work is placed on a height block and moved past the cutter while it bears firmly against the guide post. This demonstrates a fairly typical application for the peripheral jig.

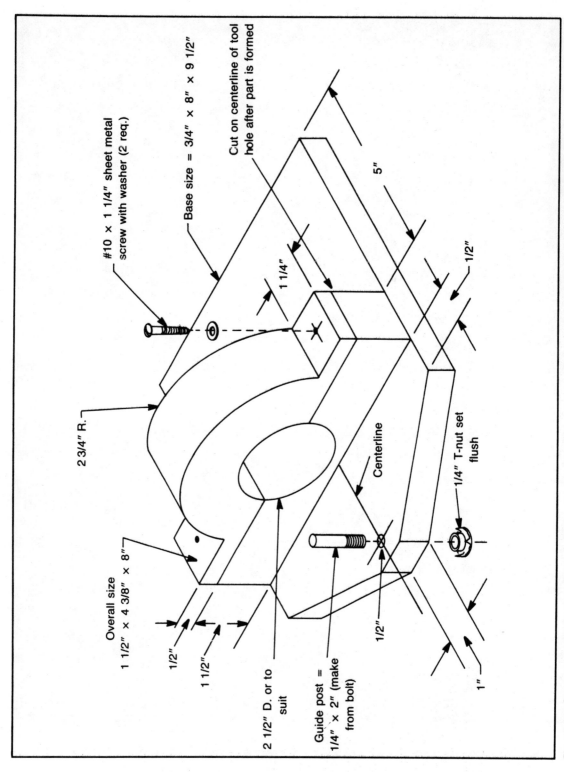

#10 × 1 1/4" sheet metal screw with washer (2 req.)

Base size = 3/4" × 8" × 9 1/2"

Cut on centerline of tool hole after part is formed

5"

1 1/4"

1/2"

2 3/4" R.

Centerline

1/4" T-nut set flush

Overall size
1 1/2" × 4 3/8" × 8"

1/2"

1 1/2"

2 1/2" D. or to suit

1/2"

1"

**Guide post =
1/4" × 2" (make
from bolt)**

Fig. 10-18. Construction details for a typical peripheral routing jig. The tool hole must be sized to suit the diameter of the router's motor.

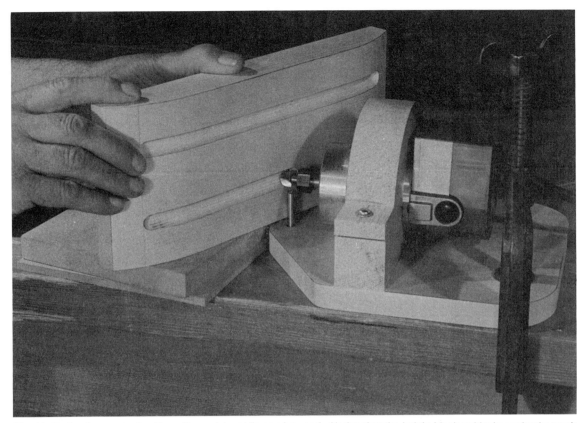

Fig. 10-19. Another example of how the peripheral jig can be used. Notice that the height block or blocks under the work must raise it enough so its bottom edge clears the top surface of the jig's base.

mounted on pivots so the tool can be swung in an arc (Fig. 10-22). Because the tool can be rotated as well as swiveled, decorative surface cuts (Fig. 10-23) are easy to produce.

The jig must be made very carefully for cuts to be precise and have correct radial alignment. Notice, in the construction details shown in Fig. 10-24, that the top of the platform is a two-piece assembly. The diameter of the circle in the top part is 9 inches, while the bottom piece has an 8-inch circle. When the parts are assembled, the difference in the diameters supplies a 1/2-inch ledge for the indexing plate to rest on.

Make the indexing plate with care so the only movement it can have in the platform is a circular one. To reduce the bulk of the jig, the toolholder is sized to suit the motor of a laminate trimmer rather than the motor of a full-size

router. A jig of this type can also be made to suit a Moto-Tool or a high-speed grinder.

When laying out the index marks, be sure that the first ones are exactly on the perpendicular diameters of the platform and the indexing plate. Other marks can be located with a protractor. Accurate marks are crucial because they are used to control the radial alignment of the cuts. Also, be sure the toolholder is centered perfectly inside the index plate.

Typical cuts that can be produced with the swivel jig are shown in Figs. 10-25 and 10-26. Results depend on the number of cuts, their spacing, the depth of the cuts, and the router bit that is used. Experiment with a bit like a V-groove cutter before researching effects that can be achieved with straight bits, core box units, and pilotless decorative bits.

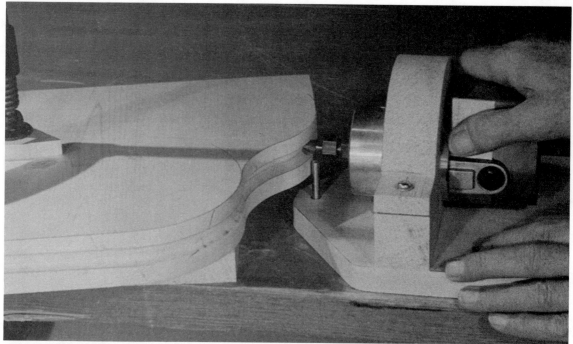

Fig. 10-20. The jig can also be used this way. The work is clamped in place; the jig is moved to make the cut. The guide post acts something like a pilot to control the depth of the cut.

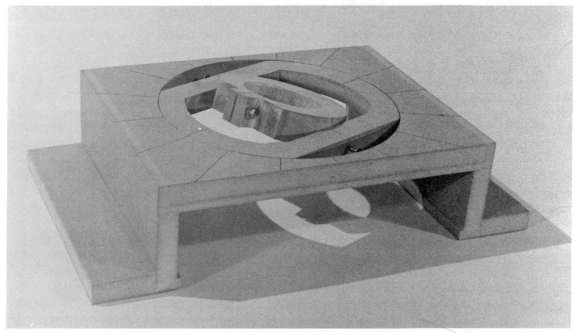

Fig. 10-21. The swivel jig consists of a substantial base that supports an indexing plate and a pivot-mounted clamp for a router's motor.

Fig. 10-22. The motor can be swung in an arc and rotated to cut on various radii. If you make a mistake, and the index plate has any play, use a small C-clamp to keep it in position for each of the cuts you make.

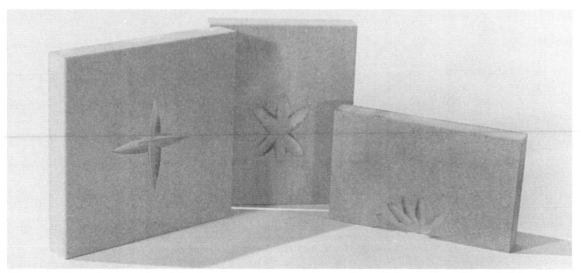

Fig. 10-23. Just a few examples of the decorative surface cuts that can be made by working with a swivel jig.

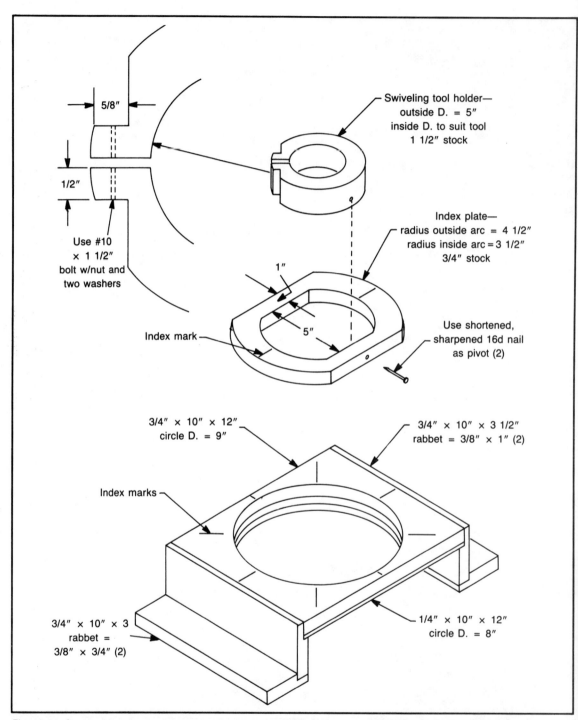

5/8"

1/2"

Use #10
× 1 1/2"
bolt w/nut and
two washers

Swiveling tool holder—
outside D. = 5"
inside D. to suit tool
1 1/2" stock

Index plate—
radius outside arc = 4 1/2"
radius inside arc = 3 1/2"
3/4" stock

1"

Index mark

5"

Use shortened,
sharpened 16d nail
as pivot (2)

3/4" × 10" × 12"
circle D. = 9"

3/4" × 10" × 3 1/2"
rabbet = 3/8" × 1" (2)

Index marks

3/4" × 10" × 3
rabbet =
3/8" × 3/4" (2)

1/4" × 10" × 12"
circle D. = 8"

Fig. 10-24. Construction details of the swivel jig. The jig performs perfectly only if all the parts are made to mate correctly. The swiveling tool holder should fit snugly in the opening of the index plate. The index plate should fit almost tightly in the hole that is required in the top part of the platform.

182

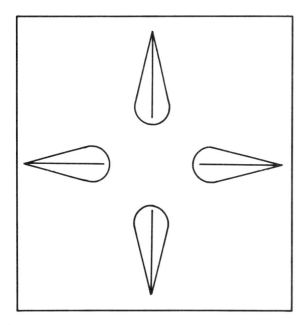

Fig. 10-25. Cuts made with the swivel jig can be stopped to produce patterns like this. These cut designs are produced by using bits like the V-groove cutter.

Fig. 10-26. Elaborate designs like this are possible when you use the swivel jig. It's wise, though, to experiment with simple designs with cuts spaced 90 degrees apart before going on to more intricate patterns.

Chapter 11

More Router Applications

THE MORE FAMILIAR YOU BECOME WITH THE router, the more useful and interesting applications you will find for it. The procedures that follow are part of the router story.

PATTERN ROUTING

Although the words "template" and "pattern" are often used interchangeably, there is a basic difference between cutting done with a template and work done by following a pattern. Essentially, a template is a guide that is made to be followed by the router when it is equipped with an accessory template guide. A pattern might be an actual project component or a specially made unit so the router, generally with a piloted bit, can be used to form one or more duplicate pieces. Also, the pattern might be shaped to provide just part of the configuration that is required on the workpieces (Fig. 11-1).

When the pattern is a complete unit used to produce duplicate parts, it is the same size and shape as the pieces needed. When the pattern is used for a partial cut, say a particular curve on one edge of components, then it can be oversize in unimportant areas that, if nothing else, can make the pattern easier to work with.

Workpieces are oversize to begin with and can be attached to the pattern in various ways—by clamping, spot gluing, or tack-nailing (Fig. 11-2). Figures 11-3 and 11-4 show the type of bits that can be used for pattern routing. Because piloted bits are used, the edges of the pattern must be smooth and flawless.

PIERCING

Piercing is a term usually associated with the jigsaw and straight cutting tools like the table or radial arm saw, but there are several ways the router can be used to do similar operations. The technique is often used to create small or large decorative panels, like those displayed in Figs. 11-5 through 11-7.

The idea is simple. Set the projection of the

Fig. 11-1. The pattern indicated by the arrow can be the full size and shape of the project, or it can be made to supply the shape for a limited area.

router bit to a little more than half the thickness of the stock. Make a series of cuts on one surface of the material. Then, invert the workpiece and make a second series of cuts that cross the first ones. Openings through the work appear wherever the cuts cross. Variations, which are limitless, are affected by the following factors: the number and spacing of the cuts; whether the cuts cross at right angles or obliquely; and the shape of the bit. Some very intriguing patterns result when pointed decorative bits are used, but be sure the thickness of the stock permits necessary depth of cut. Another idea is to work with a pivot guide to make circular grooves (with var-

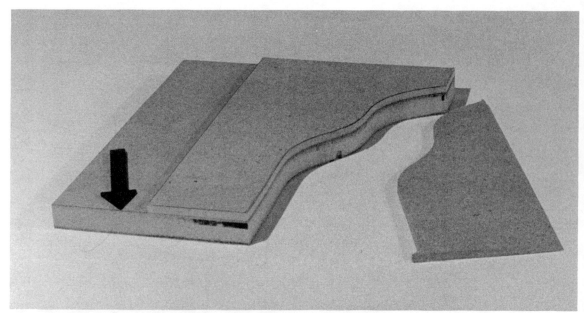

Fig. 11-2. The part that is formed will be an exact duplicate of the pattern.

Fig. 11-3. Straight bits with integral or add-on pilots can be used for pattern routing. The pilot follows the pattern religiously so be sure the bearing edge is smooth and free of flaws.

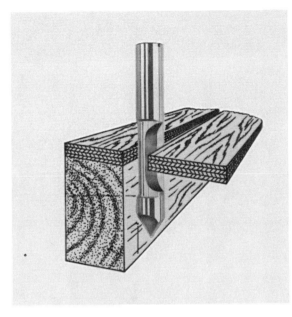

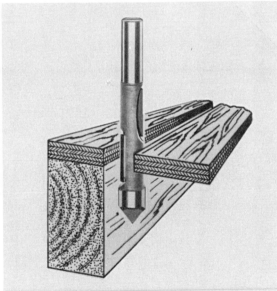

Fig. 11-4. These pilot panel bits can penetrate like a drill and are also used for pattern routing. They are especially useful for making internal cutouts. Both can be used for plunge cutting. The one on the bottom is a "stagger tooth" design.

ious center points) or to make straight or angled cuts on one surface and circular ones on the other side. It's also possible to make stopped or blind cuts for trivet-type projects like the store-

bought item shown in Fig. 11-8.

The shape of the openings depends on how you plan the cutting. Similar, equally spaced cuts that cross at right angles create square openings. If the cuts cross at oblique angles, then the openings appear as diamonds. Arc-type openings result if you make wide, straight cuts on one side and circular grooves on the opposite surface. Experimenting to check results can waste material; it's best to preview possibilities by working on paper with a straightedge and a compass.

Another type of piercing work where through cuts rather than grooves are involved is demonstrated in Fig. 11-9. The example shows how a pivot guide can be used to form perfect circular openings or discs, but the system also works when a pattern is used. Straight, pilotless bits are used when the router is directed by something like the pivot guide. When piercing by following a pattern, use plunge-type bits like those that were shown in Fig. 11-4. Figure 11-10 shows how piercing can often result in two components, although not necessarily for the same project.

HOLLOWING

Hollowing applies to the contained recesses required for the store-purchased products shown in Fig. 11-11 and the original plan in Fig. 11-12. The concept is simple: to reduce the thickness of stock between perimeter areas so cavities of optional depth and shape will be formed. Because the router has to be moved in a rather erratic cutting pattern to cover all areas, the tool should be equipped with a special subbase to adequately span across the edges of the project and provide good support for the tool regardless of where it is cutting (Fig. 11-13).

How deep to cut on a single pass depends, as always, on the horsepower of the tool, but a light-duty model can accomplish as much as a heavy-duty machine simply by repeating cut patterns with bit projection increased for each one. The outline of the cavity can be followed by moving the router freehand along marked guidelines.

187

Fig. 11-5. This type of piercing calls for making cuts on both sides of the stock. Openings occur wherever the cuts cross because depth of cut is a bit more than half the stock's thickness.

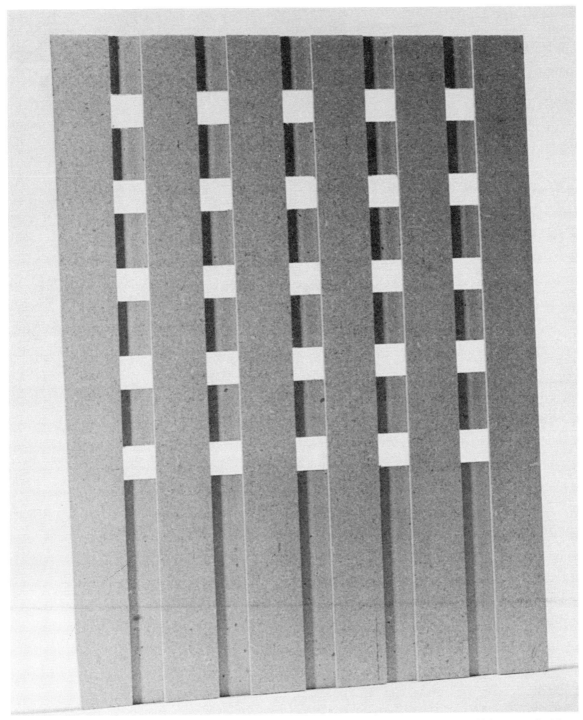

Fig. 11-6. Various effects can be created by the number, position, spacing, and width of the cuts. Using a smaller bit on one side will result in rectangular openings.

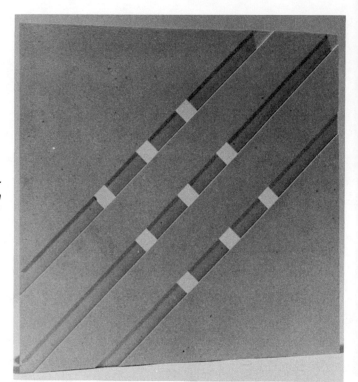

Fig. 11-7. These openings are square but appear as diamonds because the cutting was done at an angle across the panel. The effects you can create are limitless.

Fig. 11-8. Stopped or blind cuts can also be used for pierced projects. Here the technique was used for a trivet.

Fig. 11-9. Piercing also applies to operations like this. Because the bit passes through, the work must be elevated on out-board support blocks or placed on a scrap piece.

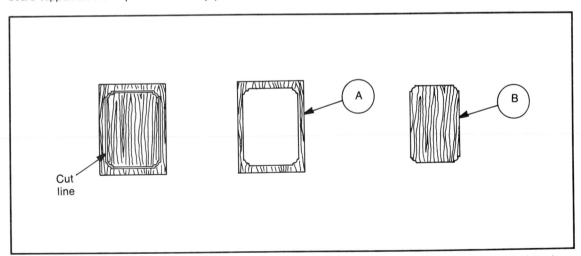

Cut
line

Fig. 11-10. It's often possible to make use of the waste piece that is left after a piercing operation. Here pierced work produces a frame (A) and a panel (B) which, for example, can be used as a plaque for a sign.

Fig. 11-11. Projects like these store-bought servers are formed by using hollowing procedures. In many cases, it's best to shape perimeters after the cavities are formed.

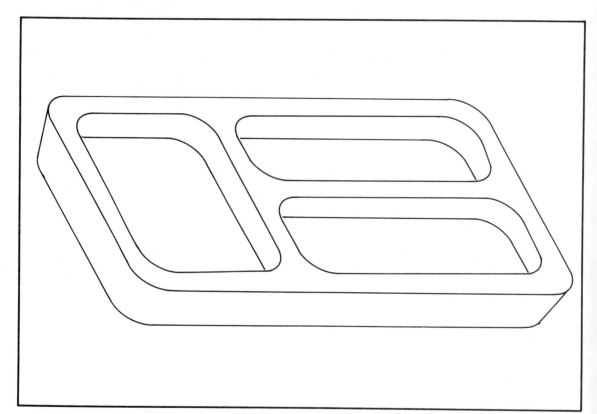

Fig. 11-12. Partitioned cavities can be formed freehand, but it's easier to get perfect results if you equip the router with a guide and make outline cuts by using a template.

Fig. 11-13. For most hollowing jobs it's necessary to equip the router with a special subbase so the tool can be supported over the entire cut area.

This is the way to go when you want informal or rustic results. Any slight deviations from the marked lines only contribute to the appearance you envision.

If you want a more formal appearance—straight lines rather than wavey ones—use a template/template guide setup to outline the cavity. The template does not have to be elaborate. Strips of wood with straight edges or curves depending on how the cavity must be shaped, will serve as a template when they are tack-nailed to the project material (Fig. 11-14).

There is another factor to consider. If the router is equipped with an extra-long subbase and is to be used with a template guide, then the auxiliary subbase must accept the guide so that only the sleeve of the guide projects (Figs. 11-15 and 11-16). This calls for a normal hole for the guide to pass through, plus a counterbore so the accessory is seated flush with the bottom surface of the base when it is installed.

Fig. 11-14. It's often possible to create a template for outline cuts simply by tack-nailing strips of wood. The strips can have curved edges as well as straight ones.

Fig. 11-15. When using templates for hollowing jobs, the special subbase must be made to accept a template guide.

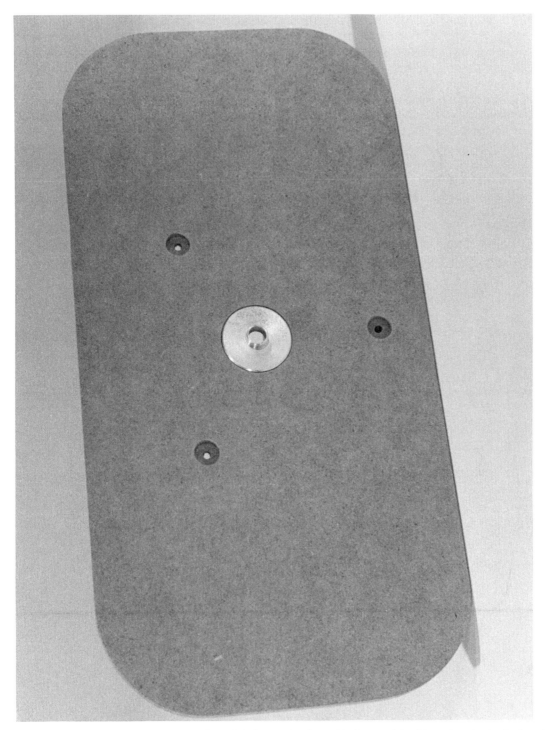

Fig. 11-16. A counterbore as well as a pass-through hole must be formed in the special subbase in order for the template guide to seat correctly. The text suggests several methods that can be used to form the counterbore.

There are various ways to accomplish this, the easiest depending on the workshop equipment you have. If you have a set of Forstner bits you can use one size to drill a hole of limited depth (actually a circular groove) for the counterbore and a second size for the through hole. The same procedure can be followed if you have a set of hole saws. In each case counterbore first. These are quickie methods. If you lack the equipment, you can achieve the same results by using the router and straight bits. Make one template with a hole to suit the outside diameter of the counterbore and a second one for the through hole.

Cutting is started by following the template to outline the cavity and then moving the router between outline cuts to remove waste material (Fig. 11-17). You can make parallel cuts, moving the router in ideal fashion so the bit is cutting into the work, or you can move the router erratically. Chances are that you will use both cutting procedures. Just be sure to keep the sub-base flat on the surfaces of the template and that you make repeat passes, when necessary, to achieve the full depth of cut you need. The procedure works fine for partial cavities as well as total ones (Fig. 11-18).

A special type of hollowing procedure is required when the cavity must slope in a particular direction. This applies to project components like chair seats (Fig. 11-19) or to units like cutting boards where you might want to channel

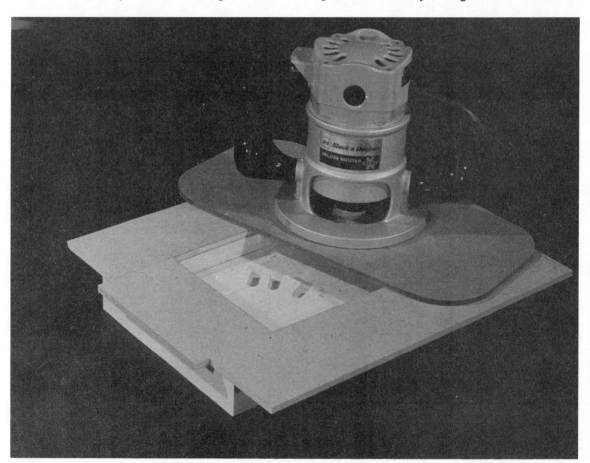

Fig. 11-17. Start a hollowing job by making outline cuts and then moving the router about to clean out waste. On very deep cuts, make repeat passes increasing bit projection for each. The last pass should be a very light, shaving cut.

196

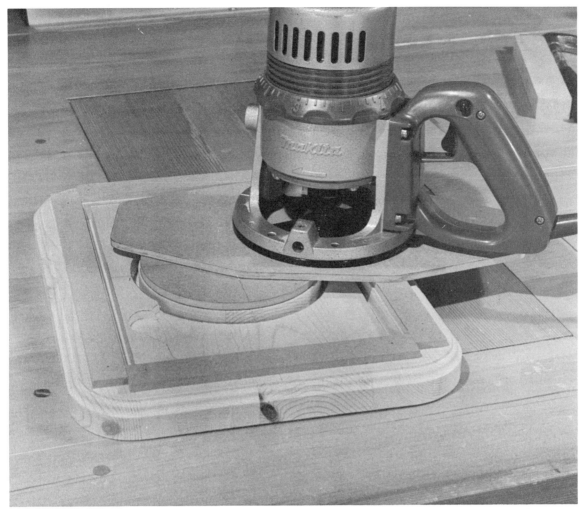

Fig. 11-18. Partial cavities result when you tack-nail a template to an inside area. The template can be any shape.

meat juices to a collection area. The answer is to make a profile template like the example in Fig. 11-20. Because the forward edge of the template is higher than rear areas, the router will cut progressively deeper as it approaches the template's back bearing edge.

Make the first pass, following the template's edge, with a large round-bottom bit. This develops the outline of the shape you need and forms a neat cove around the base of its perimeter. Then switch to a large-diameter straight bit to remove the waste between the cove cuts. A special subbase that is long enough to support the router in whatever area it is working on will be needed.

Whether you can shape top edges of cavities with the router will, to some extent, depend on the depth of the cut. There is no problem on deep cuts because a piloted bit can be guided by the shoulders of the cavity (Fig. 11-21). Solutions must be based on the particular facets of the project on hand. It might be possible to work with an edge guide riding outside edges, or by making a special secondary template that can be attached over the area or areas that are already formed.

Fig. 11-19. Chair seats are often tapered from front to back. This is a hollowing job that is accomplished with a special template.

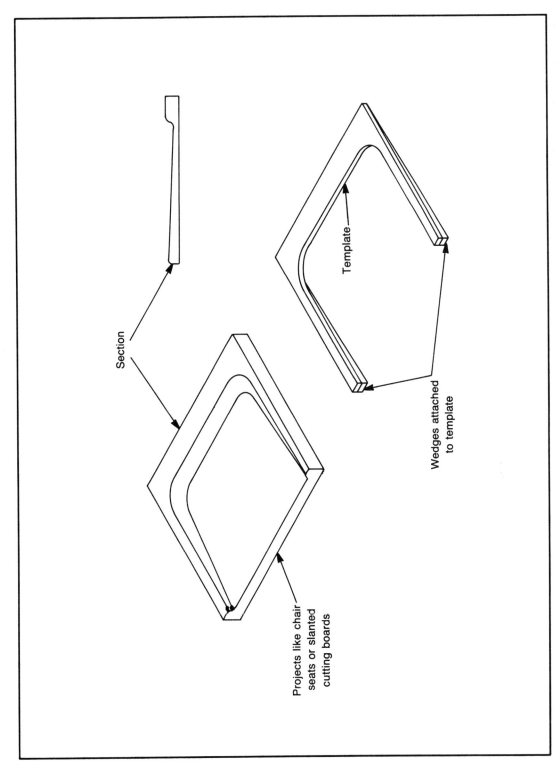

Section

Template

Wedges attached
to template

Projects like chair
seats or slanted
cutting boards

Fig. 11-20. The template for a chair seat, or similar projects, should look like this. The router cuts progressively deeper as it approaches the back edge of the template.

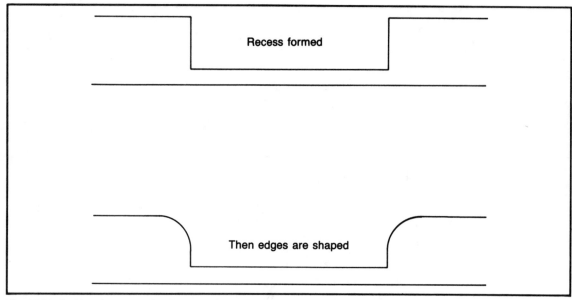

Fig. 11-21. Inside edges can often be shaped with the router after hollowing is complete.

There is no all-purpose solution. This is where router wisdom enters the picture. You examine the situation, review other router procedures and then attempt to arrive at the best method for getting the job done. You'll be surprised, as you go along, how you will start thinking "router fashion."

LEVELING AND SURFACING

After boards have been glued together as slabs for tabletops, workbenches, cabinet sides, and similar project components, it is often necessary to work with tools like scrapers, hand planes, or sanding machines, to bring the assembly to a true level surface. The extra steps are needed, not because of carelessness when gluing and clamping, but because individual parts usually have flaws like a crossgrain cup or a lengthwise bow. No matter how minor the defects, they can't be eliminated by clamping. The end result is a less-than-perfect surface.

You can rectify discrepancies by working with a hand plane or a belt sander or by using both tools, but results will be better and easier to achieve if you set up to do the job with a

router. By working with the jig that is shown in Fig. 11-22, you'll have mechanical control of the operation so the possibility of high and low spots, that can easily occur when planing or sanding, will be eliminated.

The jig is a track assembly that spans across the work and rides on strips that are temporarily attached to the slab with a few nails. The top edges of the bearing strips should be below the surface of the slab by a bit more than the thickness of the track connectors. Setting the strips correctly is an important part of the operation. Check with a level to be sure their top edges are on the same plane so that when the jig is placed, it will be at the same height over all areas of the work.

Work with the largest straight bit or mortising bit you have and adjust the bit's projection so it will just touch the work at its lowest point. Cutting is done by moving the router to and fro over the slab as the jig is moved from one end to the other. The distance between the tracks should be an inch or so greater than the diameter of the router's base. This allows you to make a few overlapping passes each time the jig is shifted.

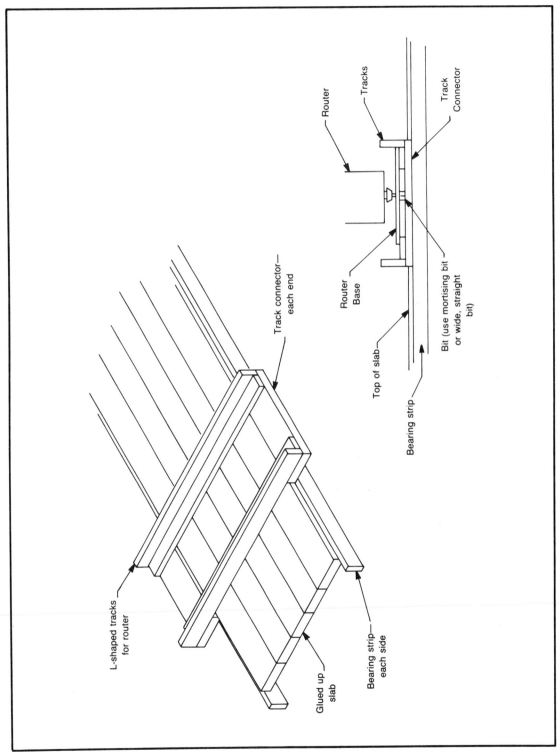

L-shaped tracks
for router

Track connector—
each end

Glued up
slab

Bearing strip—
each side

Router

Tracks

Track
Connector

Router
Base

Top of slab

Bearing strip

Bit (use mortising bit
or wide, straight
bit)

Fig. 11-22. A slab leveling jig like this makes it fairly easy to smooth and level surfaces of new or existing projects.

201

A jig of this type doesn't have to be limited to new construction. It is just as practical for renovating an existing surface, like the top of a much-used workbench. Nor does the jig have to be discarded after it has served its primary purpose. It can still be used for router jobs like cutting straight grooves.

SURFACING SLABS

A similar technique can be used to flatten the ends of small logs that you wish to mount in a lathe or use as a pedestal. It can also create a smooth surface on a rough slab that will be used as the top of a bench or coffee table. In both cases (Figs. 11-23 and 11-24), a special cage

or holding jig must be made to suit the size and shape of the material.

A cage can be made oversize if you contemplate much of this type of work, and wedges or pieces of scrap can be used to keep the work secure. The same idea holds true for a holding jig because various size workpieces can be secured by impaling them on nails driven up through the base of the jig, or by using scrap pieces between the work and the jig's sides.

The router must be equipped with a special subbase that is more than long enough to span across support areas of the jigs. The auxiliary bases do not have to be fancy; long, straight boards with a hole for the bit to pass through are good enough. The thickness of the board dic-

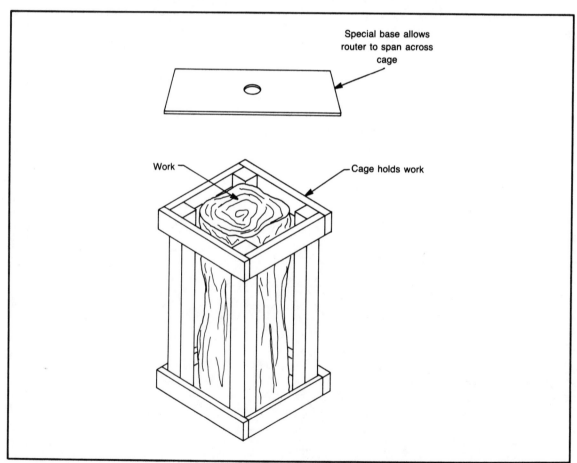

Special base allows router to span across cage

Work

Cage holds work

Fig. 11-23. Flattening the ends of logs called for a special "cage" that holds the work securely in vertical position.

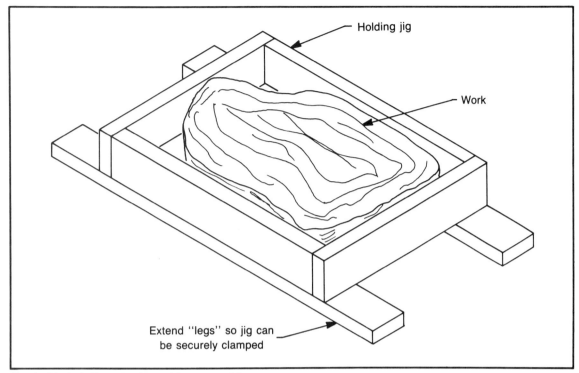

Holding jig

Work

Extend "legs" so jig can
be securely clamped

Fig. 11-24. A similar setup is used to secure slabs.

tates whether you must use attachment screws that are longer than the standard ones. Results are best and the work goes fastest when you cut with the largest straight bit or mortising bit available.

SOME FREEHAND WORK

"Freehand" router operation simply means that cutting is done without mechanical guidance of any sort—no straightedges, no templates or template guides or patterns, no jigs. Results depend totally on how the operator "sees" and how he manipulates the tool. It's an area of router work that is very intriguing, but one whose importance relates directly to user interest and work scope. There are professional sign makers, wood-carvers and wood sculptors, for example, who can handle a router with enviable artistry. They can carve letters and numbers of exclusive design and create bas-relief plaques or figures in the round in an almost matter-of-fact way. But any

one of them will tell you that the apparent ease with which they accomplish such work is misleading. The talent comes with practice—a lot of it.

One of the problems to overcome when doing freehand work is the tendency of the router bit to volunteer a cut direction and to follow grain lines. When practicing, it is wise to select a material that presents the fewest obstacles to smooth cutting; for example, soft pine or redwood as opposed to any wood species that has the hard and soft areas of Douglas fir. A test project can be something like the initial in Fig. 11-25 where the appearance is rustic and a few irregularities contribute to rather than detract from the project's appearance.

Another test possibility is recessing the background of a figure that has already been accurately outlined using a template (Fig. 11-26). You can still get careless here, but the possibility of cutting into the figure is minimized because of the outline groove. If you work with a straight

203

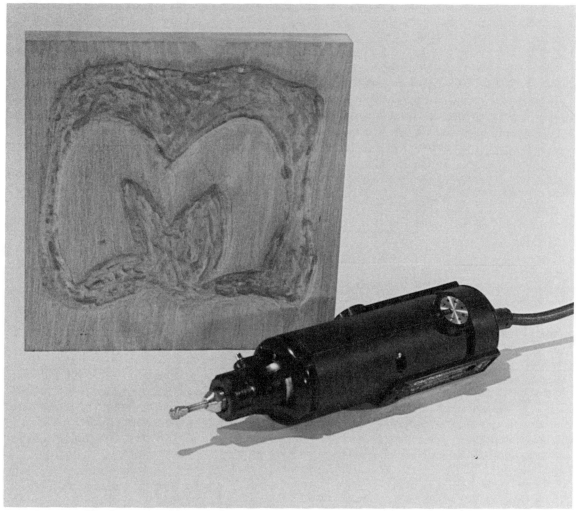

Fig. 11-25. A Moto-Tool was used to texture the background of this letter plaque. Informal designs are good projects to work on when you wish to try freehand routing.

bit you can achieve a smooth, flat background. You can use a round end or veining bit, for example, to create interesting textures. On work like this it's best to start cutting at the perimeter of the work so that as you move toward interior areas, the router will be supported by the figure. In all cases it's important for the tool to be held on a level plane.

When working freehand, it's often necessary to break the standard feed direction rule; that is, moving the router so the bit cuts *into* the work. The grip on the tool should be firmer than ever, and feed speed should be lessened. I find that it's sometimes practical, especially when following a line, to deliberately break the rule. The bit will tend to move away from the line rather than cross it.

Practice sessions should include quite a bit of cutting across or obliquely to the grain. When you can make cuts like this while accurately following a line, you'll be well on your way to free-hand expertise. Start with small bits and shal-

Fig. 11-26. Recessing the background of a figure that has been outlined with a template is another way to practice freehand routing. The idea is to get to know how to control the router when it isn't being used with guides.

low cuts. Equip the router with a subbase that has an oversize hole for the bit or, better still, install a see-through subbase so you'll get better views of layout lines. Another secret of good freehand work is anticipating how the router should be moved to follow the lines that are ahead. This is easier to do when you can see more of the lines than a standard subbase allows.

CARVING WITH A ROUTER

Freehand work doesn't have to be limited to bas-relief projects. If you view the router without its base, you can see that it can be gripped somewhat like the handpiece on a flexible shaft or used like a high-speed grinder. This particular application is more feasible with small routers or, preferably, with the motor of a laminate trimmer. It would be a bit far out to suggest handholding the motor of a big, 3-horsepower unit! Even here the idea is applicable, but only if the motor is in a fixed, stable position to apply the work to the cutter, not the reverse.

One way to secure a motor is with the type of jig that is shown in Fig. 11-27. Because of its extended base, the jig can be clamped securely to a workbench to apply the work to the cutter (Fig. 11-28). *Don't attempt to do this kind of work with standard router bits!* They can dig in and pull the work from your hands no matter how carefully you work. It's dangerous for your hands to come anywhere near those cutting edges. Even with the type of cutters that should be used for this application, rotary burrs and mills and files and such, great care should be taken with hand placement. These tools don't cut like router bits, but they do cut! Be sure the cutters that you use have the correct shaft diameter for the collet and that they are specified for safe use at the speed and horsepower of the router's motor.

Construction details for a typical motor-holding stand are shown in Fig. 11-29. To make one, follow the instructions that were outlined for the peripheral jig in Chapter 10. The only difference between the two units is in the shape of the base.

Projects "in the round," like the sculpture shown in Fig. 11-30, can be accomplished partially by working with the router in a fixed position and partially by clamping the work and applying the router. It's often possible to minimize the amount of waste that must be removed with cutters by presawing the stock to its basic form (Fig. 11-31). If you have a band saw, this kind of preparation can be done by using the technique called *compound sawing*, which is often used to shape project components like the cabriole leg. The profile of the work is drawn on two adjacent sides of the work. After one profile

Fig. 11-27. A jig of this type can be used to secure the motor of a router or laminate trimmer for jobs that can be done more conveniently by hand-holding the work.

Fig. 11-28. Shaping "in the round" is feasible with a router when the work can be done this way. Work only with cutters like rotary rasps—not with router bits!

is sawed, the waste pieces are tapped back in their original positions to give the workpiece a flat surface to ride on when the second profile is cut (Fig. 11-32).

LETTERS AND NUMBERS

Letters and numbers of just about any size and shape can be formed with a portable router, either by using the tool freehand or by working with templates. It takes practice to get optimum results when working freehand, but the method allows a good deal of liberty in terms of design. Freedom of expression is the prime reason for working without guides. Any style of numbers and letters you sketch on the workpiece, whether standard or original, can be carved out with the router. Professional signmakers often work freehand because they can turn out a one-time product that is especially right for a particular establishment.

Workers who might make a set of house numbers or a name plaque just once can do the chore more easily by working with templates. Commercial templates are available, but there are ways to work that reduce costs and that don't limit you to the particular letter and number style that is offered. The letter plaque shown in Fig. 11-33 was made by using the letter "E" from a store-bought cardboard sign as the design for a template. Hardware stores and home supply centers carry many cardboard or plastic ready-to-use signs and sets of numbers in various sizes and styles. It might be hard to find a sign that contains all the letters you need, but there are also complete alphabets with letters available in-

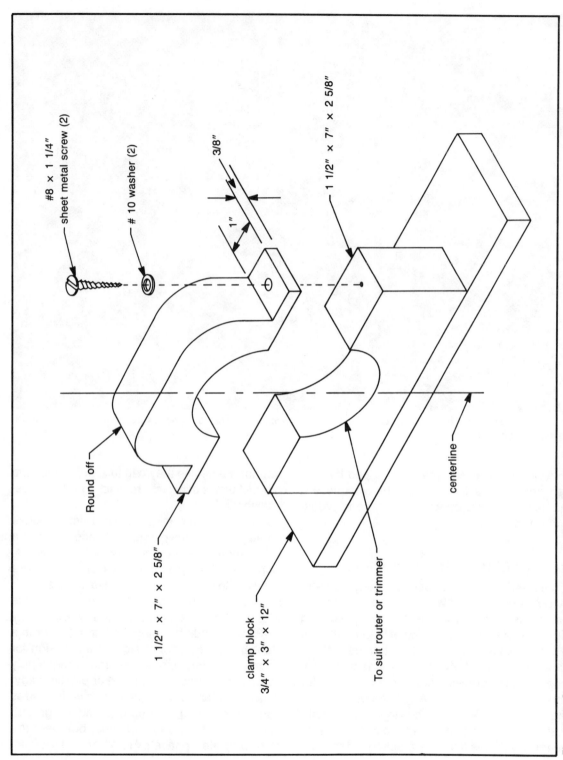

#8 × 1 1/4"
sheet metal screw (2)

10 washer (2)

3/8"

1"

1 1/2" × 7" × 2 5/8"

Round off

1 1/2" × 7" × 2 5/8"

clamp block
3/4" × 3" × 12"

To suit router or trimmer

centerline

Fig. 11-29. Construction details of a motor-holding stand you can make.

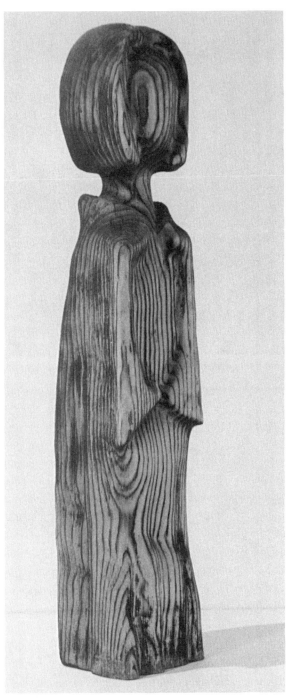

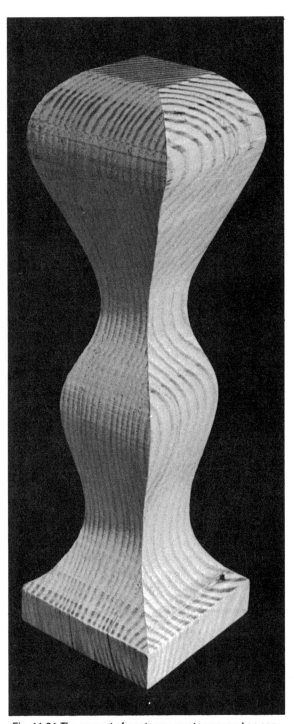

Fig. 11-30. Wooden sculptures like this can be accomplished entirely with a router motor. The motor can be secured in a stand or, with the work secured, used like a high-speed grinder.

Fig. 11-31. The amount of waste you must remove when carving figures and similar projects can be minimized by preshaping the workpiece.

Fig. 11-32. Compound sawing on a band saw is a quick way to preshape stock for carving. When pieces are small, say in the 2-inch square area, you can do the same kind of work with a jigsaw.

Fig. 11-33. Letters or numbers in various sizes and styles can be purchased at home supply centers and used as patterns to create templates for router use. Notice here that the background cutting has left irregular ridges that contribute to the motif and make the cut seem deeper than it really is.

dividually. This also holds true for numbers (Fig. 11-34).

Another way is to use headlines and titles in newspapers and magazines as sources for template material (Fig. 11-35). They can be enlarged at a copy shop to the size you want. There might be the problem of finding all the letters you need in a particular style, but you can fill in by drawing missing ones. If nothing else, printed material can be a source of type styles.

You can also be as creative as you please by designing your own alphabet and numbers. The examples shown in Fig. 11-36 were drawn with drafting instruments. Tools you can use include compasses, circle templates, French curves, and so on. When letters or numbers are to be made as individual units and are designed somewhat along the lines of those in Fig. 11-36, much of the waste material can be removed before routing by boring holes.

Whichever way you go, the pattern for the letter or number is attached to the template material with tape or an adhesive like rubber cement, and the figure is sawed to shape (Fig. 11-37). This can be done on a jigsaw or with a coping saw or, if you choose to work freehand, even with the router. At this point, because you already have the letter, you might ask—why go further? It depends on how you wish the project to appear and whether you wish to save the unit for possible future use. Formed letters can be overlayed on a shaped plaque or a plain board, or used as guides for bas-relief work.

Figure 11-38 shows one arrangement that allows for recessing the background to "raise" the letter, which is the technique used for the plaque in Fig. 11-33. The template and the straight pieces that are guides for the outline cuts are tacked-nailed or spot-glued to the workpiece. The first step is to move the template guide along all edges to form outlines for the figure and frame, then work to remove the material between the first cuts. When making a sign, the frame pieces are moved for proper spacing after each figure is formed.

You can often save time and effort when making individually shaped letters or numbers by using the following technique. Do the routing on stock that is twice or even three times thicker than the thickness you need for the parts.

Fig. 11-34. Ready-made letter and number designs can be purchased in sets or as individual pieces. They are made for use as is, but you can view them as patterns for templates that can be followed by a router.

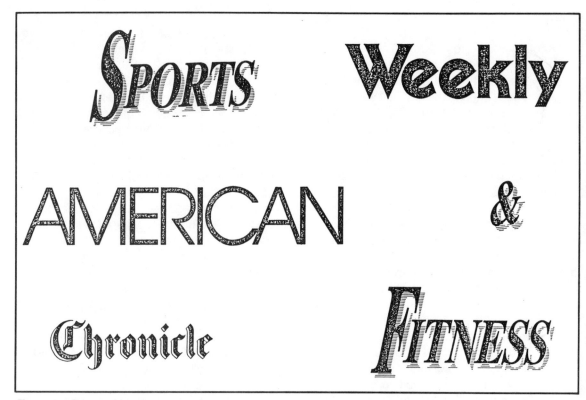

Fig. 11-35. Titles and headlines from magazines and newspapers are another source of letter and number designs.

Then resaw to get exact duplicates (Fig. 11-39). The idea is practical because a letter or number sign often needs more than one figure.

Figures 11-40 and 11-41 show some ideas you can consider for signmaking. Incised figures can be filled with a contrasting material like a wood dough or a plastic metal. A script-type lettering, accomplished by piercing with the router, can be overlayed on a contrasting backing.

Anyone who wants signmaking to be a fairly straightforward procedure or who anticipates a lot of work in this area either for fun (making signs as gifts) or for profit, should check out an accessory like the Sears Rout-A-Signer (Fig 11-42). The unit comes complete with alphabets, sets of numbers, and a carousel to store the stencils systematically and conveniently (Figs. 11-43 and 11-44).

The accessory works something like a pantograph. The letter or number template is se-

cured in a special holder at one end of the machine. A stylus is moved to follow the bearing edges of the template (Fig. 11-45). The router, mounted on a special subbase, duplicates the motions by means of an arrangement of tubes and bars that have specific swivel points. Essentially, it's how you select the swivel points that makes it possible to use the jig for letter and number sizes that range in height from about 1 inch to 4 1/2 inches while still using the templates that are supplied with the unit. The workpiece, by means of an adjustable integral clamping arrangement, is secured at the rear of the accessory and moves longitudinally for spacing between figures. The correct spacing is assured if you follow the instructions supplied with the jig, which is the answer that makes optimum results with accessories a foregone conclusion.

Black & Decker offers another system for accurate routing of nameplates, signs, and

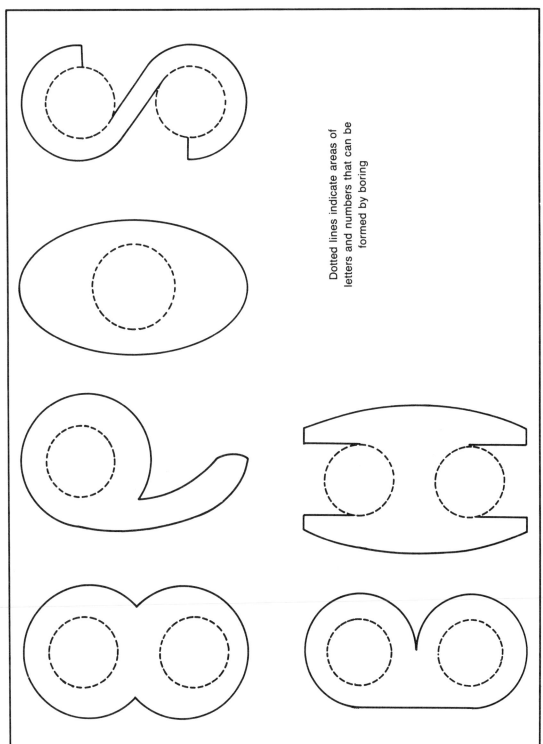

Dotted lines indicate areas of letters and numbers that can be formed by boring

Fig. 11-36. You can create your own style of letters and numbers by working with drafting tools like circle templates and French curves. It's often possible to reduce the amount of router work by boring holes to remove waste material.

213

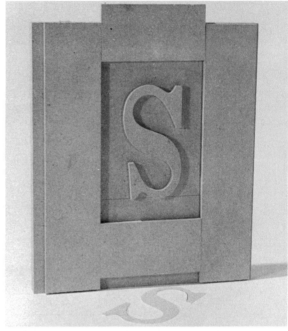

Fig. 11-37. The letter or number that you have selected or created is attached to the template material that is then sawed to profile shape. This can be done on a jigsaw, a band saw, or by hand with a coping saw.

Fig. 11-38. After the template is formed, it is attached to the workpiece by tack-nailing or spot-gluing. The arrangement shown here, with strips of material used as a template, provides an outline cut.

Fig. 11-39. The piercing technique can be used to form letters or numbers. You can produce a number of parts by doing the initial cutting on stock that is thick enough to be resawed into separate, duplicate pieces.

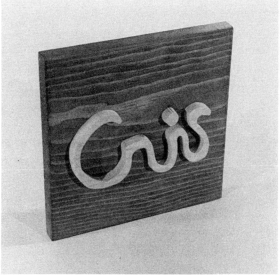

Fig. 11-40. Figures that are recessed will have more impact if the grooves are filled with a contrasting material. The filler can be a colored wood dough or a plastic metal.

Fig. 11-41. Another idea is to use the router freehand to create script-type lettering and then adhere the project to a contrasting background.

Fig. 11-42. The Sears Rout-A-Signer should interest anyone thinking of producing letter or number signs in quantity. The accessory gets you there, accurately and automatically.

215

Fig. 11-43. *How the tool is arranged allows you to produce letters or numbers ranging from 1 inch to 4 1/2 inches with the one set of stencils (or templates) that are supplied with the unit.*

Fig. 11-44. *The carousel of the Rout-A-Signer stores stencils conveniently. Symbols on its perimeter make it easy to select a particular letter or number.*

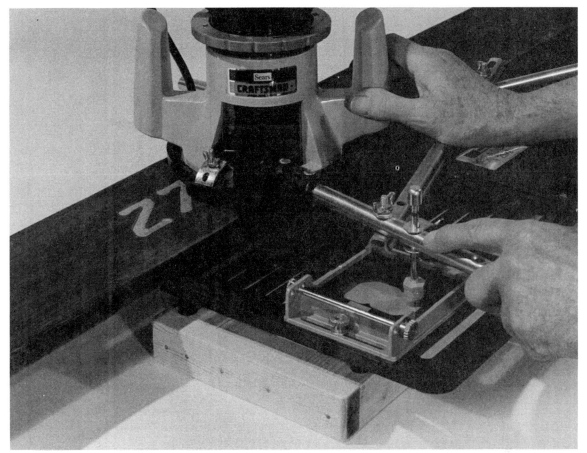

Fig. 11-45. A stylus is moved to follow the bearing edges of the template that is secured in a special clamp-type fixture at one end of the jig. Because of a pantograph-type action of the accessory, the bit in the router follows the movements of the stylus.

house numbers (Fig. 11-46). The kit includes complete sets of 1 3/4 and 2 1/2-inch size letters and numbers, and a holding device that has a built-in clamp, for the templates. The workpiece is clamped securely; the template holder is moved at a spacing of your choice for each of the figures you cut. The concept calls for using a router that is equipped with a template guide. Working with V-groove bits or straight bits is a standard procedure. Any router that you own can be used with router guides of this nature. How deep the figures will be incised is optional. If you arrange the work in an elevated position and work with a straight bit, you can "pierce" the figures right through the workpiece.

PANTOGRAPHS

Pantographs, like the Black & Decker example in Figs. 11-47 and 11-48, allow the router to duplicate just about any design or letter or number that you can draw or cut, for example, from a magazine or newspaper. Reductions of 40, 50 and 60 percent are possible. A good degree of operator control is required with units like this because it's how you guide the stylus along the lines of the pattern that affects results. If you acquire an accessory of this nature, do some practicing by making shallow cuts with a V-groove bit or a small diameter straight bit. The way to go wrong is to try to work quickly. Move the stylus slowly so you can accurately follow the lines

Fig. 11-46. Black & Decker's idea for accurately producing letters and numbers in sizes of 1 3/4 and 2 1/2 inches consists of templates secured in a special holder that can be clamped anywhere on the project. The cutting is done with a router equipped with a template guide.

you wish to reproduce. If you go "off," so will the router.

This particular unit can be used with any router having a 6-inch diameter or smaller base. It comes with 40 sheets of patterns for letters and numbers and a variety of figures and designs. The accessory must be mounted to a sheet of 3/4-inch plywood or directly to a bench. The plywood mounting is more practical because you will be able to save bench space by storing the unit when it is not in service.

INLAY WORK

The most common type of inlay work calls for forming specially shaped recesses in a surface to accommodate ready-made practical or decorative veneer assemblies (Fig. 11-49). These intriguing products are composed of dozens of pieces of contrasting species of wood and colors and run the gamut from border strips to complete scenics. Fraternal emblems, signs of the zodiac, chess and card symbols, birds and bees and flowers, and purely decorative motifs that can add an artistic touch to any project. They are readily available, all set for installation, from supply houses like Constantine's in New York.

Many of the assemblies are held together with tape on the face side, and this is the surface that should be "up" when the units are glued in place. There are two methods you can use to form the necessary recess. Make a template by using the inlay as a pattern and cut by

Fig. 11-47. Black & Decker's Router Pantograph and Design Maker can be used for relief-carved wood signs, plaques, and decorations in 40- 50- and 60-percent reductions from the original pattern.

Fig. 11-48. The bit in the router duplicates the lines that are followed by the stylus. V-groove or small diameter straight bits should be used, at least to start with. The unit can be attached directly to a bench, but a plywood base is better because it allows storing the tool when it isn't in use.

Fig. 11-49. Inlay borders are available for work that ranges from the restoration of antiques to modern furniture projects. They are usually sold in 36-inch lengths and in various widths. There is much variety in wood species and color.

working with a template guide, or use the inlay to mark the work and do the recessing freehand. The latter method is faster but calls for very careful handling of the router. The best procedure is to incise the outline with a sharp knife, using the inlay as a template. Then, with a medium-size straight bit, say 1/4 inch, and with depth of cut set to match the thickness of the inlay, clean out the waste between border lines. If the inlay has sharp corners, the job will have to be finished with a knife or, as many experts do, with a very small hand tool called a *router plane*. If you have many similar pieces to install, it's probably wise to take the time to make a special template. The recess should have clean lines and a smooth, level bottom (Fig. 11-50). If you are installing inlay borders or good-size pieces that are square or rectangular, make the border cuts by working with tack-nailed or clamped straightedges.

After the inlay is in place and the glue has dried (special glues are available), remove the paper by moistening it with a damp cloth. You'll find if you wait a minute or two that the paper peels off easily. Sand and finish when you're sure that the inlay and adjacent areas are dry.

Another type of inlay work is shown in Fig. 11-51. Here, homemade strips of material are installed in grooves formed with the router. The joints where strips cross will be perfect if you form the grooves for crossing pieces after the first strips have been glued down. The system was used to make the top for the chess table shown in Fig. 11-52. Squares were formed by using the router to make parallel grooves that were filled with strips of contrasting material. Then a second set of parallel grooves running at right angles to the first ones were cut and filled. First form a test groove in some scrap material to judge how to size the inlay strips. When

the work is done carefully, the intersecting pieces will look like a preassembled inlay (Fig. 11-53).

MORTISING FOR HINGES

Mortises required for door hinges are recesses that match the thickness and the width and length of one of the hinge leaves. How you go about accomplishing the cuts depends primarily on frequency of use. Professionals, or amateurs who might be building a house or doing extensive remodeling work, buy or rent equipment that facilitates the work and guarantees accuracy from door to door. An example is the Porter Cable product shown in Fig. 11-54. It is a set of templates that are adjustable longitudinally along an extrusion that is secured to the edge of the door. Once the templates are positioned for the number of hinges and the spacing between them, the hinge butt template can form accurate hinge mortises on any number of doors. Also, the same setup is used to form the compatible recesses that are required on door jambs.

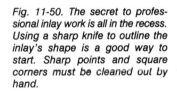

Fig. 11-50. The secret to professional inlay work is all in the recess. Using a sharp knife to outline the inlay's shape is a good way to start. Sharp points and square corners must be cleaned out by hand.

Fig. 11-51. Inlay strips can simply be pieces of contrasting material. Joints will be perfect if you form grooves for crossing strips after the first pieces have been installed.

Fig. 11-52. The chess area of the table was made by forming grooves in a plywood panel and then filling them with contrasting strips.

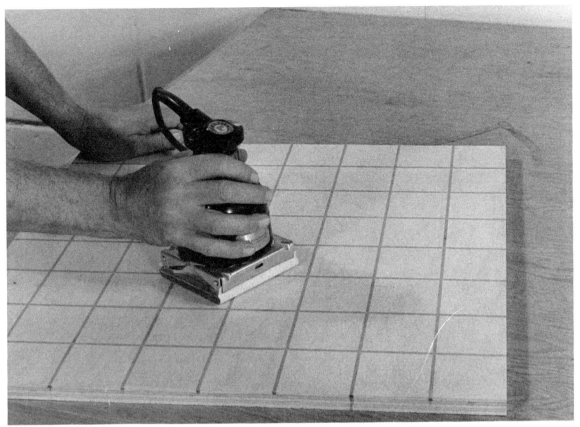

Fig. 11-53. *Every joint is perfect when the second set of grooves is formed after the first inlay strips have been glued down. "White" squares were covered with shellac before the "black" squares were stained.*

For those of us who encounter this phase of router use infrequently enough to justify purchasing or even renting a hinge butt template, there are other acceptable solutions. One of them is simply to use the hinge as a pattern to mark the edge of the door and then make the recess by using the router freehand. For better results you can make a template that eliminates the possibility of human error because the router can be used with a template guide. The template can be tack-nailed to the work (Fig. 11-55) or can be attached to a strip so that clamps can be used to hold the template in place (Fig. 11-56). Results can be just as good as those achieved by other means, but working with homemade templates does make you responsible for the dis-

tance between mortises.

Cutting is done with a straight bit that leaves rounded corners. Some hand work with a knife or chisel is required if the hinges have square corners, but hinges with round corners are available. If you seek them out you'll be ready for hinge installation as soon as routing is complete.

Figure 11-57 illustrates some facts pertaining to efficient door hanging. Although two hinges are acceptable on interior doors, which are light because they are usually hollow core, it's becoming more common to use three hinges on all doors.

You can buy individual butt hinge templates in 3 1/2- and 4-inch sizes. If you want to avoid making your own, and have units on hand for

223

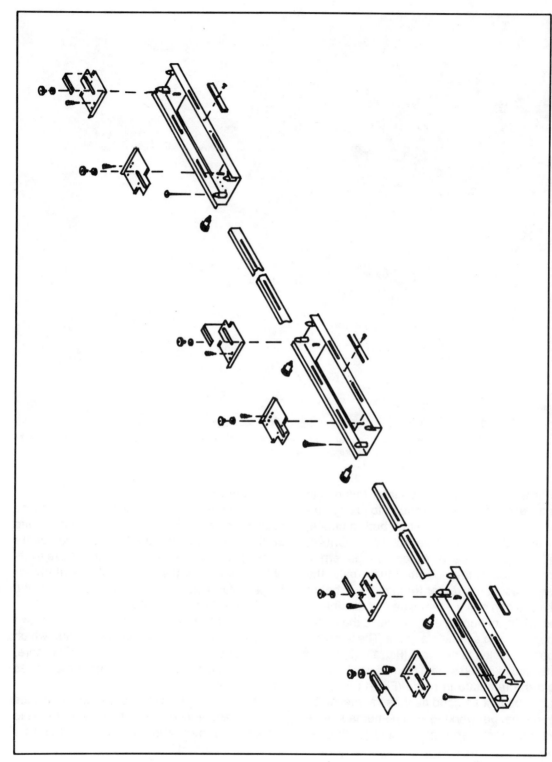

Fig. 11-54. The hinge butt template consists of three adjustable guides placed anywhere along an extrusion that is clamped to the edge of a door. Once set, the jig can be used on one or a hundred doors.

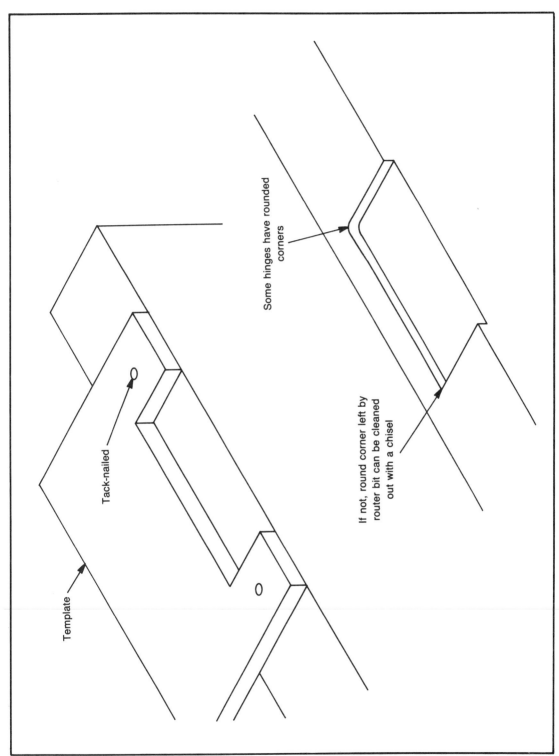

Template

Tack-nailed

Some hinges have rounded corners

If not, round corner left by router bit can be cleaned out with a chisel

Fig. 11-55. A homemade template for hinge mortising can be used when the work must be done on only one or two doors. This concept calls for tack-nailing.

225

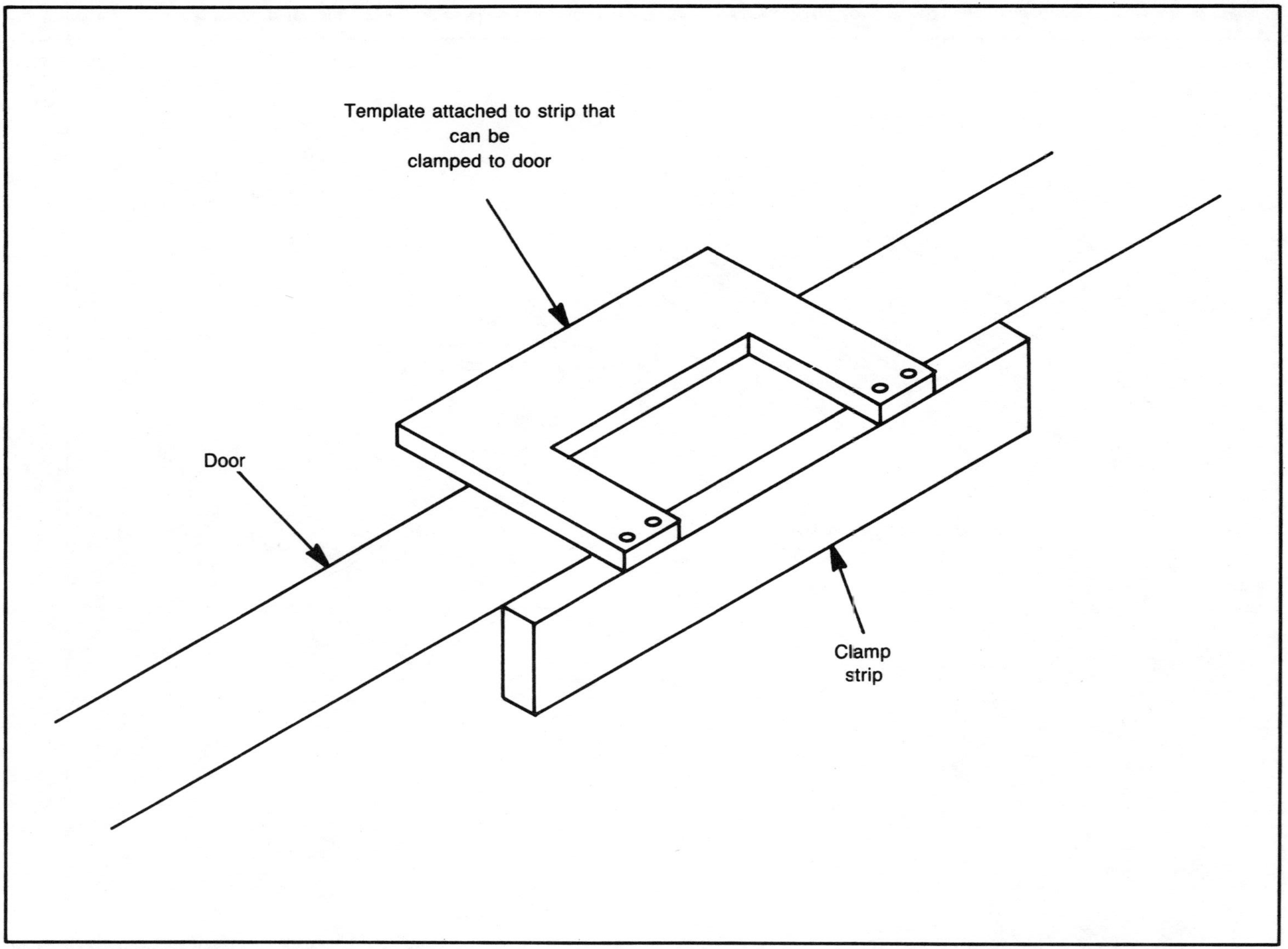

Template attached to strip that can be clamped to door

Clamp strip

Door

Fig. 11-56. Another version of the hinge mortise template has a clamp strip.

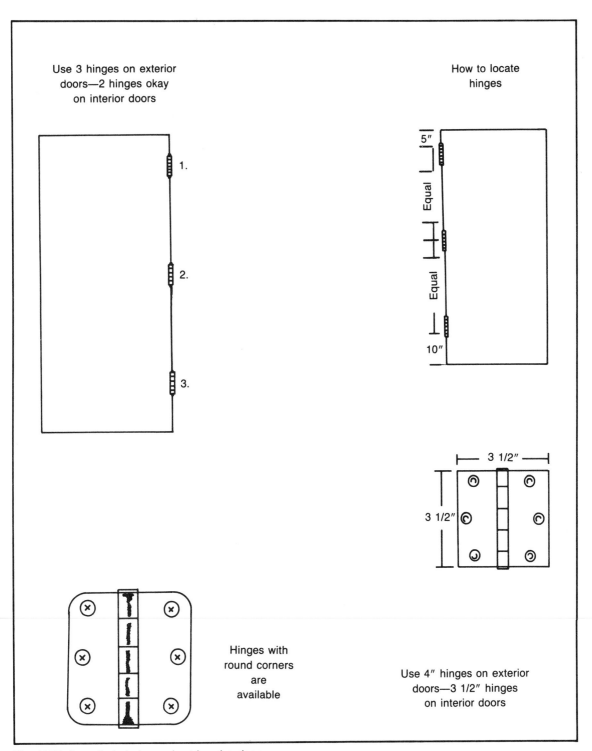

Use 3 hinges on exterior doors—2 hinges okay on interior doors

How to locate hinges

5"

Equal

Equal

10"

3 1/2"

3 1/2"

Hinges with round corners are available

Use 4" hinges on exterior doors—3 1/2" hinges on interior doors

Fig. 11-57. Some facts to know about hanging doors.

227

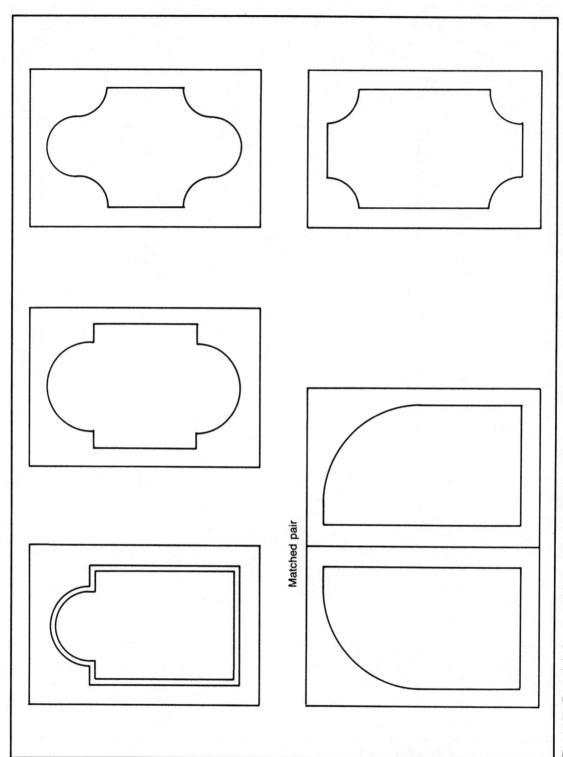

Matched pair

Fig. 11-58. Routed designs on cabinet and furniture doors can follow traditional lines or be a one-of-a-kind design.

future use, this might be the way to go.

PANEL DECORATING

Panel decorating refers to the decorative grooving that is commonly seen on cabinet doors and sides, and on drawer fronts (Fig. 11-58). There are many different types of accessories for the router that make this kind of work easy to do. But the average router user who is not involved in this activity to a great extent can get by economically and efficiently by making a special template for the job on hand (Fig. 11-59). The template can be a one-piece unit or an assembly of straightedges, quarter-round parts, and other pieces that have concave or convex arcs. The latter idea, which forms a template when the various pieces are clamped or tack-nailed to the work, was demonstrated in Chapter 8. Working with an assortment of shapes makes the template variable in size and in the groove-shapes that can be produced. When the situation doesn't permit clamping, a disadvantage is that the pieces must be secured by spot-gluing or tack-nailing, and these might not be acceptable.

The advantages of commercial accessories are that they are designed to accommodate panels of various size. Built-in clamps or holders of some sort to secure the work and a variety of corner templates that just snap into position are supplied. The Sears Door and Panel Decorating kit (Fig. 11-60) might be of interest to amateurs, or professionals for that matter, because it can be used on workpieces up to 36 × 36 inches and it's in the $80.00 price range. The guide rails are extruded anodized aluminum that are secured to the work with eight clamps. Assuming that all the parts you need to work on are the same size, the assembly needs no further adjustment after it has been organized for the first piece of work.

Seven four-piece sets of corner templates (Fig. 11-61) and an extra "blank" set that you

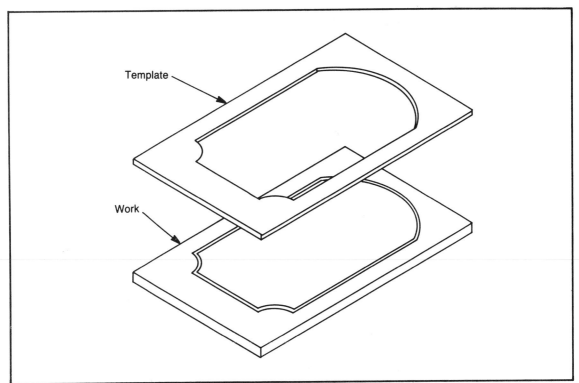

Fig. 11-59. A conventional template that you make can be used to guide the router.

Fig. 11-60. *The Sears Door and Panel Decorating Kit consists of aluminum straightedges and corner templates that just snap into place. The advantage of the jig is that it can be adjusted to suit various size doors or panels.*

can shape for a particular design are part of the kit. An adjustable radius arm is also provided so the tool can be used for forming arcs.

On a grander scale is the Decorout-Or-Planer, also offered by Sears, that is shown in Fig. 11-62. The unit requires you to supply a mounting board of 3/4- × -39- × -67-inch plywood and accepts workpieces up to 21 × 42 inches in thicknesses up to about 1 3/8 inches. The router, which can be any unit with a 6-inch or smaller diameter base, is attached to a carriage assembly that rides on rails over any part of the real working area. Because the router is maintained on a constant level, the accessory

can be used for planing surfaces as well as for decorative grooving.

A good-size owner's manual comes with the unit. The instructions should be followed to the letter, not only when workpieces are being set up, but when doing the initial assembly work required. Figures 11-63 through 11-66 show some of the details of the Decorout-Or-Planer.

THE ROUTER AS AN EDGE PLANER

If you have ever used a hand plane to smooth or joint edges or to reduce the width of a board, you'll appreciate how much easier and more

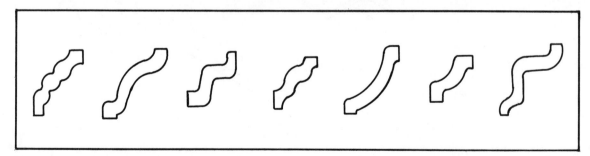

Fig. 11-61. *Corner templates come in sets of four. Seven designs are provided, in addition to a blank set that you can use for an original design.*

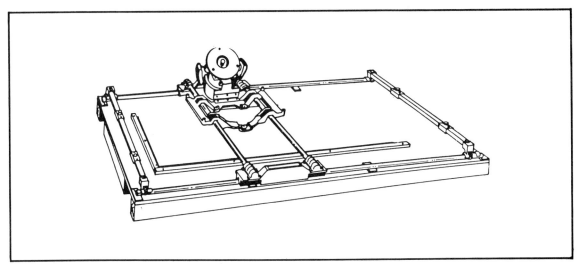

Fig. 11-62. The Decorout-Or-Planer is a larger tool that accepts work up to 21 × 42 inches. Parts must be assembled and mounted on a plywood panel you supply. It can be used with any router that has a 6-inch or smaller base.

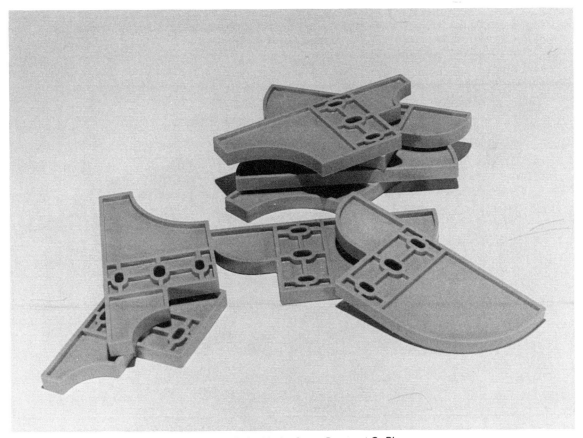

Fig. 11-63. Some of the corner templates supplied with the Sears Decorout-Or-Planer.

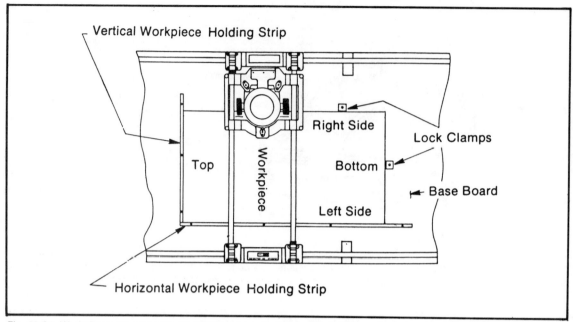

Fig. 11-64. Workpieces are secured with holding strips and lock clamps before planing or decorative routing is done. The carriage that holds the router rides on rails and can be moved in any direction.

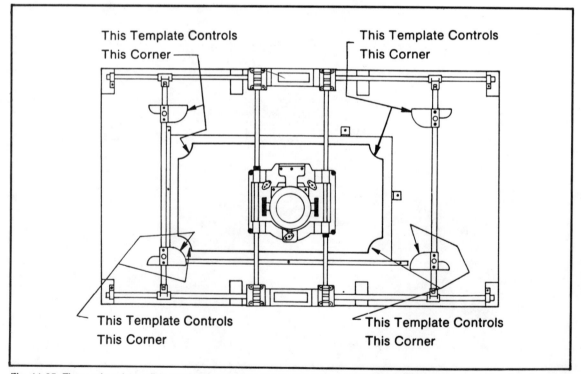

Fig. 11-65. The carriage has rollers at each corner that bear against the templates. Template placement is optional, so you do have control over designs.

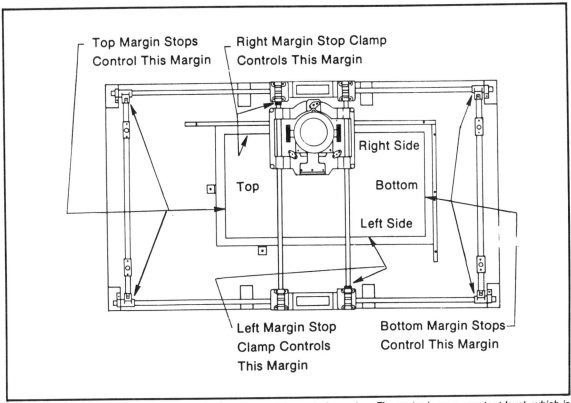

Top Margin Stops Control This Margin

Right Margin Stop Clamp Controls This Margin

Right Side

Top

Bottom

Left Side

Left Margin Stop Clamp Controls This Margin

Bottom Margin Stops Control This Margin

Fig. 11-66. Top view shows the stop clamps that are used to control margins. The router is on a constant level, which is why the jig can also be used to plane surfaces.

quickly that kind of work can be done with a router without its base and mounted in a power plane attachment (Fig. 11-67). Special cutters, like the spiral types shown in Fig. 11-68, are used in place of regular router bits.

Notice that I use the word *edge* planer. The disadvantage, if you want to look at it that way, of the router/plane setup is that it can't be used to smooth down or level broad surfaces. Only regular power planes (Fig. 11-69) can be used for that kind of work.

Plane attachments are adjustable for depth of cut with the maximum setting of about 3/32 inch. That's a pretty hefty cut for a plane and it can be handy when you wish to remove a lot of material. In my mind, though, it's how little you can shave off an edge that is the major attribute of the arrangement. Shaving a sliver from the edge of a door so it will fit perfectly is an operat-

ion the router with plane attachment can do with finesse. Results are better when you limit cut depth to about 1/32 inch, even if you must make repeat passes to get the job done.

Most of the attachments have an adjustable fence to bevel or chamfer edges as well as square them. Start cuts by placing the front edge of the attachment firmly on the work. As cutting progresses, maintain downward pressure equally with both hands. Apply more pressure with the hand at the rear of the tool as you approach the end of the pass.

To avoid the breakout or feathering that inevitably occurs at the end of cross-grain cuts and when working on plywood, use the techniques shown in Figs. 11-70 and 11-71.

Because plane attachments are not interchangeable among all brands of routers, purchase units from the same manufacturer. Be

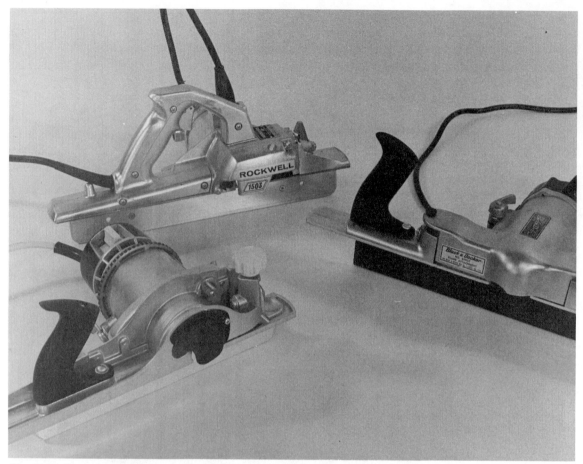

Fig. 11-67. Examples of attachments that allow the router to be used as an edge planer.

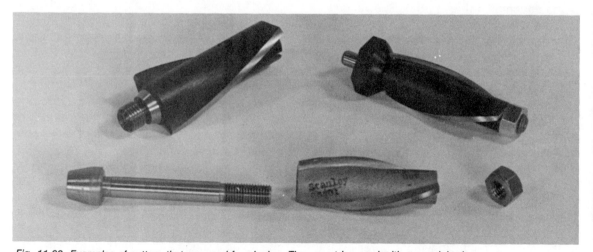

Fig. 11-68. Examples of cutters that are used for planing. They must be used with a special arbor.

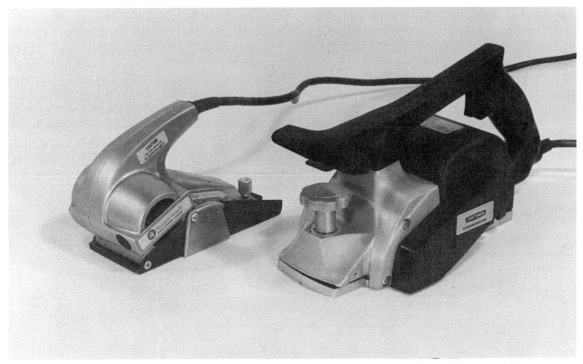

Fig. 11-69. These are regular, individual power planes that can also be used on broad surfaces. That's something the router with plane attachment can't do.

Fig. 11-70. To avoid the breakout that usually occurs at the end of end grain passes, clamp a scrap block to the end of the workpiece. Keep depth of cut on jobs like this to a minimum.

careful to follow instructions when installing the router motor. There are few adjustments required, but they must be done right for the tool to function precisely. Be cautious when working. Always keep both hands topside. Turn off the motor at the end of a cut and wait for the motor to stop before setting the tool down. Always let the motor come up to full speed before starting to cut.

WORKING WITH PLASTIC LAMINATES

Plastic laminates are as common in the modern home as an automobile on the driveway or a TV set in the family room. There was a time when the material was accepted merely as a long-lived covering for a kitchen countertop, but it is now found on furniture and cabinets, on walls and shelves, and even in moisture areas like stall showers. The reasons for increased usage include improvements in the material, better installation methods that are not beyond the scope of amateurs, and the ever-increasing variety of colors and decorative patterns and finishes. Grain patterns and tones of many wood species, butcher block effects, solid colors, slate and marble simulations that can fool the eye, the choice of a high-gloss, suede, satin, or textured finish all contribute to plastic laminate excitement. One of the newest innovations is a solid-color product that has no dark substrate. The joints on edges and corners are almost invisible and can be surface decorated like any solid material (Fig. 11-72).

Fig. 11-71. Two methods you can use to eliminate breakout when planing plywood. Use a scrap piece, or plane a piece that is slightly oversize and then saw off the imperfection.

236

Fig. 11-72. A recently introduced plastic laminate has solid color throughout. This eliminates dark lines in joints and makes it possible to surface decorate the material. Current trade names are Wilsonart's "Solicor" and Formica's "Colorcore."

If you see the sheets of plastic laminate as a veneer that is adhered to a core material, you can accept installation as a three-phase oper-

ation. The sheet is first cut to approximate size, then it is glued down by following a certain procedure, then it is trimmed to match the size and

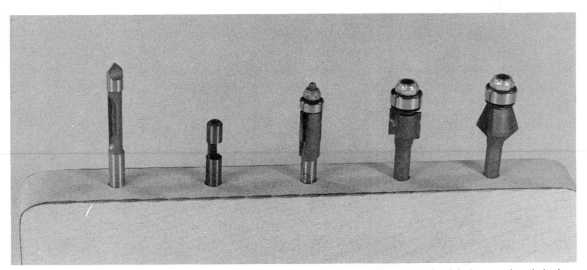

Fig. 11-73. Types of router bits that are commonly used on plastic laminates. The one on the right leaves a beveled edge; at the left is a plunging design. The bits are solid carbide or have tungsten carbide blades.

shape of the substrate. The trimming is the operation that requires some finesse, but because it can be done with a router that is equipped with the kind of bits shown in Fig. 11-73, it's a chore that can be accomplished by anyone with professional results just about guaranteed. The secret of the bits is that the pilot, whether it is ball bearing or integral, must match the diameter of the bit's cutting circle. As long as you keep the router level, and the pilot in contact with the bearing surface, you can't go wrong. The trimmed edge will be perfectly flush with the adjacent surface (Figs. 11-74 and 11-75).

In step-by-step fashion, the overall procedure is as follows: The surface and edges of the core material (particleboard or plywood) must be smooth and clean. Fill any voids in the core edges before going further. Because most applications call for the surface laminate to cover the top edges of side pieces, edges must be covered first. Cut strips about 1/4 inch wider than the edge they will cover. Attachment is a gluing job. Because conventional liquid glues require much clamping and a lot of time to dry, it's become standard practice to work with a contact cement. The only disadvantage is that the cement bonds on contact, so care must be taken to register mating pieces correctly before you press them together. Read the directions on the container. The length of time it takes for the cement to touch-dry, which it has to do before you join parts, can vary. The instructions will suggest

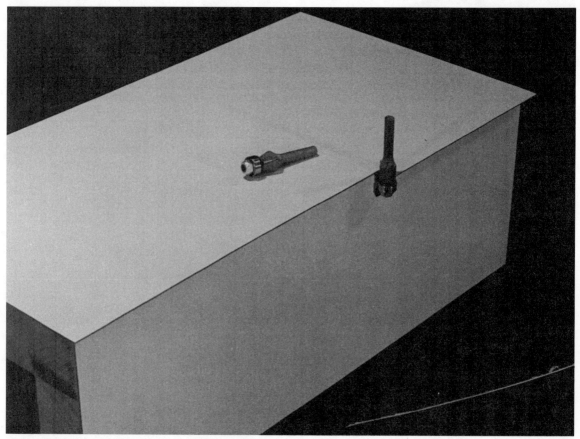

Fig. 11-74. Bits used for trimming do an excellent job because the bearing has exactly the same diameter as the bit's cutting circle.

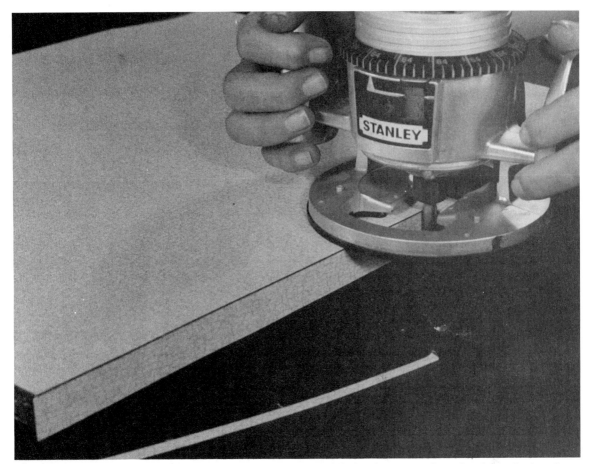

Fig. 11-75. Perfect joints are assured if you keep the router level and the bearing constantly against the work edge. Some professionals coat the bearing edge with wax or petroleum jelly as a guard against marring. This is probably needed more when a bit with an integral rather than a ball-bearing pilot is used.

a test, a common one being to touch a cemented surface with a piece of wrapping paper. If the paper doesn't stick, the cement is dry enough to work.

Place the edge pieces so the excess projects above the surface of the core. Then trim the top edge flush with the surface of the core by working with a router or a laminate trimmer (Fig. 11-76). The next step is to cut the surface cover so it is about 1/4 inch greater on all edges than the substrate. After applying the contact cement and waiting for it to dry, place the cover in position but with strips of wood or dowels between it and the core (Figs. 11-77 and 11-78).

This ensures correct registration before the cover is pressed into place. Remove the separation pieces as you go along. Be sure to apply pressure over the entire area, either by tapping with a hammer and a length of hardwood or by using a roller. An idea that works is to use an ordinary rolling pin. The last step is to work with the router to trim off excess material (Fig. 11-79).

One of the more ticklish aspects of plastic laminate cutting comes when it is necessary to join pieces end to end or when the covering must make a 90-degree turn. The mating edges of the joint must be perfect in order for the project to appear seamless. One system you can use for

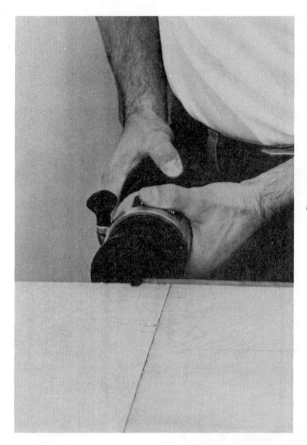

Fig. 11-76. Edges of core material are covered first. The router, in this case a laminate trimmer, cuts the strip so it is flush with the core's surface. Photograph courtesy of Formica Corporation.

Fig. 11-77. Strips of wood are placed between the cover material and the core to avoid contact until the cover is correctly aligned. Photograph courtesy of Formica Corporation.

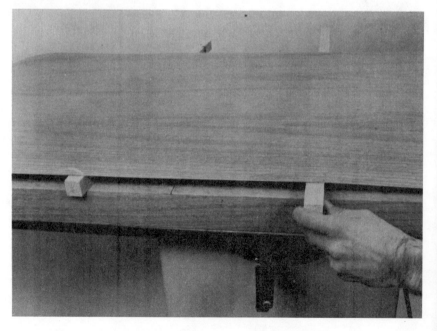

Fig. 11-78. Remove the strips, in this case dowels, as the cover is pressed down. When full contact is made, immediately apply pressure over the entire area. Do this with a hammer and a strip of hardwood, or something like a rolling pin. Photograph courtesy of Formica Corporation.

Fig. 11-79. The last step is to trim the laminate so it will be flush to the edges. Photograph courtesy of Formica Corporation.

perfect butt joints is shown in Fig. 11-80. The two parts are elevated on boards or pieces of plywood and placed so the edges to be joined are separated by less than the diameter of the straight bit that will do the cutting. The router is guided by a straightedge that is secured parallel to the cut line. Another way would be to overlap the edges and guide the router for the cut by clamping a straightedge on each side of the cut line as tracks for the tool.

Miter joints can be cut in similar fashion (Fig. 11-81). You must be sure to place the pieces so the cut angle will be exact. In this case, the mating pieces are placed together face side

to face side. When the cutting is carefully done, the joint will be tight and invisible (Fig. 11-82).

Figure 11-83 shows examples of how you can work with plastic laminates as if they were wood veneers. Often, scrap pieces can be utilized this way on projects like small tables, boxes, clock faces, and so on.

THE ROUTER AS A THREADING TOOL

Cutting threads in wood may seem like a far out hobby, but the technique has many practical applications (Figs. 11-84 through 11-86). There is nothing wrong with getting into some areas of

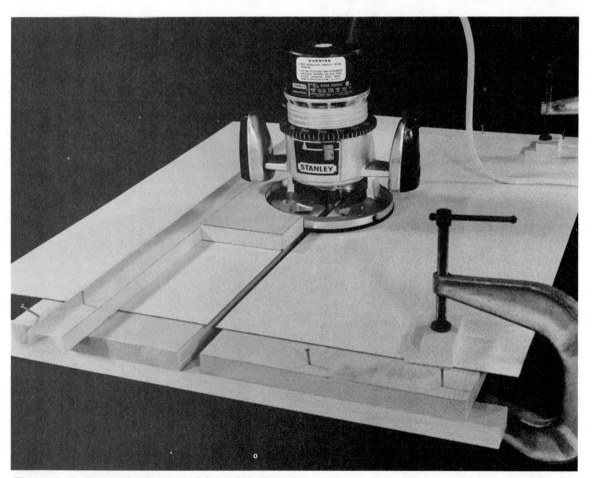

Fig. 11-80. You'll get perfect butt joints if the mating edges of the pieces are trimmed at the same time. I put together this temporary jig because I had many pieces to cut.

Fig. 11-81. Use a similar system for miter joints. In this case the parts to be joined are held together face side to face side. Be sure the pieces are clamped in place at the correct angle.

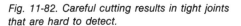

Fig. 11-82. Careful cutting results in tight joints that are hard to detect.

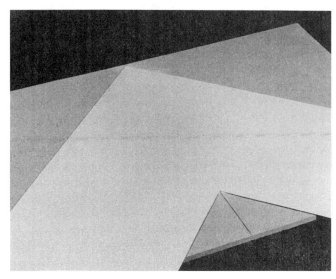

Fig. 11-83. Plastic laminates can be worked almost like wood veneers so interesting inlay effects are possible. Scrap pieces can often be used to make panels for small projects.

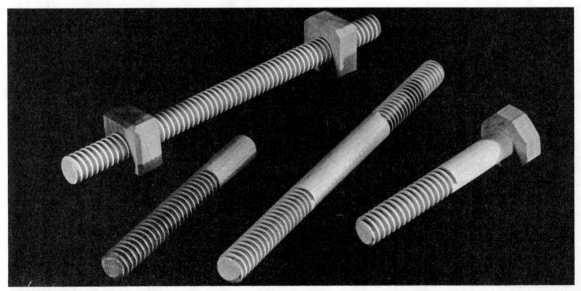

Fig. 11-84. You can form wooden nuts and bolts when the router is organized for threading operations. Projects like this can provide intriguing details on some assemblies. Think of them, for example, as fasteners on outdoor furniture.

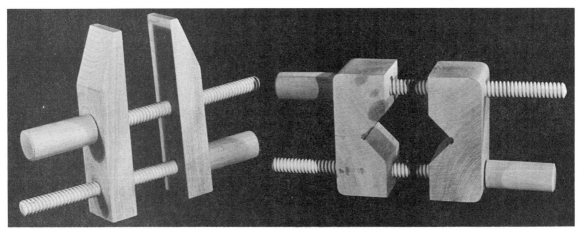

Fig. 11-85. Other projects include light-duty, conventional, or special application clamps.

Fig. 11-86. My book binding jig uses threaded dowel to apply pressure.

245

shop work just for the fun of it. Often adding a threaded post or securing an assembly with nuts and bolts made of wood can provide eye-catching details to a project.

This type of work is usually done with special thread boxes that are used by hand, but a recent innovation allows quick and precise thread forming in wood, and even in some plastics, by using a router. The accessories required (Fig. 11-87) are offered by The Beall Tool Company and can be used with any router. The parts can be purchased individually or as a complete kit that includes threading equipment (for outside threads) and taps (for inside threads) in sizes of 1/2, 3/4, and 1 inch.

The threader, which serves as a base for the router (Fig. 11-88), is bolted to a block of wood that is then secured in a vise or clamped to a benchtop. Special dies are used in the base so that after the cut is started, feeding the work through at the correct speed is automatic. The router bit supplied is a HSS double-ended, three-flute spiral type that was specially designed for the purpose of forming threads.

The only crucial adjustment that is required of the worker is the projection of the bit. A little trial and error is required before the threads are perfect, but once the cut depth is established, you can turn out threaded pieces by the yard.

The dowels to be threaded should be

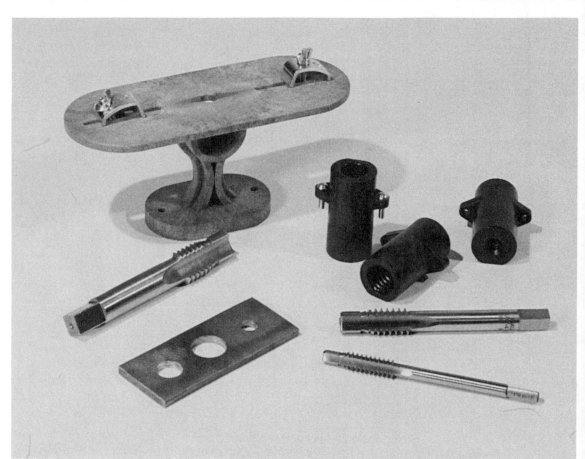

Fig. 11-87. The Beall Tool Company threading tools can be used with a router and can be purchased as the set shown here or as separate components. Outside threads are formed with a special router bit. Inside threads are formed by hand with specially designed taps.

Fig. 11-88. *The router mounts on a special base that is secured to a block of wood. Threads are formed by moving the dowel through special dies that, after contact with the cutter is made, control the speed with which the work is fed through.*

selected with care. Reject any that are undersize or more oval than round. Dowels that are slightly oversize can be made perfect by driving them through the sizing plate. Internal threads are formed in fairly routine fashion with the taps. The taps that are supplied were specially designed with long pilots to keep them vertical in the hole and assure perpendicular threads.

CHAIN-MAKING TECHNIQUE

Using the router to form links for wooden chains might not be of interest to all router users, but the techniques involved are very intriguing and might come in handy for small project components requiring special setups, or when making rings like those in Fig. 11-89. It's another activity that demonstrates the flexibility of the router and one worth knowing even if rarely used. The procedure is explained as follows:

Step 1. Prepare the number of pieces required for the links by sawing. Make a cardboard template to mark the outside and inside shape of the links on each piece. Shape the outside

Fig. 11-89. The chain-making techniques that follow can be used to form rings. You may never use the router for projects like this, but the procedure is very interesting and can prove useful for other applications.

with a handsaw, a jigsaw, or band saw. Sand the outside edges smooth. Remove the bulk of the waste from the interior area by boring overlapping holes (Fig. 11-90).

Step 2. Make the holding fixture shown in Fig. 11-91. The frame provides a tight fit for the

link block. The opening through the base, which serves as a template, is sized to suit the inside shape of the link. Use a straight, piloted router bit to finish shaping the inside of the link.

Step 3. Use the same holding fixture from Step 2 to hold the link while rounding over the

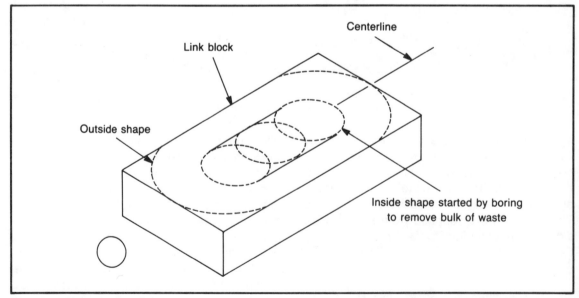

Fig. 11-90. Blanks for the links are cut to size and shaped to outside form. Remove the bulk of the inside waste by boring overlapping holes.

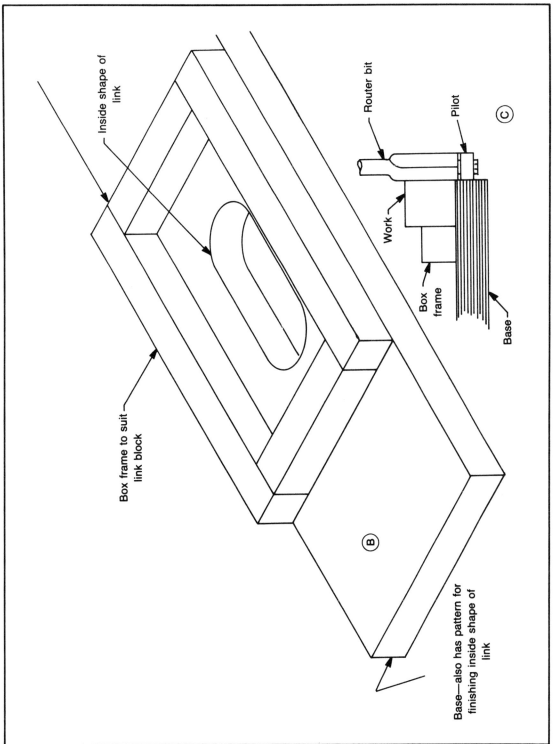

Inside shape of link

Box frame to suit link block

Base—also has pattern for finishing inside shape of link

Ⓑ

Router bit

Work

Box frame

Pilot

Base

Ⓒ

Fig. 11-91. The next step is to make a box frame that serves as a jig so the inside of the links can be routed to final form. A straight, piloted bit is used.

249

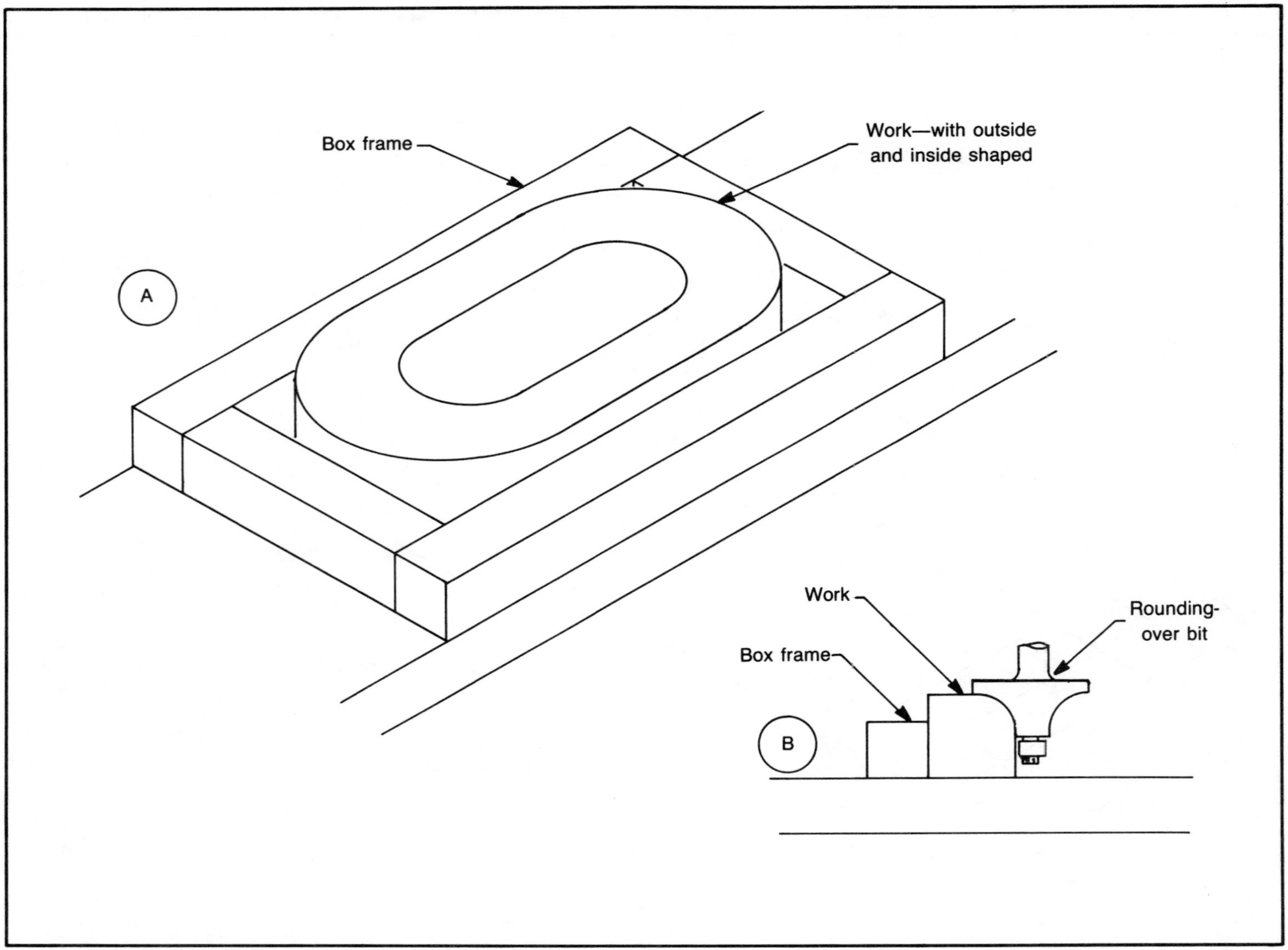

Work—with outside
and inside shaped

Box frame

A

Rounding-
over bit

Work

Box frame

B

Fig. 11-92. The same jig is used to hold the work to round over inside edges.

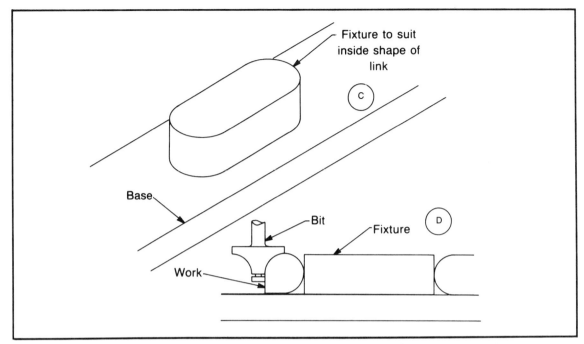

Fixture to suit
inside shape of
link

Base

Bit

Fixture

Work

Fig. 11-93. For the final step another fixture with a plug that suits the inside shape of the link is needed. The rounding-over bit is used to shape the perimeter of the links. Because a piloted bit is used, the links will have a flat area on inside and outside edges. You can live with this or eliminate it by doing some sanding.

inside, top, and bottom edges (Fig. 11-92).

Step 4. Make a holding fixture that exactly suits the inside shape of the links (Fig. 11-93). Use the rouding-over bit to shape the outside edges of the links.

A factor that is not shown in the illustrations is that the piloted bit must have some bearing surface. This means that the inside and outside edges of the links will have a "flat." You can live with this or do some sanding to get rid of it. Half of the links will have to be split on the center-line before all links can be connected (Fig. 11-94). You can do this with a knife or a thin-bladed saw. A coping saw with a very fine blade will do if nothing else is available. Reassemble the parted links after they have been inserted through full links by coating mating edges with glue and holding them together with small clamps or heavy rubber bands.

THE ROUTER AS A LATHE ACCESSORY

If you own a lathe, you can view the portable

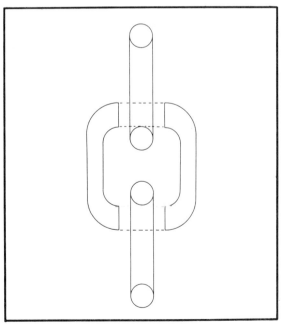

Fig. 11-94. Alternate links must be split on a centerline so they can interlock with full links.

Fig. 11-95. It's easy to do fluting or reeding on a lathe-mounted spindle when a trough-type jig is installed because the router can be guided longitudinally over the centerline of the work. The spacing of the cuts is no problem if the lathe has an indexing device.

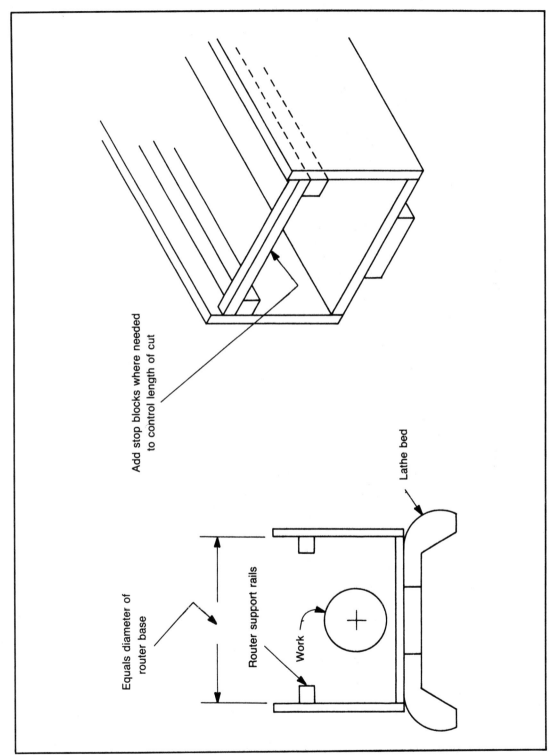

Add stop blocks where needed to control length of cut

Equals diameter of router base

Router support rails

Work

Lathe bed

Fig. 11-96. This type of lathe jig provides tracks for the router. It must be made so the bit doing the cutting and the workpiece have the same vertical centerline. Stops placed across the side members of the jig are used when you wish to limit the length of the cuts.

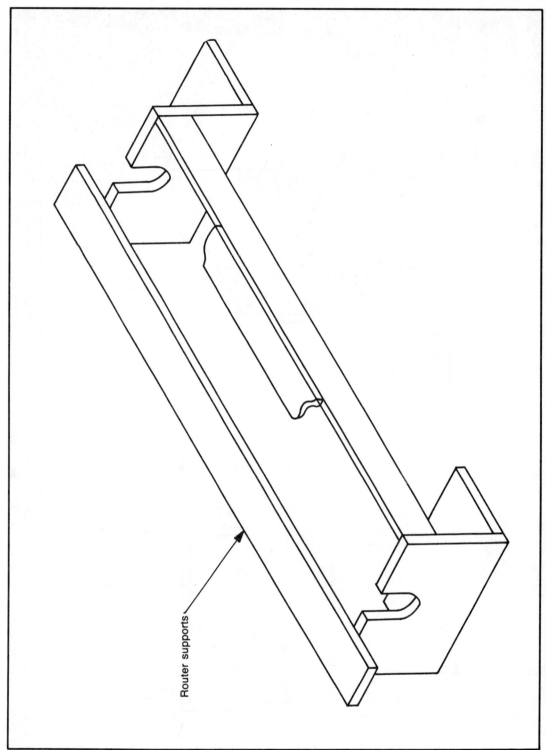

Router supports

Fig. 11-97. Another design for a lathe jig you can make to use the router like a motorized lathe chisel. In this case the jig supplies support areas. You can control the cutting path of the router by using an edge guide.

Fig. 11-98. The router is equipped with a special subbase so it easily spans the open area between support surfaces. Notice that the auxiliary base is a 1/16-inch thick piece of aluminum. This is not crucial for the application, but it does demonstrate that various materials can be used for subbases that you manufacture.

router almost as if it were a motorized lathe chisel. The router is suitable for the technique because homemade jigs allow the router to be moved longitudinally on the lathe's working axis for forms like reeds and flutes or held still for circumferential cutting. If you recall the fluting jig described in Chapter 10, you'll recognize the similarity between that jig and the lathe arrangement shown in Fig. 11-95. The jig for the lathe can be designed with raised sides that serve as tracks for the router or with separated support areas to hold the router level while it moves ac-

Fig. 11-99. Peripheral shaping is done with the router in a fixed position. Both the router bit and the workpiece are turning. Depth of cut can be set with the bit centered over the workpiece or by presetting it and then moving the router to make contact. Cuts like this can't be made with piloted bits.

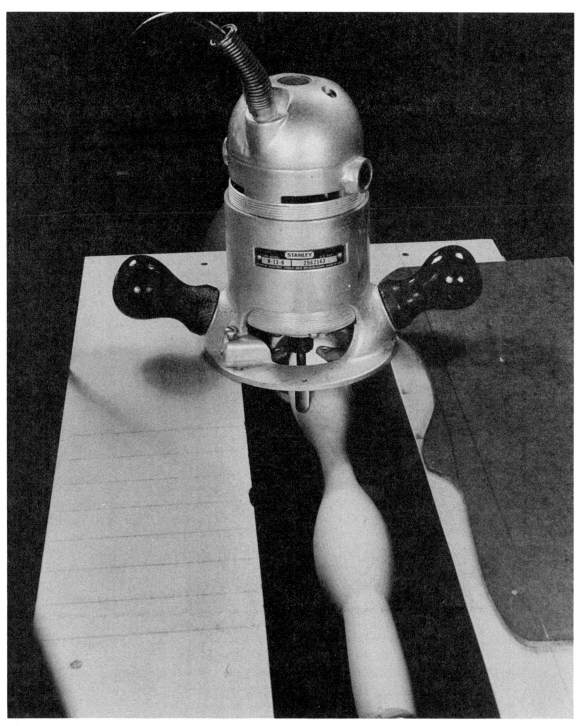

Fig. 11-100. Contours on spindles can be shaped by using templates to guide the router. Situate the template slightly forward of the spindle's vertical centerline for cutting. Work with rotary rasps and burrs instead of regular router bits.

curately using an edge guide (Figs. 11-96 and 11-97).

Most lathes have indexing devices to maintain spacing between longitudinal cuts (Fig. 11-98). If the lathe does not have this feature, you can still work accurately by using the strip of paper system that was described in Chapter 10.

For cuts on the circumferences of spindles, you can hold the router in a fixed position by using clamps or by bracing it against a stop fixed to the jig (Fig. 11-99). The cut depth can be controlled by adjusting the bit's projection while both spindle and router bit are turning or by adjusting bit projection beforehand and then sliding the router to make contact. There is opportunity here for experimentation. One idea is shown in Fig. 11-100. The spindle is formed to a particular shape by using the template to guide the movements of the router. This is a good way to work when you need many similar pieces. Fluting and reeding cuts are made with the work in a fixed position and only the router working. Peripheral cuts are made with both the lathe and the router turning.

Chapter 12

The Router as a Shaper

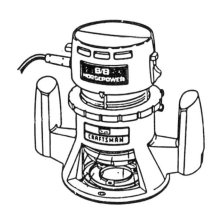

THE PORTABLE ROUTER AND THE STATIONARY shaper are two different tool concepts. They have enough in common, however, that a router secured in an inverted position in a special stand is so much a counterpart of the other that the differences in appearance and use are minimal (Figs. 12-1 and 12-2).

Too often, though, the router is organized for stationary shaper work by mounting it under a slab of plywood that has a hole through it for the router bits. A clamped-on strip of wood serves as a fence. Working this way handicaps anyone who wants to get the most out of the idea. For one thing, the fence should consist of individually adjustable *infeed* and *outfeed* sections. Then when the cut removes the entire edge of the stock, for example, the outfeed fence can be brought forward to provide support for the work *after* it has passed the cutter (Fig. 12-3). Another factor is that edges on curved pieces can't be shaped by working against a fence. A regular shaper provides *fulcrum pins* for this facet of shaping, and so should a homemade

version (Figs. 12-4 and 12-5). The function of the pins is to provide a brace point for the work so it can be held firmly while it is advanced slowly to make contact with the cutter. Freehand work on a shaper is done with the workpiece bearing against collars that are mounted on the spindle along with the cutter (Fig. 12-6). When a router is used, the bearing surface for the work *must* be provided by a pilot on the router bit (Fig. 12-7).

APPLICATIONS

There isn't much you can't do with a router/shaper setup. By working with conventional router bits, you can form decorative edges on straight, round, or curved workpieces, do rabbeting and dadoing, joint edges, cut grooves, form tenons, and more. Even more exciting is that you can work with the new types of bits being produced—bits designed for practical purposes, but which can't be used in traditional router fashion. They can only be used when the router is mounted in a stand. Most of the newcomers make it possible for router users who

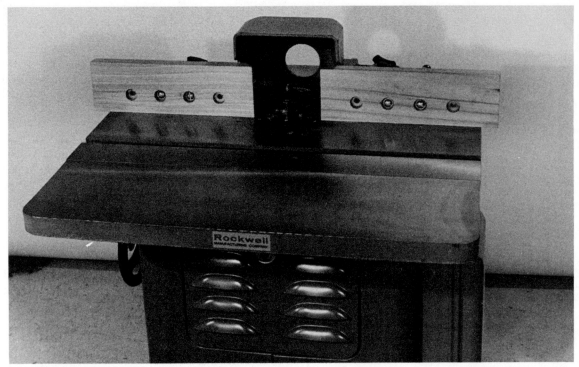

Fig. 12-1. Anyone interested in making a router/shaper stand should think in terms of imitating the features of a good-size, regular shape like this Rockwell (now Delta) industrial tool.

add a shaper table to do work like panel raising and forming those intriguing mating configurations like cope and stile cuts that are required for frame and panel constructions. Doors (Fig. 12-8) are now included in the list of projects you can accomplish with a portable router.

Bits in this category may be purchased individually or in sets. Some include extra bits like the door lip and the glue joint cutter that are included in the Freud set shown in Fig. 12-9. The glue joint cutter is handy when the door panel is made of solid wood rather than a material like plywood. For one thing, available stock might not be wide enough to suit the width of the door. Another reason is that narrow pieces joined edge to edge are less likely to warp than a one-piece board. It often happens that a board is concave (cupped) across its width. A common method used to eliminate the distortion is to saw the board into three pieces and then reassemble with the center piece inverted. Other ideas that

are used to create flat, solid wood panels are shown in Fig. 12-10. The glue joint cutter is a big help when you are involved in this kind of work.

The door lip cutter shown in Figs. 12-11 and 12-12 is used to form the edge that is often seen on doors of kitchen cabinets and similar projects. Some variation in the height of the shoulders without affecting the shape and size of the quarter-round lip is possible. You can also work (Fig. 12-12) so the top shoulder is completely eliminated. The changes from a full profile cut depend on the height of the cutter in relation to the work. Other sets of bits used with a router for paneled door construction are shown in Figs. 12-13 and 12-14.

The cutters that are used for this phase of router work must not be treated too casually. All of them have 1/2-inch shanks, which indicates that they be used only with a heavy-duty tool. Even so, it's wise to avoid excessively deep cuts

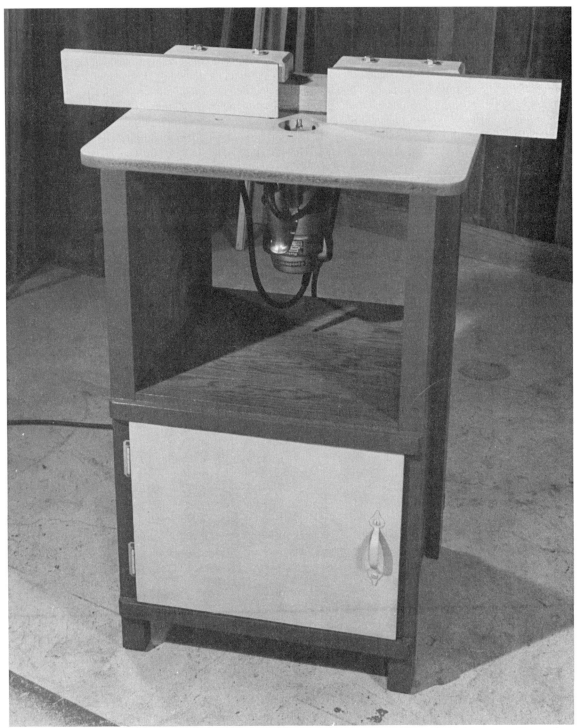

Fig. 12-2. The homemade stand should be a counterpart of the commercial version. This early model was used in my shop for a long time. It lacked, among other things, a slot for a miter gauge.

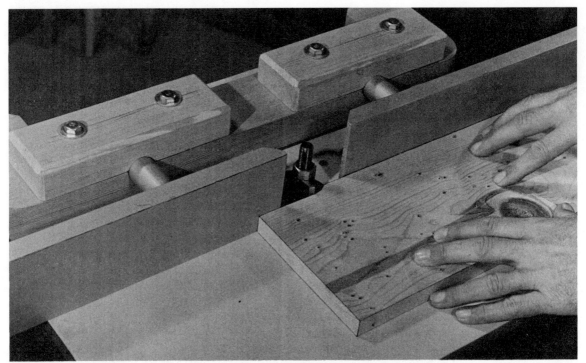

Fig. 12-3. Infeed and outfeed fences should be individually adjustable. Then, when a full-edge cut is made, the outfeed fence can be brought forward to supply support for the work after it has passed the cutter.

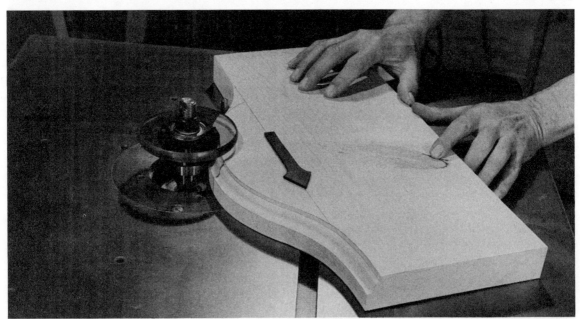

Fig. 12-4. A regular shaper provides for the installation of fulcrum pins that are needed when doing freehand shaping. The arrow indicates feed direction, which is always against the cutter's direction of rotation.

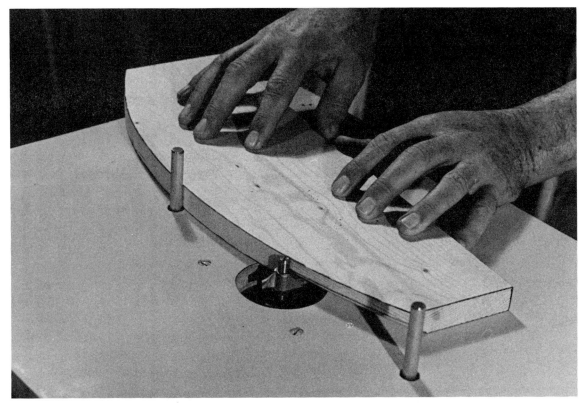

Fig. 12-5. A homemade version should also provide for fulcrum pins, one on the infeed side and a second one on the out-feed side.

and fast feed rates. The size of the bits alone should inspire respect and prompt you to use them with care and good router judgement.

Another set of bits that should be mentioned here because they must be used in a router/shaper setup, is the Sears seven-piece Crown Molding kit (Fig. 12-15). It contains all the cutters and arbors that are required for producing standard or original molding shapes. Chapter 3 has more information on the Sears cutters. If you own a Delta light-duty or heavy-duty stationary shaper, you can use it with router bits by replacing the standard spindle with the special router spindle shown in Fig. 12-16.

COMMERCIAL ROUTER/SHAPER TABLES

The Porter Cable product in Fig. 12-17 is a husky unit with a 16- × -18-inch nonconductive,

"Benelex" table. It has most of the features of a regular shaper including individually adjustable fences that can also be moved longitudinally to minimize the opening around the cutter. Various table inserts provide openings of 1 1/4, 2, and 3 inches. A feature I like is the built-in, 20-amp, lockable key-type, double-pole switch. The router is easily turned on or off without having to reach under the table. The table is available complete with a 22,000-rpm, heavy-duty, 1 1/2-horsepower router that will accept 1/4-inch and 1/2-inch shank router bits—or comes alone. The table is drilled to accept most Porter Cable routers, but new holes can be drilled by the customer when other brand routers are on hand.

The Sears table in Fig. 12-18 has a 13 1/4-inch- × -18-inch die-cast aluminum top and adjustable fences with wood facings and alumi-

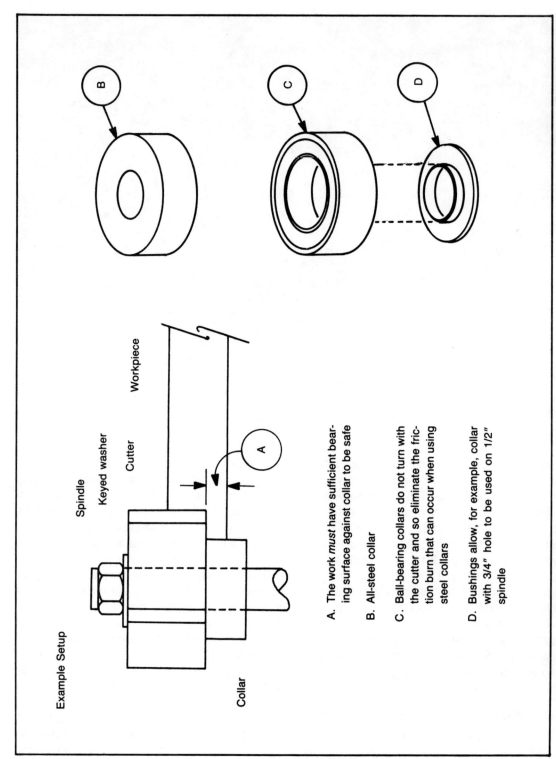

Example Setup

Spindle
Keyed washer
Cutter
Workpiece
Collar

A. The work *must* have sufficient bearing surface against collar to be safe

B. All-steel collar

C. Ball-bearing collars do not turn with the cutter and so eliminate the friction burn that can occur when using steel collars

D. Bushings allow, for example, collar with 3/4" hole to be used on 1/2" spindle

Fig. 12-6. Freehand shaping is required for circular or curved pieces because they can't be guided by a fence. Collars are used on the spindle of a shaper for work support and to control the depth of the cut.

Fig. 12-7. When freehand shaping is done on a router/shaper stand, work support and cut depth are provided by the pilot on the cutter.

Fig. 12-8. Shaping components required for paneled doors have always been a shaper operation. Now, because of special bits, the portable router can do the same work when it is mounted in a stand.

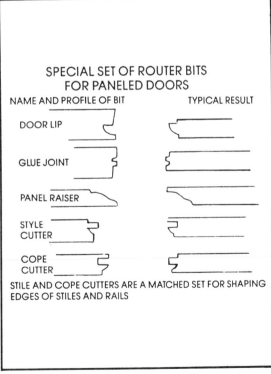

Fig. 12-9. This set of bits (from Freud) includes glue joint and door lip cutters.

265

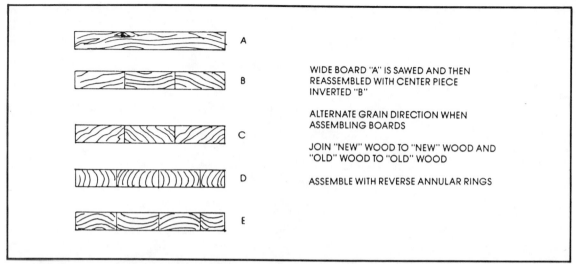

A

B WIDE BOARD "A" IS SAWED AND THEN
REASSEMBLED WITH CENTER PIECE
INVERTED "B"

ALTERNATE GRAIN DIRECTION WHEN
ASSEMBLING BOARDS

C

JOIN "NEW" WOOD TO "NEW" WOOD AND
"OLD" WOOD TO "OLD" WOOD

D ASSEMBLE WITH REVERSE ANNULAR RINGS

E

Fig. 12-10. Common methods used to guard against warpage and joint separation when door panels are made of solid wood.

Fig. 12-11. Hinged doors often have edges that are shaped this way. The cut is made in one pass by using a door lip cutter. This type of door is usually used with very simple frames.

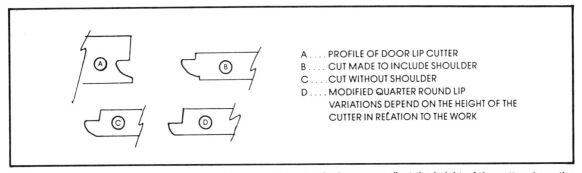

A ... . PROFILE OF DOOR LIP CUTTER
B ... . CUT MADE TO INCLUDE SHOULDER
C ... .CUT WITHOUT SHOULDER
D ... . MODIFIED QUARTER ROUND LIP
   VARIATIONS DEPEND ON THE HEIGHT OF THE
   CUTTER IN RELATION TO THE WORK

Fig. 12-12. You can vary the shape produced by a door lip cutter by how you adjust the height of the cutter above the table in relation to the work.

num bases. Accessory extensions are available should you wish to provide additional work surface. The table can be used with most Craftsman routers and others that have a 6-inch base. A miter gauge, which can accept an extra-cost hold-down clamp, is part of the package. The same table is available with a cover at the rear that can be connected to a 1 1/4-inch diameter vacuum hose.

ROUTER/SHAPER STANDS YOU CAN MAKE

There are advantages to making your own router/shaper stand. It can be designed as a floor model to use like any individual tool and can include a cabinet area or drawers for storage of accessory equipment. Table size is optional. A groove for an on-hand miter gauge can be an important factor in the concept. Also, you can make attachment arrangements that are exactly right for a router you already own.

I've made several for my own shop, each new one coming closer to an optimum design. Construction details for an early version that served for quite a long time are shown in Fig. 12-19. It did not have a slot for a miter gauge, though. I became convinced that even a homemade version should have guards to protect the operator and an electrical arrangement to turn

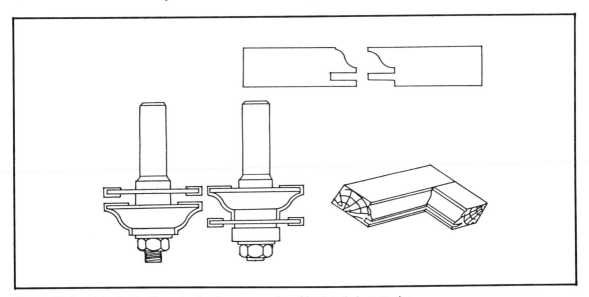

Fig. 12-13. Special sets of stile and rail cutters are produced by Grissly Imports, Inc.

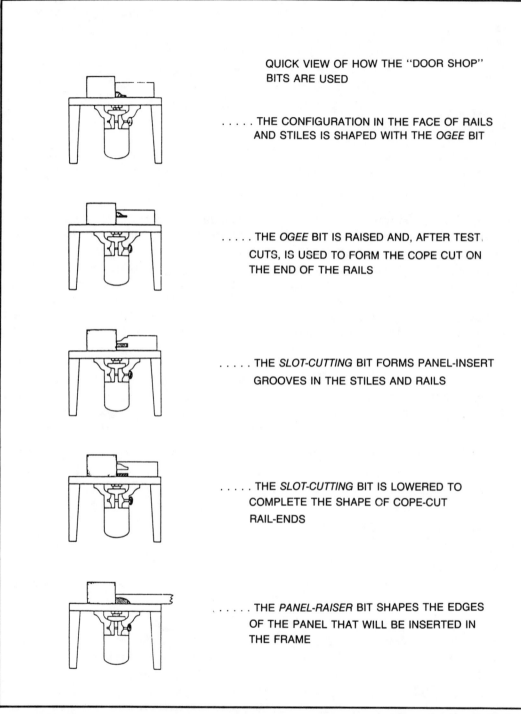

QUICK VIEW OF HOW THE "DOOR SHOP" BITS ARE USED

. . . . . THE CONFIGURATION IN THE FACE OF RAILS AND STILES IS SHAPED WITH THE *OGEE* BIT

. . . . . THE *OGEE* BIT IS RAISED AND, AFTER TEST CUTS, IS USED TO FORM THE COPE CUT ON THE END OF THE RAILS

. . . . . THE *SLOT-CUTTING* BIT FORMS PANEL-INSERT GROOVES IN THE STILES AND RAILS

. . . . . THE *SLOT-CUTTING* BIT IS LOWERED TO COMPLETE THE SHAPE OF COPE-CUT RAIL-ENDS

. . . . . . THE *PANEL-RAISER* BIT SHAPES THE EDGES OF THE PANEL THAT WILL BE INSERTED IN THE FRAME

Fig. 12-14. Some of the cutters in the Door Shop set from Zac Products, Inc., do double duty. You'll get perfect results if you follow the instructions that are supplied with the cutters.

Fig. 12-15. The cutters in the Sears Crown Molding Kit must also be used in a router/shaper setup. The cutters can be used to produce standard or original molding designs.

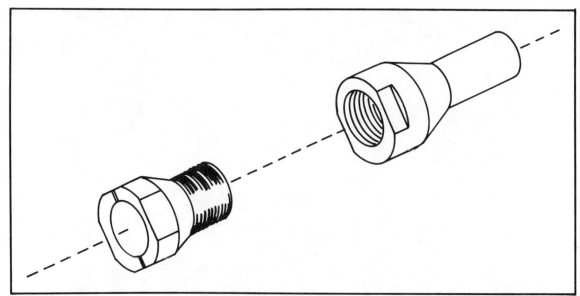

Fig. 12-16. Anyone who owns a Rockwell (Delta) shaper should check out this adapter. It allows the shaper to work with conventional router bits that have 1/4-inch or 1/2-inch shanks.

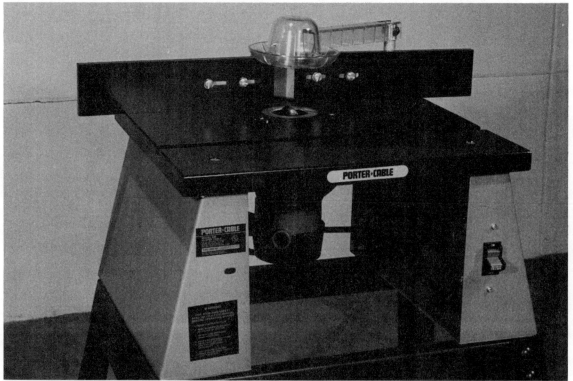

Fig. 12-17. Porter Cable router/shaper table can be purchased with or without a heavy duty 1 1/2-horsepower router. Built-in electricals make it easy to turn the router on or off.

Fig. 12-18. Sears router/shaper tables comes with a miter gauge that will accept an extra-cost hold-down. The same unit is available with a back dustcover that can be connected to a vacuum cleaner.

the tool on and off conveniently, without using the switch on the tool.

The router/shaper stand that is now standard in my shop has a good-size table and includes all the features of a good shaping machine. Large wood fences are individually adjustable and can also be moved to minimize the opening around the cutter. An adjustable guard is part of the fence assembly that is used for straight line cuts, and there is a slot in the table sized to suit a miter gauge that was already in the shop (Fig. 12-20). The design provides fulcrum pins and a second guard that is used when doing freehand shaping (Fig. 12-21). The on-off switch (Fig. 12-22) is located where it's easy to get at. Having a convenient on-off switch is also

better for the router. It's not good for the tool to keep running unnecessarily, which is likely to happen when it's a nuisance to get to a built-in switch.

Construction details for the router/shaper cabinet and its components, which include guards to make, and a list of materials are provided in Figs. 12-23 through 12-27. Unlike some commercial tables, this unit is designed to accommodate any router. The only part of the project that needs to be customized is the recess on the underside of the table, which has to be shaped to fit the router's base. Use the subbase as a pattern for the attachment holes. Screws that secure the router are driven from the top. Counterbore or countersink the holes so the

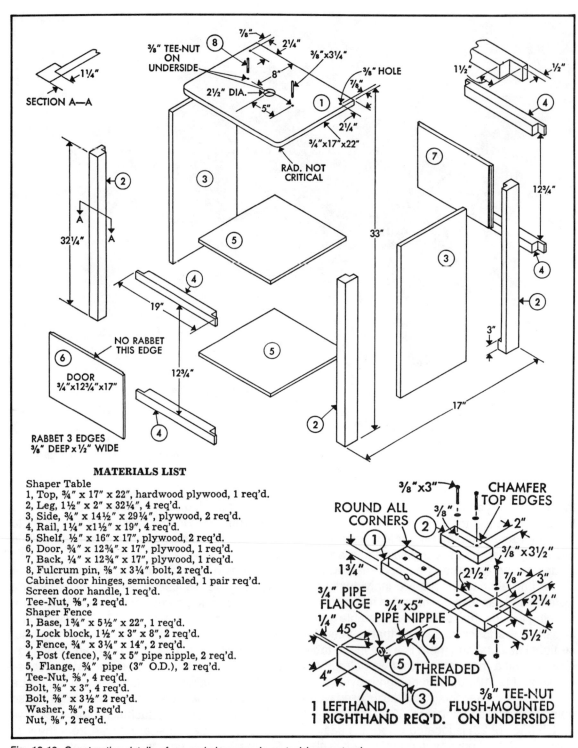

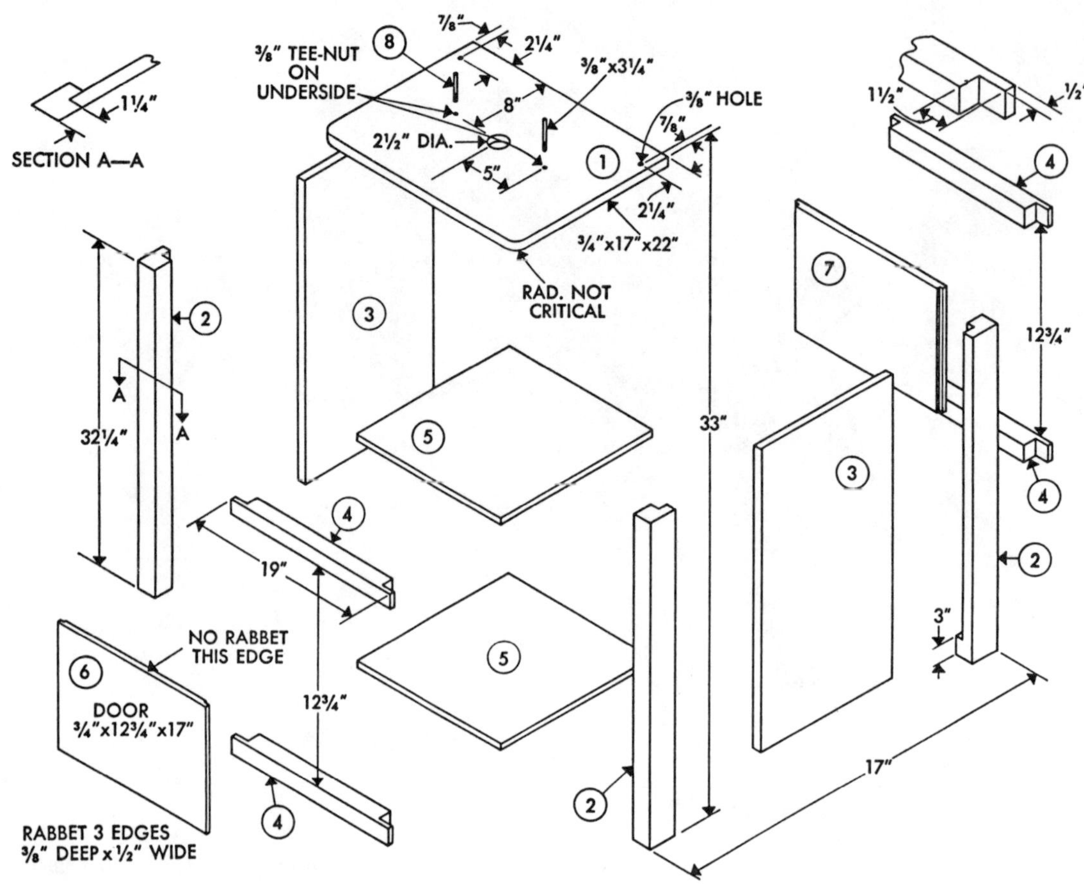
SECTION A—A
1¼"
3/8" TEE-NUT ON UNDERSIDE
7/8"
2¼"
3/8"x3¼"
8"
3/8" HOLE
2½" DIA.
5"
7/8"
2¼"
3/4"x17"x22"
RAD. NOT CRITICAL
1½"
½"
12¾"
33"
32¼"
A
A
19"
12¾"
NO RABBET THIS EDGE
DOOR
3/4"x12¾"x17"
RABBET 3 EDGES
3/8" DEEP x ½" WIDE
3"
17"
1
2
3
4
5
6
7
8

MATERIALS LIST

Shaper Table
1, Top, ¾" x 17" x 22", hardwood plywood, 1 req'd.
2, Leg, 1½" x 2" x 32¼", 4 req'd.
3, Side, ¾" x 14½" x 29¼", plywood, 2 req'd.
4, Rail, 1¼" x1½" x 19", 4 req'd.
5, Shelf, ½" x 16" x 17", plywood, 2 req'd.
6, Door, ¾" x 12¾" x 17", plywood, 1 req'd.
7, Back, ¼" x 12¾" x 17", plywood, 1 req'd.
8, Fulcrum pin, ⅜" x 3¼" bolt, 2 req'd.
Cabinet door hinges, semiconcealed, 1 pair req'd.
Screen door handle, 1 req'd.
Tee-Nut, ⅜", 2 req'd.
Shaper Fence
1, Base, 1¾" x 5½" x 22", 1 req'd.
2, Lock block, 1½" x 3" x 8", 2 req'd.
3, Fence, ¾" x 3¼" x 14", 2 req'd.
4, Post (fence), ¾" x 5" pipe nipple, 2 req'd.
5, Flange, ¾" pipe (3" O.D.), 2 req'd.
Tee-Nut, ⅜", 4 req'd.
Bolt, ⅜" x 3", 4 req'd.
Bolt, ⅜" x 3½" 2 req'd.
Washer, ⅜", 8 req'd.
Nut, ⅜", 2 req'd.

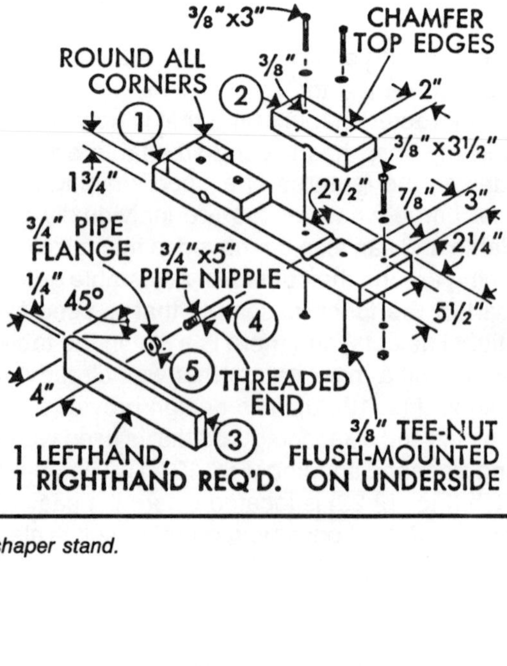
3/8"x3"
CHAMFER TOP EDGES
ROUND ALL CORNERS
3/8"
3/8"
2"
3/8"x3½"
1¾"
2½"
7/8"
3"
2¼"
3/4" PIPE FLANGE
3/4"x5" PIPE NIPPLE
1/4"
45°
5½"
4"
THREADED END
3/8" TEE-NUT FLUSH-MOUNTED ON UNDERSIDE
1 LEFTHAND, 1 RIGHTHAND REQ'D.
1
2
3
4
5

Fig. 12-19. Construction details of my early homemade router/shaper stand.

Fig. 12-20. My current router/shaper stand, which you can duplicate, evolved from earlier models. It comes as close to a regular shaper as anything can be. The miter gauge and the attached hold-down are Shopsmith items.

Fig. 12-21. The unit provides for infeed and outfeed fulcrum pins and a guard for freehand shaping.

Fig. 12-22. The router can be turned on or off without having to use the router's switch by using the external switch that is located in an easy-to-reach position on the side of the stand.

screwheads won't project above the table's surface. I chose to install two drawers, but if you wish, you can use the bottom area as a cabinet by installing a hinged door.

THE ROUTER/SHAPER AT WORK

A difference between a regular shaper and a router/shaper setup is that a shaper might have a reversible direction of rotation while a router turns only in one direction. This means that a shaper operator can choose to move work from left to right or right to left. On a router/shaper, work feed direction is from right to left. Cutting is *always* done by moving the work *against* the

cutter's direction or rotation (Fig. 12-28).

Figure 12-29 supplies important information concerning how fences should be positioned in relation to the cut being made. The bearing surface of both fences are on the same plane when only part of the work edge is removed. When the entire edge of the stock is removed, as in a jointing cut, the outfeed fence is brought forward a distance that is equal to the depth of the cut. If this isn't done, the work will have no support after it has passed the cutter. In addition to being set for the cut, the fences should be adjusted longitudinally to minimize the open area around the cutter.

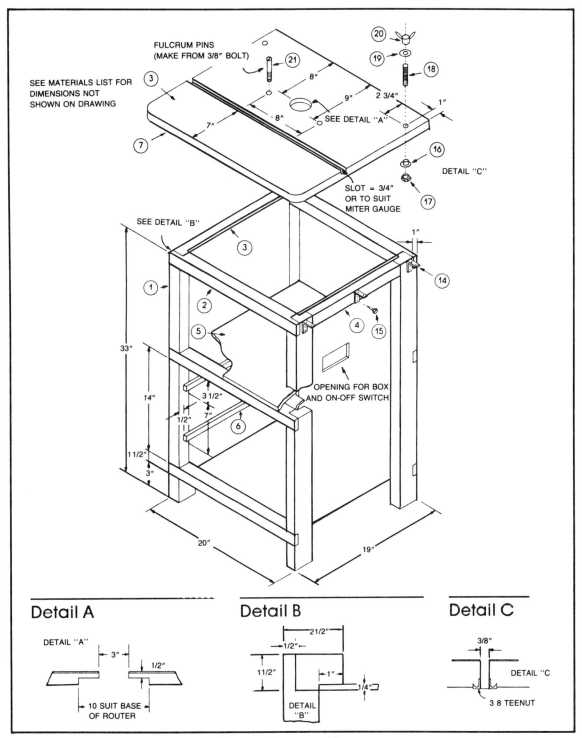

FULCRUM PINS
(MAKE FROM 3/8" BOLT)

SEE MATERIALS LIST FOR
DIMENSIONS NOT
SHOWN ON DRAWING

8"

9"

2 3/4"

1"

7"

8"

SEE DETAIL "A"

DETAIL "C"

SLOT = 3/4"
OR TO SUIT
MITER GAUGE

SEE DETAIL "B"

1"

33"

14"

3 1/2"

1/2"

7"

OPENING FOR BOX
AND ON-OFF SWITCH

11 1/2"

3"

20"

19"

Detail A

DETAIL "A"

3"

1/2"

10 SUIT BASE
OF ROUTER

Detail B

2 1/2"

1/2"

11 1/2"

1"

1/4"

DETAIL
"B"

Detail C

3/8"

DETAIL "C"

3 8 TEENUT

Fig. 12-23. Construction details of the router/shaper cabinet assembly.

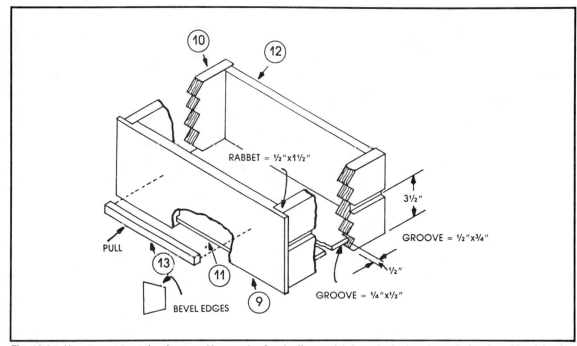

Fig. 12-24. How to construct the drawers. You can be fancier if you wish by substituting dovetails for the rabbet joint that connects the drawer front to side pieces.

It's always a good idea, when cutting across end grain, to use a miter gauge to advance the work (Fig. 12-30). There are no options when the work is narrow. Accuracy and safety demand that you move such pieces with a mechanical device. Some operators use a block of wood to advance the work, but that's a secondary choice.

It's often possible to make an end-grain cut on stock that is wide enough to accommodate the number of parts that are required. For example, if you need four rails that are 2 inches wide, make the rail-shaping cut on stock that is wider than 8 inches and then saw it into individual pieces. The only thing to remember is to leave an allowance for the saw kerfs.

Figure 12-31 demonstrates another application for the technique. It would be very difficult, let alone safe, to end-shape small parts like the one shown in the photograph, but if a large block was shaped first, it could be sawed into any number of identical pieces.

There is always some feathering or splintering at the end of cross-grained cuts. There-

fore, when shaping two adjacent edges or all four edges of a workpiece, make the cross-grained cuts first. The final cuts that are parallel to the grain will remove the imperfections.

FREEHAND SHAPING

"Freehand" should not be taken literally. It simply applies to working on circular or curved edges that can't be guided by a fence. The width of the cut and support for the workpiece during the pass are provided by the pilot, preferably ball-bearing, that is on the cutter (Fig. 12-32). You can see that a pilotless bit can't be used for this type of cutting. Always be sure that the arrangement provides sufficient bearing surface for the edge of the work (Fig. 12-33) and that you use the fulcrum pins.

The cut is started by bracing the work firmly against the first fulcrum pin (infeed side) and then very slowly advancing it until it contacts the cutter and receives support from the pilot (Fig. 12-34). Once the work has good support from the pilot, it may be swung free of the fulcrum pin.

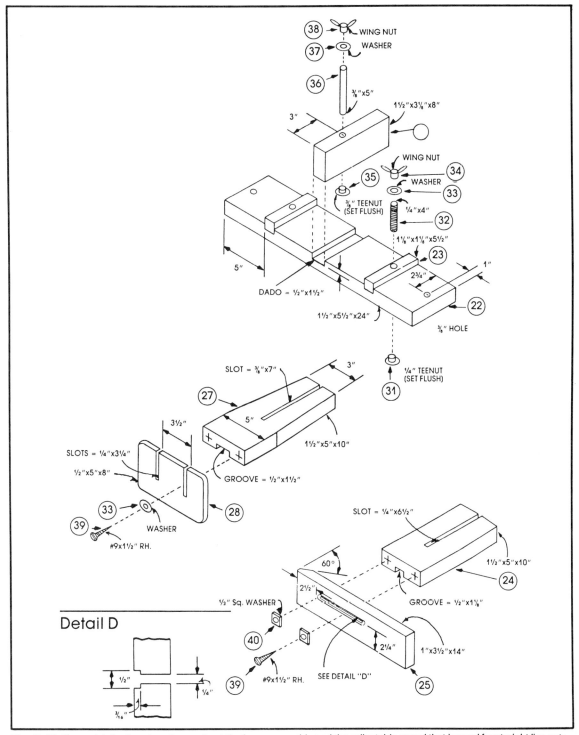

Fig. 12-25. These details show how to construct the fence assembly and the adjustable guard that is used for straight line cuts.

277

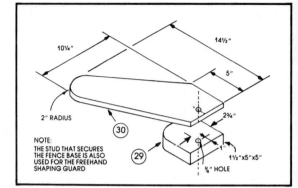

Fig. 12-26. This is how the guard used for freehand shaping is made.

2" RADIUS

NOTE:
THE STUD THAT SECURES
THE FENCE BASE IS ALSO
USED FOR THE FREEHAND
SHAPING GUARD

10¼"   14½"   5"   2¾"   1"   1½"x5"x5"   ¾" HOLE

KEY	PART	#PCS.	SIZE	MATERIAL
1	leg	4	1-1/2" x 2-1/2" x 33"	fir
2	rail	6	1-1/2" x 1-1/2" x 20"	"
3	side	2	1/4" x 16" x 20"	hardboard
4	brace	2	1-1/4" x 1-1/2" x 14	fir
5	shelf	1	1/4" x 17" x 19"	hardboard
6	guides	4	1/2" x 3/4" x 18-1/2"	fir
7	table	1	1-1/8" x 21" x 24"	(see note)
8	cover	1	025 x 21" x 24"	"
DRAWER				
9	front	2	3/4" x 7" x 18"	pine
10	side	4	3/4" x 7 x 17-1/2"	"
11	bottom	2	1/4" x 16" x 17-1/2"	hardboard
12	back	2	3/4" x 6" x 15-1/4"	pine
13	pull	2	1/2" x 3/4" x 10"	"
HARDWARE				
14	connector	6	1/2" x 1-1/2" x 1-1/2"	metal angles
15	screws	24	#8 x 1"	roundhead
16		4	3/8"	Teenut
17		2	3/8"	nut
18	stud	2	3/8" x 4"	threaded rod
19		2	3/8"	fender washer
20		2	3/8"	wing nut
21	fulcrum pin	2	3/8" x 2-3/4"	make from bolt
FENCE ASSEMBLY				
22	base	1	1-1/2" x 5-1/2" x 24"	fir
23	guide	2	1-1/8" x 1-1/8" x 5-1/2"	"
24	fence support	2	1-1/2" x 5" x 10"	"
25	fence	2 (1L/1R)	1" x 3-1/2" x 14"	"
26	guard guide	1	1-1/2" x 3-1/8" x 8"	"
27	guard support	1	1-1/2" x 5" x 10"	"
28	shield	1	1/2" x 5" x 8"	"Lexan"
FREEHAND SHAPING GUARD				
29	height block	1	1-1/2" x 5" x 5"	fir
30	shield	1	1/2" x 10-1/4" x 14-1/2"	"Lexan"
HARDWARE				
31		2	1/4"	Teenut
32	stud	2	1/4" x 4"	threaded rod
33		4	1/4"	fender washer
34		2	1/4"	wing nut
35		1	3/8"	Teenut
36	stud	1	3/8" x 5"	threaded rod
37		1	3/8"	fender washer
38		1	3/8"	wing nut
39		6	#9 x 1-1/2"	roundhead screw
40		4	1/2" x 1/2"	Sq. washer

NOTES
. . . . . table (#7) made from readymade glued-up pine slab
. . . . . cover (#8) = Wilsonart's aluminum "decorative metal" or do-it-yourself aluminum
. . . . . hardwood like maple or birch can be submitted for fir

Fig. 12-27. Materials list for the router/shaper stand. Any dimensions that are not shown on the drawing for the cabinet can be found here.

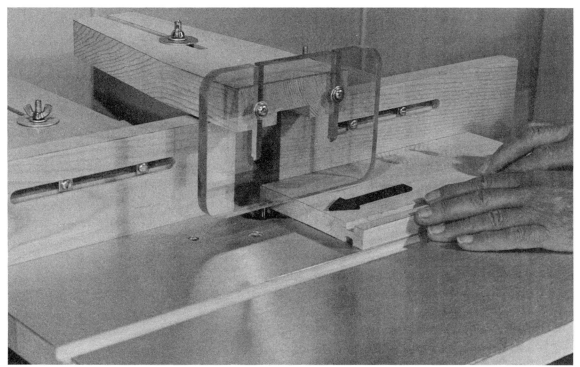

Fig. 12-28. The router has a single direction of rotation which, when viewed when the tool is inverted, is counterclockwise. Because work must be moved against the cutter's rotation, all passes (as indicated by the arrow) must be made from right to left. Position the guard so it barely clears the surface of the workpiece.

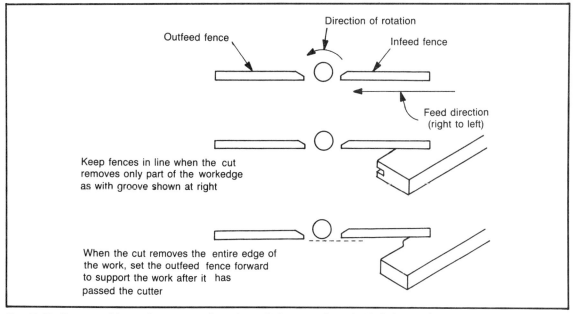

Fig. 12-29. The router/shaper fences are adjusted to suit the type of cut that is being made.

Fig. 12-30. A miter gauge makes it easier and safer to make crossgrain cuts. A hold-down can be a big help. The guard, even though it is not shown here, should be used.

Fig. 12-31. Large pieces can be shaped and then sawed into many identical parts.

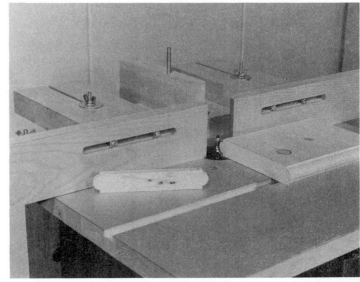

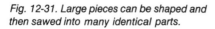

Fig. 12-32. The pilot on the router bit provides bearing surface for the work and also controls the depth of the cut.

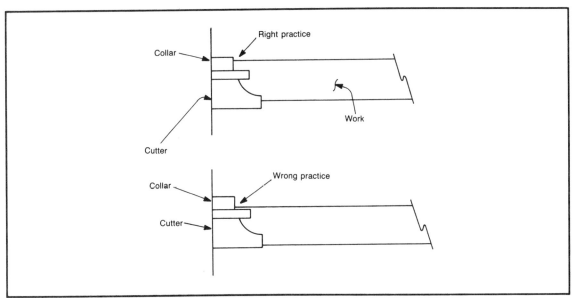

Fig. 12-33. Always be sure that the pilot provides enough bearing surface for the workpiece. Bits that do not have pilots cannot be used for this type of cutting.

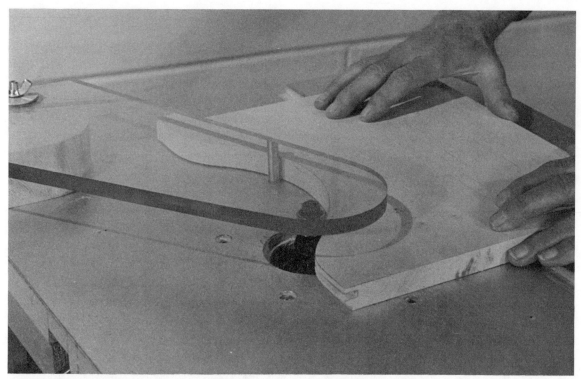

Fig. 12-34. The work, after being braced against the infeed fulcrum pin, is advanced very slowly to make contact with the bearing on the cutter. Be sure to keep the work flat on the table throughout the pass. Never allow your hands to come close to the cutting area.

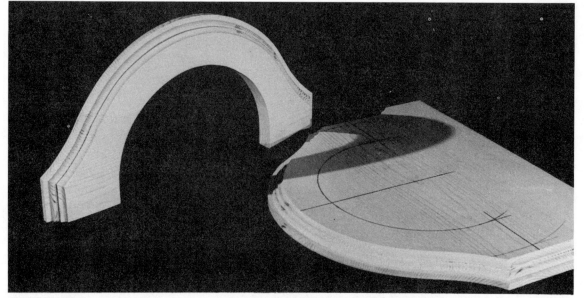

Fig. 12-35. When you need narrow parts, form the shape on a large piece of stock and then saw off the area you need.

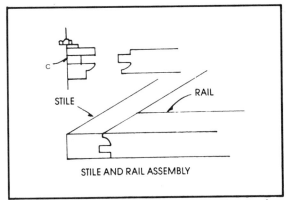

Fig. 12-36. Cope and stile cutters and other bits are often offered as matched sets. You must be very careful when setting up for each of the cuts. It's often possible to use the first cut that is made as a gauge to establish the correct position for the second cutter.

It's a moot point whether this is good practice or not. There is nothing wrong with continuing to use the pin for work support so long as the shape of the work permits it. Many operators work with both fulcrum pins installed, relying on the outfeed pin to provide support at the end of the cut. The shape of the work will have some

bearing on how long the infeed pin can provide support and whether both pins can be utilized.

Never try to shape pieces that are too small or too narrow for safety. When a narrow part is needed, form the shape on a board that can be hand-held safely and then saw off the part that is needed (Fig. 12-35).

IN GENERAL

Efficient cutting procedures call for moving the stock just fast enough for cutters to work freely. Forcing cuts will not speed production. Any feed speed or cut depth that slows the router excessively, overheats the cutter, or burns the wood is obviously poor practice. All work edges must be smooth and square to adjacent surfaces to begin with. Always work with sharp cutters and maintain pilots and bearings in pristine condition. If you don't care for your tools, they won't care for you.

While the router supplies the power and the cutters produce necessary shapes, it's the operator's responsibility to understand procedures and to establish correct cutter-to-work relation-

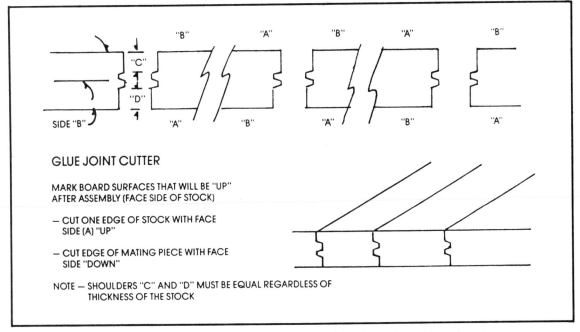

GLUE JOINT CUTTER

MARK BOARD SURFACES THAT WILL BE "UP"
AFTER ASSEMBLY (FACE SIDE OF STOCK)

— CUT ONE EDGE OF STOCK WITH FACE
   SIDE (A) "UP"

— CUT EDGE OF MATING PIECE WITH FACE
   SIDE "DOWN"

NOTE — SHOULDERS "C" AND "D" MUST BE EQUAL REGARDLESS OF
   THICKNESS OF THE STOCK

Fig. 12-37. This is the procedure to use in order to get accurate mating edges when using a glue joint cutter.

Fig. 12-38. *Having a library of sample cuts is a big help because the pieces can be used as gauges when it is necessary to duplicate a setup. The sample piece will determine the position of the fence and the height of the cutter.*

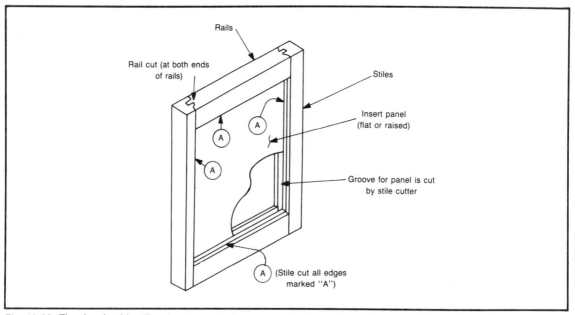

Fig. 12-39. *The drawing identifies the parts of a panel assembly and tells where various cuts should occur.*

ships. This is especially important when using matched cutters like those often supplied for stile and rail assemblies (Fig. 12-36) and for other cutters like the glue joint (Fig. 12-37).

Building a library of sample cuts, like those shown in Fig. 12-38, can considerably reduce setup time on future projects. Once you have shaped a piece correctly, cut off a small section of it and save it to use as a gauge when a similar piece is required.

A lot of the cutters that must be used in a router/shaper arrangement are designed for frame and panel constructions (Fig. 12-39). While they might be used for similar results, operational procedures will differ. Some sets have matched cutters, others include individual cutters that, in a sense, are multipurpose. They can produce various elements of a shape depending on width of cut, depth of cut, and so on. It is very important then to carefully follow the instructions that are supplied with the cutters. Most manufacturers are very generous with educational materials, but the effort is lost if you don't go to school.

Chapter 13

The Portable Router and the Radial Arm Saw

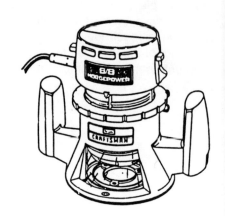

THE TITLE OF THIS CHAPTER SOUNDS LIKE THAT of a fairy tale, but there is no fiction here. When you combine the true capability of the portable router with the flexibility of the radial arm saw, you have a concept that rivals, and in some cases surpasses, what can be done with overhead and pin-routing machines. This is fact because the router is mounted in place of a saw blade to hold it still or put it through all the motions that the sawing machine is noted for. The router can be stationary while workpieces are moved, or the reverse can happen. With workpieces clamped or held by some other means, the router can be raised or lowered, swung in a vertical or horizontal arc, moved in a circular path, even positioned horizontally so the router bit is parallel to the tool's table. Standard router bits, with or without pilots depending on the operation, can be used.

Too often, though, the router/radial saw arrangement is lauded because of the intriguing surface decorating cuts it can make (Fig. 13-1). It does jobs like this in fine style, and the applica-

tion should not be ignored, but it's in more practical areas of woodworking that the setup really shines. Grooves and dadoes, stopped or blind, edge embellishments, dovetail cuts—all these and more are possible (Fig. 13-2).

MOUNTING THE ROUTER

This relatively new method of working is possible because of a unique accessory that is secured to the saw arbor end of the tool's motor. Black & Decker offers one that can be mounted on 9-, 10-, and 12-inch DeWalt radial arm saws. It can be used with most routers because the encircling clamp that grips the router securely is adjustable (Fig. 13-3). The attachment is locked between the motor's cover plate and arbor end bell in a way that provides enough adjustment room to situate the router perpendicular to the top of the saw's table (Fig. 13-4).

The Sears version provides a platform for the router (Fig. 13-5). The unit attaches only to current Craftsman 10-inch radial saws and to some specific former models. Be sure to check

Fig. 13-1. A lot of decorative surface cutting can easily be done when the router is used with a radial arm saw. Cuts have varying depth when the work is held on a slant board. V-groove, core box, and veining bits are typical router bits that are used for this type of cutting.

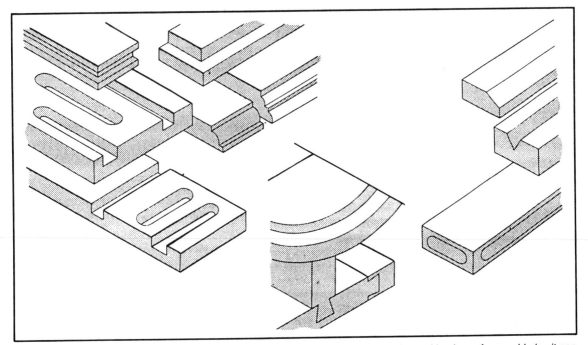

Fig. 13-2. On the more practical side are the cuts shown here. Because the router is used in place of a saw blade, it can move through the crosscutting and mitering modes of the radial tool, be locked in a fixed position, and set so the cutter is parallel to the table.

Fig. 13-3. Black & Decker's attachment for DeWalt machines locks on the saw end of the tool's motor. It is easy to adjust the router perpendicular to the table.

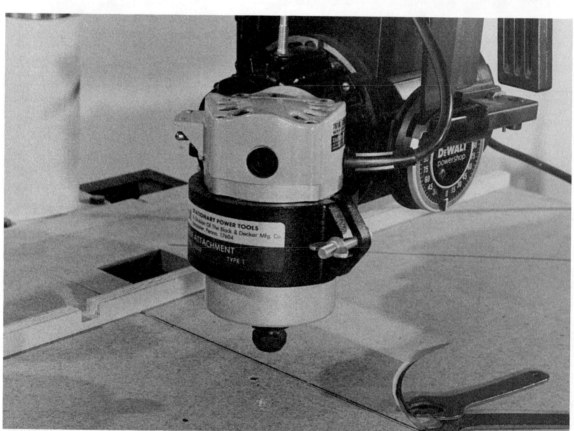

Fig. 13-4. Only the motor of the router is used. There is enough leeway in the clamping arrangement so that almost any router can be used.

Fig. 13-5. The Sears version is also secured on the saw end of the motor, but it provides a platform for the router with its base to rest on. Routers with a 6-inch diameter base can be used.

first for compatibility with the tool you own. All Sears routers and most other brand tools that have a 6-inch diameter base can be secured on the platform.

There is a solution if a commercial unit can't accommodate your needs. Make your own along the lines of the idea that is detailed in Fig. 13-6. The idea is basically simple, but you can judge that it must be dimensioned and shaped exactly for the tool you will use it on. If you are not equipped for metalworking, you can make a prototype using easily bent and drilled sheet metal and have the final product made for you by a metalworking shop. It's also possible to make a sample by using stiff cardboard. The slot for the saw guard stud must be wider than necessary to rotate the unit to position the router perpendicular to the table. Use long carriage bolts to secure the router between the clamp blocks.

The saw becomes just a carrier; don't have it plugged in when using the router. Also, situate the router's cord, possibly by threading it through the yoke of the machine, where it will be safe and won't interfere with the work. Be sure the router switch is in the "off" position before plugging it in.

CUTTING

The direction in which you move the work must always be *against* the cutter's direction of rotation. Because the router's attitude is the same as it would be if you were handholding it and looking down on it, the bit's rotation is clockwise. Feeding too fast, regardless of whether you are moving the router or the work, results in inferior cuts and can harm the tool and the cutter. On the other hand, being too cautious allows the bit to do more burnishing than cutting. Because wood densities vary, an efficient feed speed is a judgement that must be made by the operator. The usual precautions apply. If the cutter chatters or the router slows excessively, it's possible that you are cutting too deeply or too fast, or that you are using a dull bit. By this time you probably have done enough work with a router to know how it should feel, sound, and move

when being used efficiently. If not, some practice cutting will soon get you to the right plateau.

STRAIGHT CUTTING

Cuts that are made across the grain to produce forms like rabbets and dadoes are done with the saw set up in normal crosscut position (Fig. 13-7). The depth of the cut is controlled by the cutter's height above the table; the width of the cut by the diameter of the bit. The width of the cut is not limited by the size of the bit. You can get to any cut width with any bit simply by making repeat passes. How deep you can cut in a single pass depends on the density of the material and the horsepower of the router. A few light cuts, say between 1/8 and 1/4 inch, will quickly guide you along the right path.

For stopped or blind cuts (Fig. 13-8), start with the bit elevated above the work and then slowly lower it by using the tool's regular arm-height control, until it enters the work. Then move the router as you would normally. You can work to lines marked on the work, or you can control the length of the cuts by using small clamps on the tool's arm to limit how far the motor can be moved. You'll get accurate results when repeat passes are needed to deepen a cut if you start with the work clamped in position.

To do grooving or rabbeting on long edges, the router's position is secured with the tool's rip lock. The work, guided by the fence, is moved to make the cut. The setup is the same as that required when using the saw for ripping operations.

Some types of standard molding designs can be duplicated by making through or stopped cuts across stock that has been ripped to suitable width (Fig. 13-9). Many types of pilotless bits can be used on work like this, so results are not limited to grooves formed with a straight bit. Parts that are formed by using this particular technique can be used as is, but they can also serve as base stock that can be sawed to produce slim moldings (Fig. 13-10).

Straight edges can be shaped by using a fence as a guide for the work. As shown in the

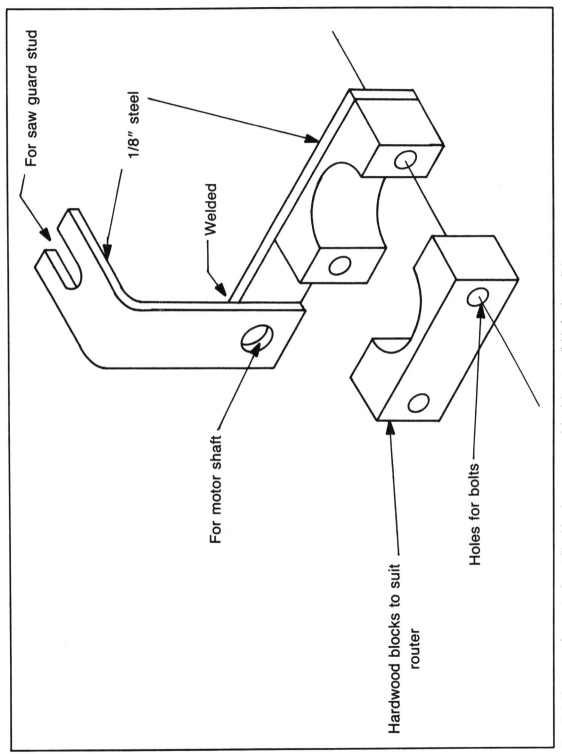

For saw guard stud

1/8" steel

Welded

For motor shaft

Hardwood blocks to suit router

Holes for bolts

Fig. 13-6. You can make an attachment like this when a commercial unit is not available for the radial arm saw you own.

Fig. 13-7. The tool is used in crosscut position for cuts like dadoes and rabbets. When the same cut is required on many pieces, use a stop block on the fence to gauge the work's position.

Fig. 13-8. Because the router can be raised or lowered by using the tool's arm-elevating mechanism, stopped or blind cuts pose no problem. The work must be held firmly. Use clamps when necessary.

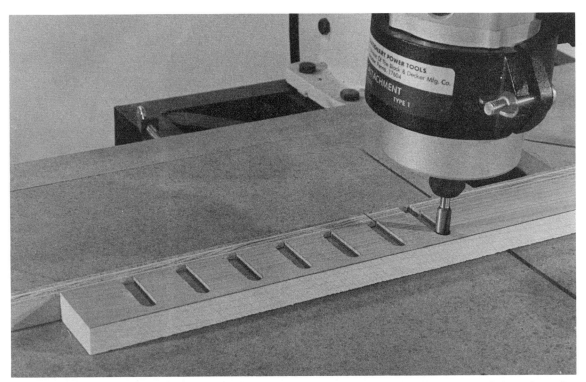

Fig. 13-9. Use the same setup to surface cut strips for molding. Results will be more dramatic if you use pilotless, decorative bits. A mark on the fence can be used to gauge spacing between cuts. Use a small clamp on the arm of the tool to limit motor travel when cuts must be stopped.

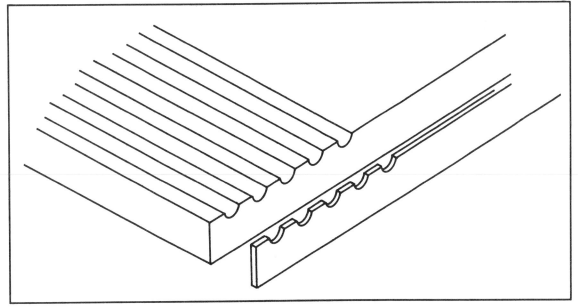

Fig. 13-10. Surface cut pieces can be sawed to produce slim moldings.

Fig. 13-11. To shape edges, lock the router in position and move the work along the fence. The work is moved from left to right. This is a good way to operate even if the bit has a pilot.

example in Fig. 13-11, the router's position is locked; the work, held snugly against the fence, is moved from left to right. You can provide for the cutter's height above the table by cutting a relief area in the fence or by working with a two-piece fence. A two-piece fence is a good idea because it can be adjusted to minimize the opening around the cut area regardless of the bit that is being used.

SHAPING CURVED AND CIRCULAR EDGES

When shaping curved and circular edges while handholding the router, clamp the work and move the router. The router on a radial arm saw is stationary; the work is moved to make the cut. The depth of the cut is controlled by the cutter's

height above the table. The work is guided by an integral or ball-bearing pilot that *must* be on the bit (Figs. 13-12 and 13-13).

Circular edges can be shaped perfectly by using the pivot guidance method that is demonstrated in Fig. 13-14. The work is impaled on a nail driven up through the bottom of a plywood support that is clamped to the regular table. After adjusting the height of the cutter, hold the work firmly and bring the cutter forward to make contact. Then, with the rip lock tightened to keep the router stationary, rotate the work—in this case in a counterclockwise direction—to make the cut.

You can use the same technique to form circular surface grooves and even to cut out discs

Fig. 13-12. Curved edges are shaped by keeping the router still and moving the work against a piloted bit. You have some control over the shape you can get from any bit because the router's height above the table is adjustable.

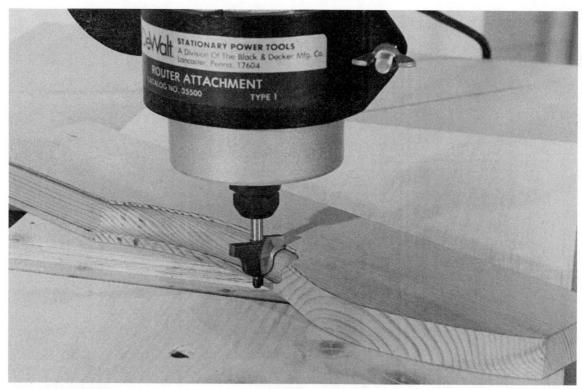

Fig. 13-13. In some cases it's necessary to elevate the workpiece. A piece of plywood with a dado cut across it will serve. The dado provides freedom for the bit's pilot.

Fig. 13-14. Circular edges can be shaped by using the pivot guide system. The work is turned clockwise, as indicated by the arrow. Always work so fingers will not be near the cutting area. It's very important to keep the work flat on the table throughout the pass.

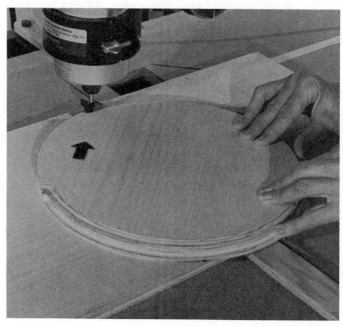

Fig. 13-15. Use the pivot technique to form circular grooves. Discs can be formed the same way, but elevate the work to keep the bit from cutting into the tool's table.

(Fig. 13-15). A groove is just a limited depth cut. For discs, use a small diameter straight bit and, if necessary, make repeat passes until the cutter is through the work. Elevate the work on some scrap material so the bit will not cut into the saw's table.

Internal routing is possible because the router is adjustable vertically by raising or lowering the tool's radial arm. This means you can raise the router and, after placing the workpiece, lower it to position the bit for the correct cut (Fig. 13-16).

work while the router is in a fixed position (Fig. 13-17). All the precautions that were suggested for this type of operation when the router is used in routine fashion apply here. Final results depend primarily on how carefully you work. Remember that the bit tends to be contrary, following grain lines and patterns rather than your directions. Grip the work very firmly and work more slowly than you normally would. It's a good idea to outline figures first by working with a small diameter bit and then remove remaining waste with a larger cutter.

FREEHAND ROUTING

Freehand routing is done by manipulating the

HORIZONTAL ROUTING

Horizontal routing is a term that can apply to the

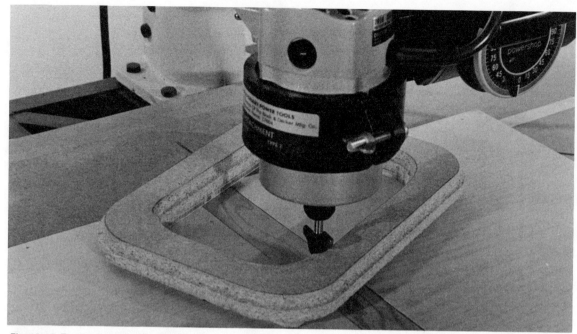

Fig. 13-16. To shape inside edges, place the work in position before lowering the router. Always move the work to cut against the bit's direction of rotation.

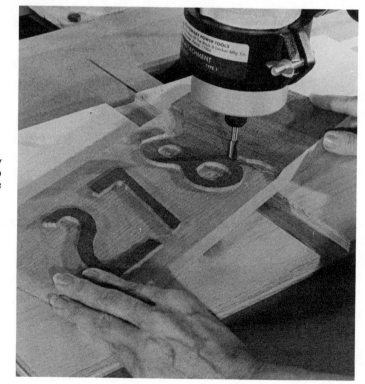

Fig. 13-17. A firm grip on the work is necessary when doing freehand routing. Practice on scrap material before starting a project. Make test cuts on hard and soft woods.

Fig. 13-18. When the router is set in horizontal position, the bit can't be positioned close to the tool's table. A special table that provides an elevated work surface is needed.

Fig. 13-19. Forming an end groove is a typical operation made possible when the router is secured in a horizontal position. The work must be held firmly or clamped. Use straight bits to form grooves, rabbets, tongues, and tenons. This is a good way to form dovetail slots and the pins that are needed with them. The pin requires two passes, one into each surface of the stock.

router/radial arm arrangement because the router can be placed in the position that is demonstrated in Fig. 13-18. Because of the way the router is mounted, there is a limit to how close to the table a cutting bit can be situated. Therefore, a special table that provides an elevated work surface and that has is own fence is needed. The fence is actually a back piece that extends below the "legs" of the table to grip it in the slot between the tool's table boards that is normally occupied by a regular fence.

Figure 13-19 is just a quick example of how horizontal routing can be utilized. The work is held or clamped to the table; the bit does the cutting when the router is pulled forward. Other cuts that can be made by using this setup include rabbets, tenons, dovetail slots, and end-grain shaping. When you consider that the router can also be tilted when in a horizontal position, you can envision many other possible applications.

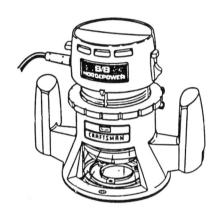

Chapter 14

Some Interesting Major Accessories

THE PORTABLE ROUTER'S VERSATILITY INCREASES when accessories utilize the tool as a high-speed driver of a host of cutting bits. Operators can devise any number of special guides, jigs, and holders to use the tool well beyond its basic concept. This also holds true for manufacturers who make routers or unique accessories that hold a router in a particular way, or supply controlled movement for the tool so it can be applied in various ways to the workpiece.

Because of the accessories, a router can be used to form various types of spirals or flutes and reeds on spindles, turn out letters and numbers on a production basis, form bowl-type projects, do bas-relief or intricate 3-D carving, and more. It isn't necessary for router owners to buy all the extras or, for that matter, even one of them. Much depends on to what length you wish to increase the scope of your router workshop. But the accessories are very interesting and you should know about them, which is why they are discussed here.

All the units come with very detailed instruc-tions for efficient use and, in some cases, for cor-rect assembly. It's crucial to study the pamphlets and to accept the information as bible. The sup-plier does want you to be happy with the product.

BOWL CRAFTER

The Sears Bowl Crafter lets you work with a router to do bowl-type projects usually done with a faceplate on a lathe. To a more limited extent, it's also possible to form some spindles (Fig. 14-1). Actually, the unit is a headstock with a built-in motor that turns the workpiece. The router is secured on a special carriage that is manipulated by the operator and serves as a mo-torized lathe chisel (Fig. 14-2).

The carriage-mounted router is guided by templates that are secured at the base of the headstock and is maneuverable for both inside and outside cuts (Figs. 14-3 and 14-4). Exclusive cutters that mount on the special, router-driven arbor must be used (Figs. 14-5 and 14-6). An as-sortment of patterns like those shown in Fig. 14-7 are supplied with the unit so the user can

Fig. 14-1. Typical projects made on the Bowl Crafter. Intriguing effects result when you make blanks by assembling contrasting woods. Note that some spindle work is also possible.

start work immediately. It's a good idea to start with one or two of the projects that are suggested. You can move on to original ideas after getting acquainted with the equipment.

Methods of preparing stock for turning are suggested in Fig. 14-8. You can use solid blocks of wood or prepare blanks by laminating separate pieces. The latter idea presents the opportunity for using contrasting woods for unique effects. To start with, use the stack method for large diameter workpieces and the sandwich method for projects or components that are long and have small diameters. It's always wise to minimize the amount of work the router must do by sawing off as much waste as possible before mounting the workpiece.

The Bowl Crafter can be used to turn projects up to 10 inches in diameter and up to 5 inches in thickness or length. The accessory is used with Sears routers and others that have a 6-inch diameter base. The router should be at least 3/4 horsepower.

THE ROUTER CRAFTER

The Router Crafter that is shown in Figs. 14-9 and 14-10 is another unit in the impressive array of router accessories that are offered by Sears Roebuck under the Craftsman brand name. As the photos indicate, the tool imitates a lathe. It has an adjustable tailstock that accom-

Fig. 14-2. The tool includes a headstock with a built-in motor that turns faceplate-mounted work at slow speed. The router on a special carriage is used like a motorized lathe chisel. Other typical projects are plates and cups.

Fig. 14-3. Cutting is controlled by a guide in the carriage that bears against a template situated at the base of the headstock. The one being used is for a large salad bowl.

Fig. 14-4. Outside contours are also established by using a template. Special router bits for inside and outside cutting must be used.

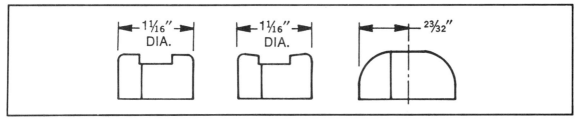

Fig. 14-5. The special router bits, from left to right, are for straight, outside, and inside-concave cuts. The bits are sold separately, individually, or in sets of three.

modates work of various lengths and a headstock that can be indexed. A major feature is that the headstock, and thus the work, can also be rotated by means of a hand crank. Because of the way the tool can manipulate a router or the workpiece—or the router and the work—simultaneously, you can do a variety of intriguing operations on spindles with mechanical precision. Very little assembly work is required before the accessory can be used. It can be secured directly to a bench, but I think a box-type structure like the one shown in Fig. 14-11 is a better way to go. By adding a simple drawer, the base could provide storage for other tools, router bits, and so on.

What makes the Router Crafter so flexible is the cable drum that is situated in the headstock. Turning the hand crank causes the carriage-mounted router to move parallel to the workpiece. Small cable-mounted clamps can be positioned to limit the length of cuts. Because of the indexing mechanism in the headstock, it's easy to divide the workpiece into 2, 3, 4, 6, 8, 12, or 24 equal spaces. Spiral cuts are made when the router is moved longitudinally while the work is rotating. It's also possible to do peripheral cutting by keeping the router still while the work is turned.

After becoming acquainted with the tool, you'll find it fairly easy to do the following operations on table legs, lamp bases, posts, and other projects or project components that are not greater than 3-inch square or more than 36 inches long:

☐ Form straight or tapered, equally spaced flutes or beads parallel to the workpiece.

☐ Do left- or right-hand "roping" or "spiraling." Diamond patterns occur when left- and right-hand cuts are combined.

☐ Do peripheral shaping by working with pilotless router bits.

☐ Form contoured spindles by organizing a setup that allows the router to follow a template that you attach to the front of the accessory.

These operations are done by following basic procedures, but you can go further by combining different types of cuts. For example, you can do peripheral cutting after a workpiece has been shaped lengthwise with flutes or reeds. Figures 14-12 through 14-15 show examples of work that can be done with the Router Crafter.

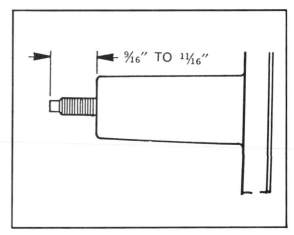

Fig. 14-6. The bits, together with guides that are provided, thread onto a special arbor that is secured to the carriage and turned by the router. Be sure that the dimension shown here is exact.

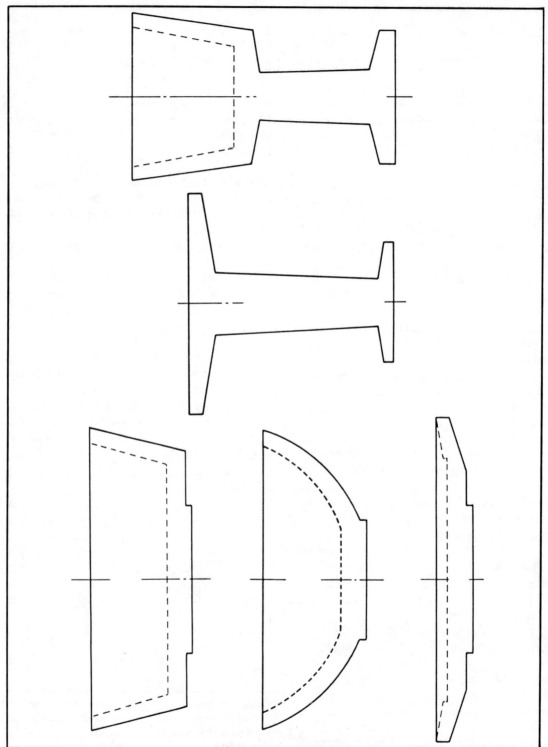

Fig. 14-7. An assortment of paper patterns that are used to make templates are provided with the tool. Get acquainted with the Bowl Crafter by using one or two of them before designing original projects.

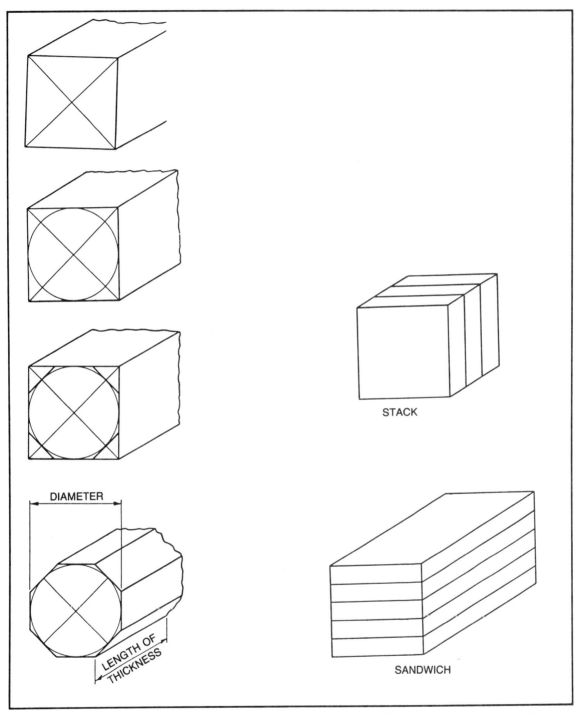

STACK

DIAMETER

LENGTH OF THICKNESS

SANDWICH

Fig. 14-8. Various ways to prepare stock for turning. Remember the tool's capacities. Maximum project size is 10 inches in diameter and 5 inches thick. Spindles should not be more than 5 inches long. Turning blanks can be solid stock or built up by using the sandwich method.

Fig. 14-9. The Router Crafter also uses a router as a motorized lathe chisel. For fluting or reeding, the work is held still while the router is moved longitudinally by means of the hand crank.

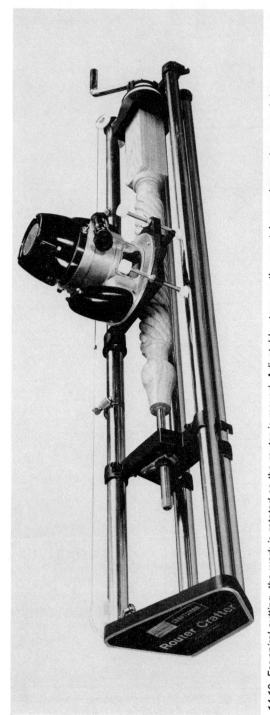

Fig. 14-10. For spiral cutting, the work is rotated as the router is moved. Adjustable stops on the rear tube can be used to control the router's travel.

Fig. 14-11. The Router Crafter can be mounted directly on a workbench, but a box-type support is more practical. It makes the unit portable and can also be used for storage.

THE MILL-ROUTE

The Mill-Route (Figs. 14-16 and 14-17) produced by Progressive Technology, Inc., works something like a pantograph but has control features that help you work with ultimate precision. The accessory can be used to produce a single project or to make a template that can then be followed by the stylus to form any number of duplicate parts. It's literally true that the router, which is counterbalanced when it is mounted, will mimic any movement of the stylus, whether it is following lines of a drawing or a template. The router has a vertical lifting action, and this ensures that all cuts will be perpendicular to the surface of the work. A nice feature is that the router automatically lifts from the work whenever the operator removes his hands from the control bar.

In addition to doing carving and forming letters and numbers, the Mill-Route can be used for grooving and for the kind of through cuts that are required when making an oval or circular frame. Moldings can be shaped by keeping the router still and moving the work past the cutter, and a similar arrangement allows edge shaping. It's recommended that the tool be mounted on a 44-inch square sheet of 3/4-inch particleboard. It's also possible to mount the unit on a special table, an extra cost accessory that is offered by the same manufacturer (Fig. 14-18). Either way,

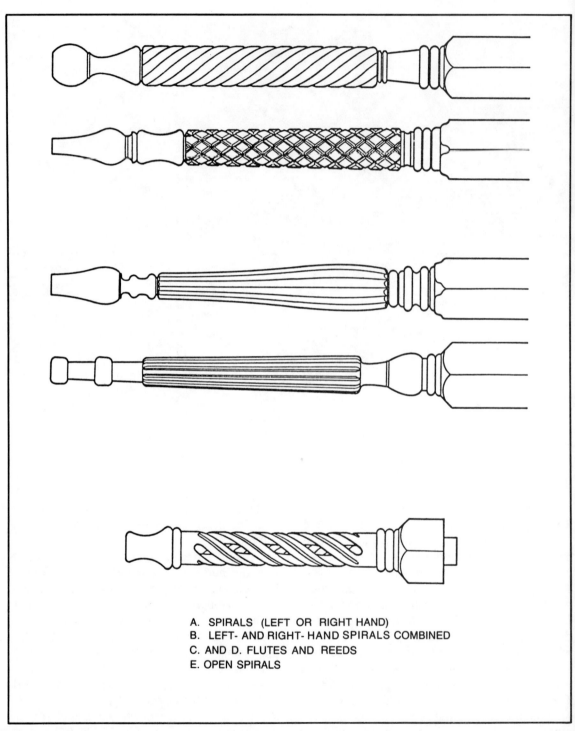

A. SPIRALS (LEFT OR RIGHT HAND)
B. LEFT- AND RIGHT- HAND SPIRALS COMBINED
C. AND D. FLUTES AND REEDS
E. OPEN SPIRALS

Fig. 14-12. Some of the work that can be done on the Sears Router Crafter. Diamonds appear when both left- and right-hand spirals are formed. Open spirals require a through, concentric hole in the workpiece.

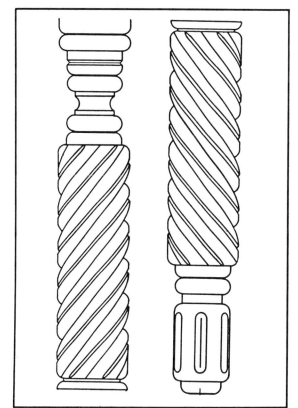

Fig. 14-13. Spirals can be formed to the left or right and can be embellished by repeating a cut with a different bit. Work can be done on tapered spindles as well as straight ones.

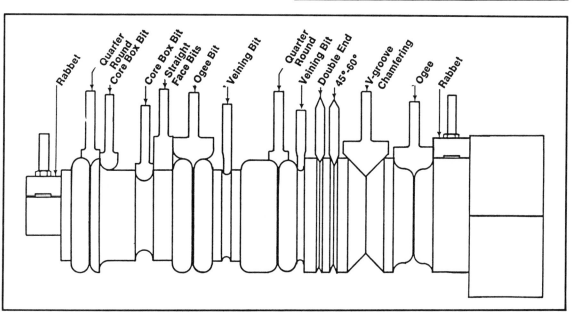

Fig. 14-14. Typical beads, coves, and flats that can be produced on the Sears Router Crafter. Usually for this type of cutting, the router is held still while the workpiece is rotated.

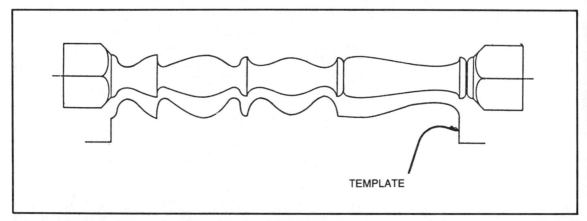

TEMPLATE

Fig. 14-15. To shape particular profiles, the router is controlled by a guide that rides against a template secured at the front of the machine. This is a good way to turn duplicate pieces.

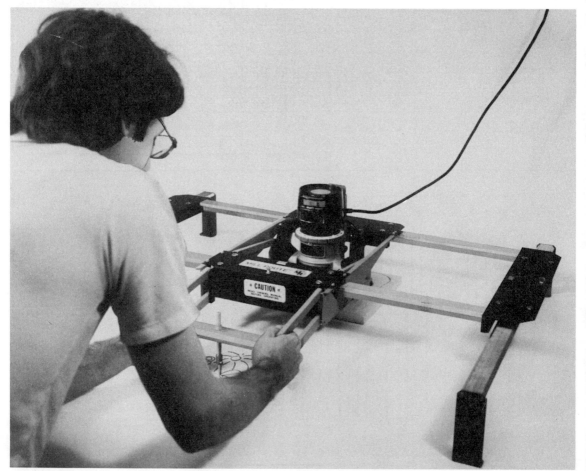

Fig. 14-16. The Mill-Route is an easily controlled machine that uses a router to follow any line that is traced by the stylus. The first project can be used as a template when duplicate pieces are required.

Fig. 14-17. Work can be done by using ready-made templates or by designing your own. Whether free or cutting, the router is always perpendicular to the surface of the work. It lifts automatically when the control bar is released.

the tool covers a 20- × -24-inch area, which is capacity enough to make large signs and work on most cabinet and door panels. The universal mounting plate is guaranteed to fit your router.

The company has started to offer ready-made templates. Some letter sets and carving templates that can, for example, be used to decorate cabinet doors, picture frames, or clock faces are currently available.

DUPLI-CARVER

The Dupli-Carver shown in Fig. 14-19 is more than a router accessory. Because it is equipped by Laskowski Enterprises, Inc., with their stand-

ard 5/8-horsepower router and a speed control, it should be thought of as a complete unit. The tool is sophisticated, but can be quickly mastered by anyone. The "secret" of the machine is the way the router can be manipulated to duplicate any configuration that is traced with the stylus. As demonstrated in Fig. 14-20, the router floats through various actions almost as if it were an extension of your hand. This, plus being able to mount workpieces on turntables, two of which are supplied with the machine, is what makes it possible to do, step-by-step, the kind of intricate 3-D carving shown in Fig. 14-21.

The Dupli-Carver is not limited to small proj-

313

Fig. 14-18. You can mount the Mill-Route on a panel of 3/4-inch particleboard or on a work table that is offered at extra cost. It's also possible to make your own separate stand.

ects. It can be organized to duplicate projects up to 66 inches long and 8 inches in diameter (Fig. 14-22). What might be of interest to anyone doing production work is that several machines can be organized in tandem so that a single operation can produce two, three, or four objects at a time and they can be as large as 32 inches in diameter and 40 inches tall. A special line of router bits is offered, many of them designed for duplication of very fine detail (Fig. 14-23).

Other accessories include a variety of let-tering templates, various sizes of styli, sanding cones, a special unit for sign making, and more.

ROUTER-RECREATOR

With the Router-Recreator pictured in Fig. 14-24, you can carve 3-D figures up to about 8 inches tall (Fig. 14-25) and also make signs, do fluting on spindles, shape edges, form uniform depth or tapered grooves, do bas-relief carving, and even do some panel decorating. It's a lot to expect from a single router accessory, but the tool doesn't let you down.

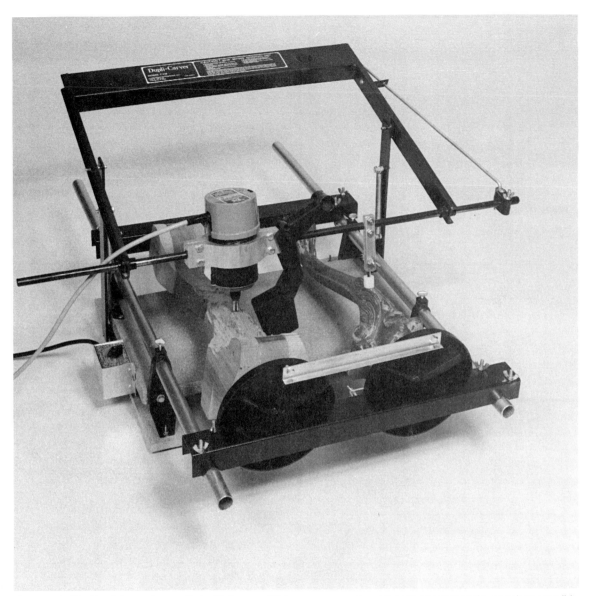

Fig. 14-19. The Dupli-Carver is supplied with its own 5/8-horsepower router. Intricate carvings in-the-round are possible when the blank and model are mounted on synchronized turntables.

Any router that has a 3- to 3 3/4-inch diameter motor body can be mounted on the counterbalanced shaft that also holds the stylus. The shaft rides on pulleys controlled with steel cables. The router can be moved backwards or forwards, from side to side, and can be tilted. The actions are controlled individually or can be combined. This allows the router bit to imitate how the stylus moves so it can follow intricate configurations. The weight that supplies the counterbalancing is adjustable, making it easy to provide a light touch regardless of the router's weight.

One way that the machine is used to do 3-D

315

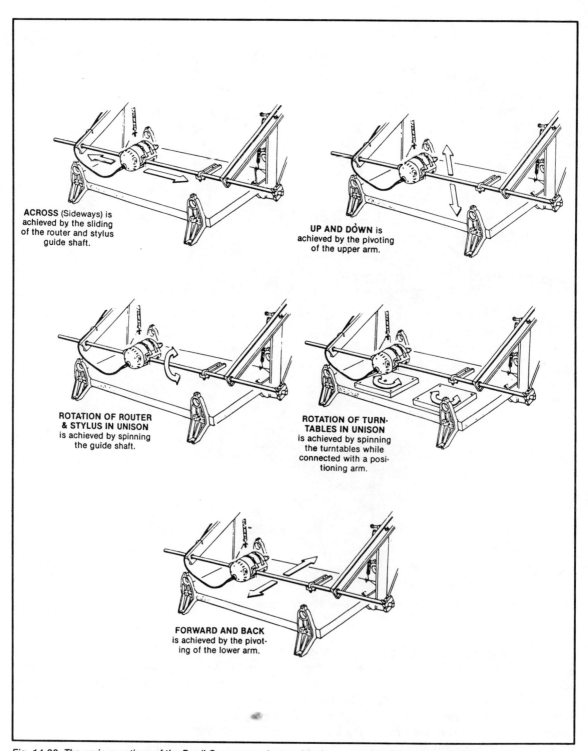

ACROSS (Sideways) is achieved by the sliding of the router and stylus guide shaft.

UP AND DOWN is achieved by the pivoting of the upper arm.

ROTATION OF ROUTER & STYLUS IN UNISON is achieved by spinning the guide shaft.

ROTATION OF TURN-TABLES IN UNISON is achieved by spinning the turntables while connected with a positioning arm.

FORWARD AND BACK is achieved by the pivoting of the lower arm.

Fig. 14-20. The various actions of the Dupli-Carver are what enable the router bit to follow intricate undercuts and contours.

Fig. 14-21. This bust of Lincoln demonstrates the various stages of roughing and adding detail to a piece of work. Results are excellent when you take your time and work carefully.

Fig. 14-22. The Dupli-Carver can handle projects up to 66 inches long and 8 inches in diameter. Among the commercial people who use the tool are gunsmiths, antique restorers, and makers of musical instruments.

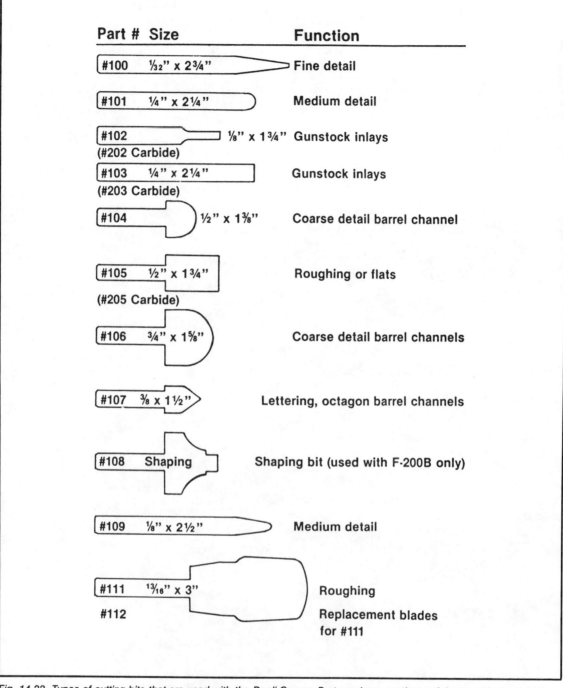

Part #	Size		Function
#100	⅟₃₂" x 2¾"		Fine detail
#101	¼" x 2¼"		Medium detail
#102 (#202 Carbide)		⅛" x 1¾"	Gunstock inlays
#103 (#203 Carbide)	¼" x 2¼"		Gunstock inlays
#104		½" x 1⅜"	Coarse detail barrel channel
#105 (#205 Carbide)	½" x 1¾"		Roughing or flats
#106	¾" x 1⅝"		Coarse detail barrel channels
#107	⅜ x 1½"		Lettering, octagon barrel channels
#108	Shaping		Shaping bit (used with F-200B only)
#109	⅛" x 2½"		Medium detail
#111	¹³⁄₁₆" x 3"		Roughing
#112			Replacement blades for #111

Fig. 14-23. Types of cutting bits that are used with the Dupli-Carver. Part numbers are those of the manufacturer. All are high-speed steel.

Fig. 14-24. The Router-Recreator works with a router and stylus that mount on the same counterbalanced shaft. The shaft rides on wheels that are controlled with steel cables.

carving is demonstrated in Fig. 14-26. Both the model and the blank are secured on mounting blocks that can be rotated 360 degrees. They must be turned in unison. This is accomplished by following the corresponding marks on the mounting blocks and the tool.

Many types of conventional router bits can be used with the Router-Recreator, but for carving operations, it's wise to buy the special set shown in Fig. 14-27. The set is available on its own or with the machine. Buying the products together is a good idea because the price is less than if the tools were purchased individually. Also available for the machine is a foot-actuated switch that lets you keep both hands free to control the router. Figures 14-28 through 14-33 show

some ways this interesting router accessory can be used.

THE EDGE-CRAFTER

Ever wonder how the fancy edges often found on drum tables (Fig. 14-34) and similar projects are created? The first thought would be that after the disc was formed and its edges bulked with a circular strip, shaping would be accomplished by using the freehand technique on a shaper or a router/shaper stand. That's a good judgement, but the same kind of work can be done in a more controlled fashion, using a Craftsman accessory designed specifically for mounting on the router tables available from Sears (Fig. 14-35). With some tinkering, however, the unit could easily

319

Fig. 14-25. Plaque was made by using a chess piece as a model. Figures in-the-round up to about 8 inches tall are possible.

be adapted for use on any router/shaper table, whether store bought or homemade.

Basically, the accessory works by providing a central pivot point and an assortment of templates that bear against an adjustable roller guide after they have been secured to the workpiece. The pivot controls how the work is rotated and the templates relate to the shape of the work. The roller guide that provides bearing surface for the template allows the cutting to be done without the need of collars on a spindle or a pilot on the cutter.

A simple project that serves as an example of work that can be done is the oval picture frame shown in Fig. 14-36 together with the template that was used to create it. Shapes that are

more complex are in the scope of the Edge-Crafter whether they are formed with the templates supplied with the tool (Fig. 14-37) or whether you decide to create original ones. It's important to remember that the size of the workpiece is not limited by the dimensions of the template. A case in point—the oval template, which measures about 11 and 15 inches on its long and short axes, can be used for solid ovals or open frames up to about 25 × 30 inches.

Original templates can be made from 1/4- or 3/8-inch hardboard or plywood. Squares and rectangles, hexagons and octagons, and other geometrical forms are possible. It's wise to avoid points and sharp corners and abrupt changes in contours. As always when using a router bit,

Fig. 14-26. Model and blank are mounted on blocks that can be rotated 360 degrees. It's important for the blocks to be turned in unison.

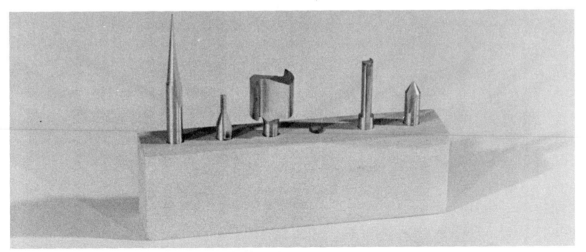

Fig. 14-27. Many types of router bits can be used with the Router-Recreator, but for carving purposes, it's essential to have the cutters in this set.

Fig. 14-28. Some panel decorating is possible. The stylus, indicated by the arrow, follows the outlines of a template; the router duplicates the moves.

322

Fig. 14-29. To create a raised panel area, you can switch to another stylus tip and a larger diameter bit.

Fig. 14-30. Straight fluting can be done by moving the stylus along kerfs cut into a piece of wood. You can follow a marked line, but the kerfs provide more control. For tapered cuts, place a height block under one end of the workpiece.

Fig. 14-31. Sign making is another possibility. You can guide the stylus with stencils or with templates.

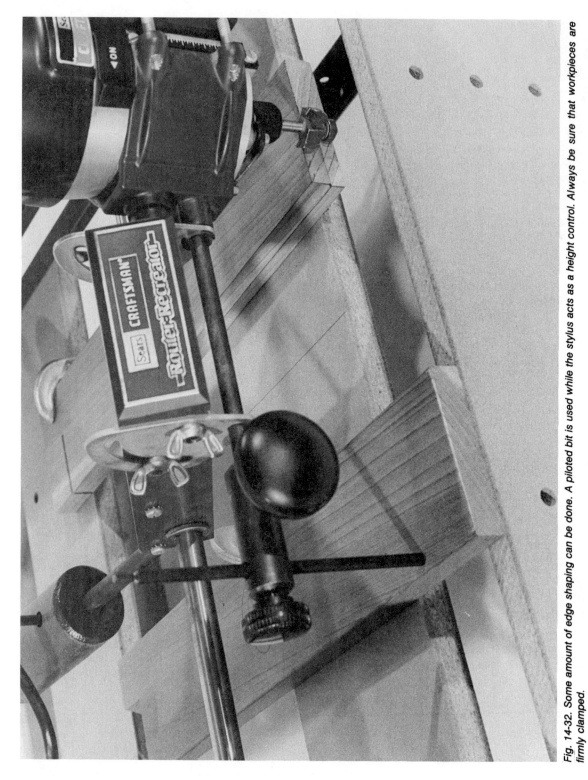

Fig. 14-32. Some amount of edge shaping can be done. A piloted bit is used while the stylus acts as a height control. Always be sure that workpieces are firmly clamped.

Fig. 14-33. Fluting can also be done on spindles. Here too, the stylus acts only as a height control. Note the C-clamp being used to secure the work.

Fig. 14-34. Fancy raised edges on tabletops and other projects like trays and end tables, can be shaped by using the Edge-Crafter. The fluting on the post and the legs can also be done with a router by using techniques that were demonstrated in other chapters.

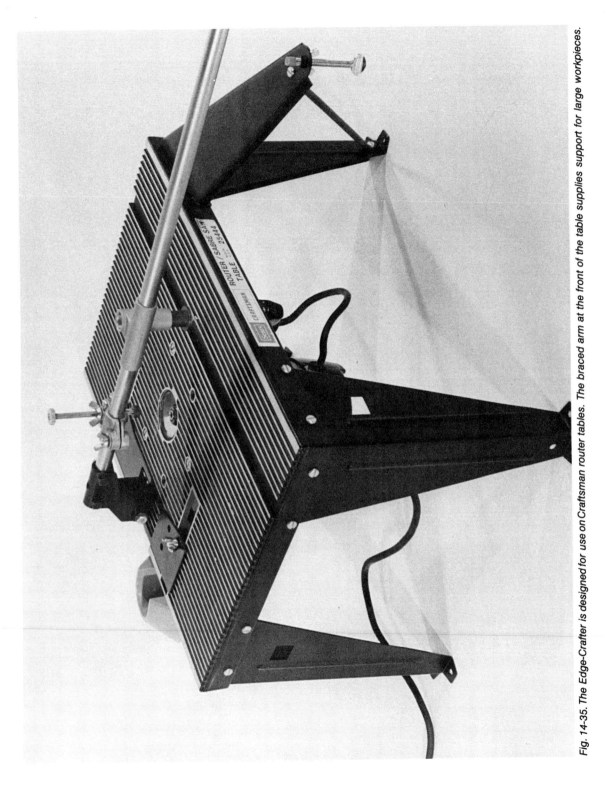

Fig. 14-35. The Edge-Crafter is designed for use on Craftsman router tables. The braced arm at the front of the table supplies support for large workpieces.

Fig. 14-36. The shape of the oval frame was determined by the plastic template. Workpieces of this nature are cut to rough shape and then mounted on plywood for inside and outside cuts.

Fig. 14-37. These are the templates that are supplied with the tool, but you can design original ones. The size of the project is not limited by the size of the template.

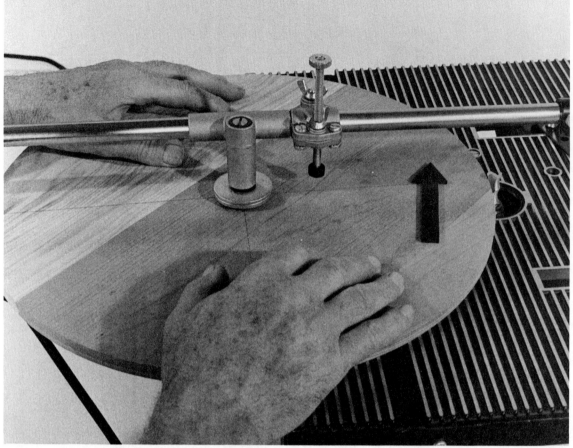

Fig. 14-38. Round workpieces can be edge-shaped without using a template. The Edge-Crafter, with the guide assembly locked to conform to the diameter of the work, acts as a pivot guide. The arrow indicates correct rotation for the project.

you can't shape a sharp corner; plan for any inside or outside turn to have a radius that is at least 1/4 inch.

Circular projects can be done without a template because the work is turned on the central pivot and the depth of the cut is controlled by the position of the guide clamp assembly (Figs. 14-38 and 14-39). To mount the work, locate its center by drawing intersecting lines and then use a compass to draw the circumference. Rough cut the work to approximate the size. After using an awl to form an indent where the lines cross, mount the work good side down, as shown in Fig. 14-40. A long screw passes through the guide to serve as a pivot point.

Various ways to use the Edge-Crafter are demonstrated in Figs. 14-41 through 14-47. The current model, shown in Fig. 14-48, might differ a bit from the unit that I have been using in my shop, but the operational procedures remain the same.

Well, it's time to stop. One of the problems with router shop talk is that it can go on forever. New ideas and new applications are daily events. Probably by the time this book is in print there will be more accessories, more bits, more router innovations. The information included here, however, should have you prepared for whatever comes along. Until next time then, safe and happy woodworking.

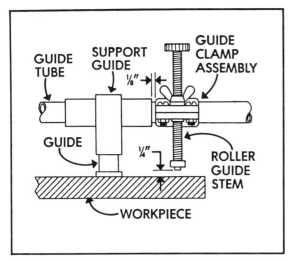

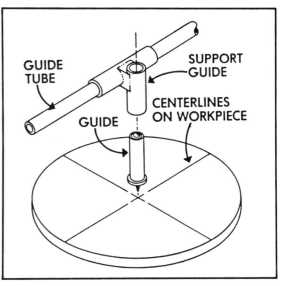

Fig. 14-39. The roller guide stem, which is part of the guide clamp assembly, is brought into play only when templates are used. Work is moved while keeping constant contact between the roller on the stem and the bearing edge of the template.

Fig. 14-40. A long screw passes through the guide and serves as a pivot point. The guide tube slides through the sleeve on the support guide.

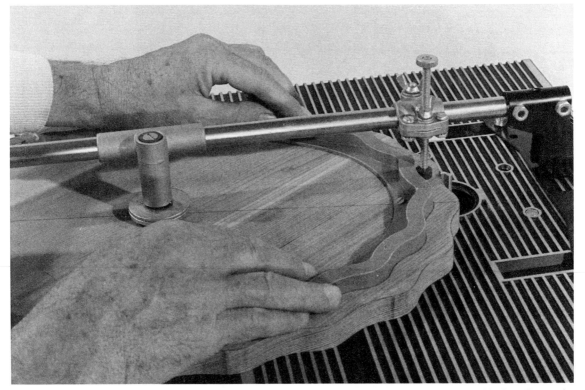

Fig. 14-41. Templates are attached to the work with small screws. Keeping the template in contact with the roller on the guide stem is what controls the cut. A straight bit is used to cut the work so it will conform to the shape of the template.

Fig. 14-42. A raised rim for a project is started with the workpiece attached to a piece of plywood on which the template is fastened. This step is producing the outside shape.

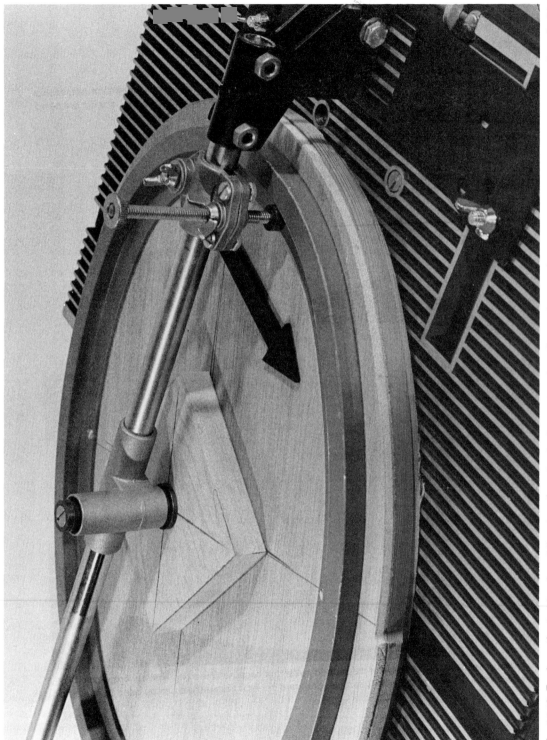

Fig. 14-43. To shape the inside edge of the rim, the setup is changed so the roller on the stem bears against the inside edge of the template. In this operation, the cutter can't be seen. Note, as indicated by the arrow, that the work is now rotated in a clockwise direction.

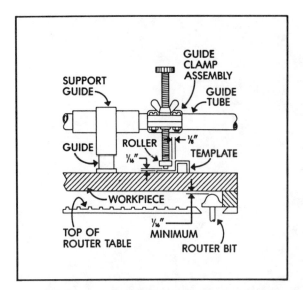

Fig. 14-44. This cross-sectional view shows the relationship between bit and work when inside edges of a rim are being shaped.

Fig. 14-45. The guide tube slides easily in the sleeve of the support guide, but because of working with various stock thicknesses, it doesn't always remain parallel to the work's surface. Standard 5/8-inch flat washers can be used to make adjustments.

Fig. 14-46. After a workpiece has been brought to basic shape with a straight cutter, its edge can be embellished by changing to another bit. The cut is still controlled by contact between template and the roller on the guide stem.

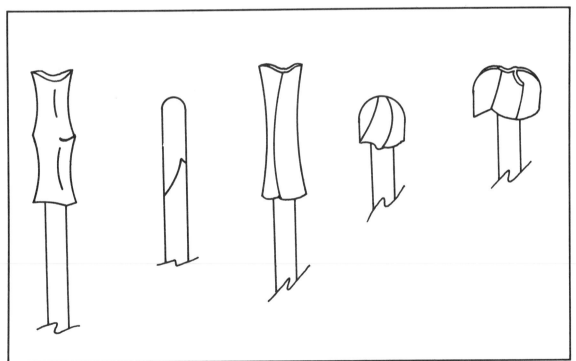

Fig. 14-47. Many types of pilotless router bits can be used with the Edge-Crafter, but this set is recommended, at least to start with. It includes a 1/2-inch core box, 1/4-inch veining, 3/4-inch ogee end-cutter, 1/2-inch edge-rounding, and a 1/2-inch double-bead edging bit.

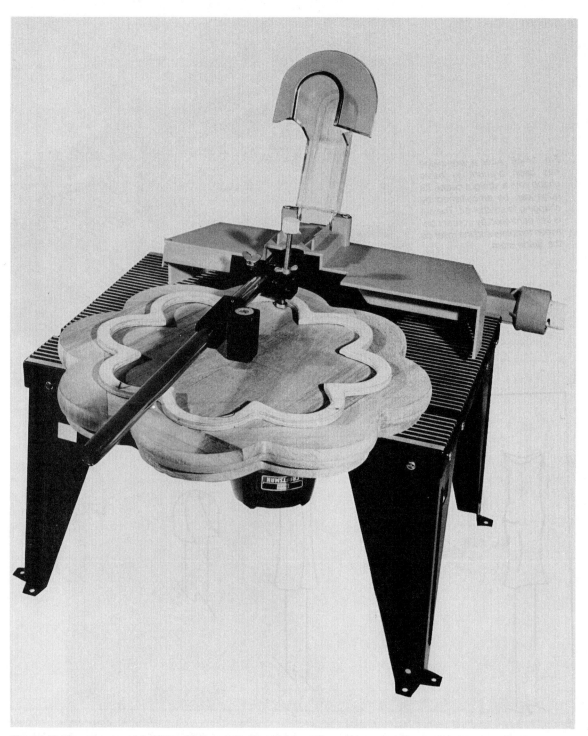

Fig. 14-48. The current model of Edge-Crafter might differ a bit from the unit that was photographed for this book, but operational procedures remain the same. This Craftsman router table has a cover that can be hooked to the hose of a vacuum cleaner.

Index

Index

Other Bestsellers from TAB